Structures of Prejudice

Structures of Prejudice

Carlyle Marney

Abingdon Press   new york   nashville

STRUCTURES OF PREJUDICE

Copyright © 1961 by Abingdon Press

Library of Congress Catalog Card Number: 61-8411

Quotations from *Back to Methuselah* by George
Bernard Shaw, are used by permission of the
Public Trustee and The Society of Authors.

SET UP, PRINTED, AND BOUND BY THE
PARTHENON PRESS, AT NASHVILLE,
TENNESSEE, UNITED STATES OF AMERICA

TO ELIZABETH

Lux lucis benigna

Contents

7

CONTENTS

9

The Padded Cell

The armadillo and the snail, the rabbit and the porcupine, crave security. Nature answered with cartilaginous cases to hide in, long back-leg muscles for a running start, and quills for defense attached to hinder parts. All living nature craves security.

Man is part of living nature and craves his securities too. He can think about tomorrow; he can recognize his ultimate enemy, death. The day he began to anticipate his own tomorrow he became an anxious man. This is the facade of anxiety out of which all his slaveries, old and new, arise. The relief of our anxieties and the possession of security are one and the same—and the satisfaction of this urge is the main work of civilization.

Hence we live our lives with locks on doors and windows. We shatter the nerves of our hard-working burglars with electrical alarms. We lock the secrets of our adolescent years from the prying eyes of parents in the dubious safety of diaries with keys. This is a world of shotguns and pistols, moats, drawbridges, and railroad detectives. The mantle of security is thrown over our furs and good woolens with cedar-lined

11

closets; we cover our heads with tile roofs, wind insurance, and portable bombproofs that once upon a time were storm cellars. We project this thrust for security with life insurance policies, investment houses, bank vaults, armed guards, old-age retirement plans, and family foundations.

The nation, too, craves its securities and builds tariff walls, alliances with most favored nations, keeps its blood pure by way of immigration quotas, borrows from itself with bonds, and paradoxically postpones and guarantees its bankruptcy by artificially supporting prices. The good solid burgher shaves in front of a medicine cabinet that bulges with panacea and believes in lightning rods, electric stock fences, and slats under his bedsprings. Sometimes, if he is hefty, he wears a belt and suspenders, too.

And our fears? Cancer, a cardiac condition, wild sons, adultery, plane wrecks, new bombs, the Russians, and for our jobs. Credit, debts, suits, courts—these are heavy concerns. God reigns, if at all, with a hammer, and we live our lives, arms upraised against the coming blow, ready to duck into any temporary shelter. The old order changes, and this is too much for Aunt Fanny in *Lanterns on the Levee*, so she has to have her genteel dose of morphine daily. The drive is for security. Give us status, security, even the safety of slavery, and guarantee it. Make sure life turns out right!

In order to accomplish this security we carry around with us a swarm of comfortable notions which follow us, as Bertrand Russell has said, like flies on a hot day. We are a "chosen people"; we speak of Protestant unity, as if no other cleavages exist; we support some private Zion and find security in claiming to be antilabor, anti-Jewish, anti-Catholic, and antiforeigner. We proclaim the superiority of a particular racial minority; we expect the invincibility of American arms; we extol the virtue of American character and the worthwhileness of business. We believe in the material, the temporal, and the future, and our goal is happiness; make sure life turns out right. If the going gets too rough there is always a portable padded cell into which and out of which one can dodge for security. We have our pads for the semi-insane, protection from the sharp edges of reality. And if we cannot upholster life's corners with prejudiced notions we have all sorts of chemical substitutes for padded ideas.

This unhappy spectacle Unamuno called "the rule of Whirligig, the King." In the center of prosperity and development our nerves are shot, and we reach for chemical diversion to allow us to endure the frustrations of prosperity. "Have you got a Miltown on you?"

This is the new padded cell which comes into use where our structures of prejudice fail to support us. We use barbiturates to sleep on, caffein to wake on, and tranquilizers to calm down on.[1] We use Manhattan bombers to create a party and tomato juice with Worcestershire sauce to get over one. Pepto-Bismol slows down your stomach juices and hydrochloric acid speeds them up. We carry aspirin for minor insulation and Demerol for a blackout. Marijuana is for kicks, mickey finn gives oblivion; beer will break the ice, and vodka will melt it. This is the padded cell, standard equipment in the new slave pens we have built for ourselves.

And God? He is no longer standard equipment. He has become the great accessory to whom there is little occasion to turn save as one wants to get or forget something. While in the mess of pornography piled just inside the drugstore one can always pick up copies of Norman Vincent Peale or Mickey Spillane who do very well the selfsame job. They are guaranteed to insulate us during the reading from our own reality. If television in the corner is not disturbance enough, we carry a portable with us on vacation and to football games, lest we miss a good thing. But this is a surface view.

By and large, we are immersed in materialism, provincialism, institutionalism, and individualism. The first is a metaphysical error, a perversion of reality; the second is an epistemological error, a false limitation of knowledge; the next is the ethical error implicit in our satisfaction with lesser values; and the last is theological madness, the denial of personality. Each participates in the rest, few of our prejudices belong to one structure of culture alone; they combine in texture and strength to form a net, a cage, a cell—a padded cell!

I

We are committed to the material world; until someone can show us a better than material world, this is it. Out of five hundred years of our

---

[1] In a clinic at Austin State Hospital, the discussion was about the effectiveness of tranquilizers in the treatment of mental patients. A young psychiatrist gave a glowing report in terms of how many "new" patients were being released in sixty days with the help of tranquilizing drugs. At this point a huge, fine-looking priest of the Roman Church leaned over my shoulder to whisper, "Oh, yes, tranquilizers are wonderful! We are putting them in the communion wafers at my place, and it just does away with *sin!*"

life and work in a world of machinery we have learned to expect things to go right. We now demand the same tireless, efficient, energetic output from our livers and lights that once we could get only occasionally from gadgets. Surgeons must perform successfully like automatons. Friends must answer instantly like telephone operators. Marriage is an automatic and mechanical harnessing of personal powers. Salesmen exist for output. Recreation is measured in quarts and sizes. Profits are guaranteed. Sons and daughters are plastic toys. God, the great God, is a mechanic, and what is infinitely worse, mechanics are gods. The great high priest is the service man, who, like God, is on duty twenty-four hours a day, and whom only God can help if he is in automobile or television service and not available, and good!

In the padded cell the distinctively human is swallowed up in the distinctively mechanical. Theism's ancient anthropomorphic God is done away. He is dead and can no more walk in a garden in the cool of the day. But mechanism's god is here, and bells ring, lights flash, circuit breakers click, and the total comes out of the IBM, for mechanism's god, just as Streeter says, is mechanomorphic.

This is not just the relativism of Protagoras; this is more than *anthropos metron*; this is less godly than that, for this is *mechano-metron*, which means that the idol has come alive to measure its creator. This is worse than the automatic evolutionism of the nineteenth century; this is more deadly than ambition or *hubris* or our infantile worship of the colossal. This is more deadly even than the current rebirth of the attempt to structure ethics into a calculus. This is the deadly triumph of the dead. Everything is reduced to energy and stuff, from which a return is expected. And this is about all the human that remains—the expectation of getting something back.

Herodotus claimed that the bitterest sorrow a man can know is to aspire to do much and to achieve nothing. Not so: the bitterest sorrow is to aspire to do much and to do it, and then to discover it was not worth the doing.

II

We are, all of us, limited by the provincial. This is an epistemological problem, for the ways we arrive at new knowledge are barred from us by walls we have set up. By and large, all of us expect the world to be

14

an enlarged version of our own back yards. We would make the world like ours, if we could. "No Jews in my village," said the farmer to his Jewish seat mate on a train. "And that's why it's a village," said the Jew in reply.

Like cartographers in ancient times who peopled the land beyond their boundaries with fearsome creatures we carry nonsensical notions in our heads as if they were gospel. In my boyhood Huns had horns and Charles Darwin wore a tail and was cloven-hoofed. A neighbor from my beloved Saxon mountains, after two weeks in Pensacola, asked "to see a Catholic" as if he expected to be bitten if he got too close. I was not alone in believing oysters were an aphrodisiac—even if I could not spell it. And I knew one could feed his brain with fish and buttermilk.

"What bubbles we do blow," cried MacNeile Dixon in his Gifford Lectures. The Fijians had their prejudices too, and thought a seventeenth-century European was hardly fit to eat, while all white men were too tough and salty unless parboiled. We all have these silly ideas in some form or another, and they block our way to new knowledge. Representative Durham and the House Committee on Military Affairs blocked the distribution of a pamphlet done for the Armed Forces by Margaret Mead on Races of Mankind because Adam and Eve were pictured with navels, reports Bergen Evans, but the real reason must have had something to do with Dr. Mead's teaching about race. Jim Peal overheard a man say in a New Orleans elevator, "Two things I can't stand: these people who discriminate and a dam' nigger!" In Asunción a man told me he had heard of Texas; it was a place in Chile. While in North Carolina a man burned his copy of the Revised Standard Version of the Holy Scriptures as an instrument of Satan. I know preachers in the mountains who have said that television aerials are horns of the devil, while a friend visiting in prewar Germany was censured for riding a trolley to his preaching appointment on the Sabbath, but offered beer for a bracer just before the sermon.

Tibideaux's houseboat broke its moorings and floated out in the Gulf at night. When Tibideaux discovered his plight at daylight he cried, "Brisconne, wake up! We ain't here no more." This is where we are. Fettered to our respective provincialisms, we are "bundles of prejudice"

15

and do not know who or where we are. We are all, thus, victims of Kierkegaard's "thoughts which wound from behind."

Provincialism may be geographical, cultural, political, ideological, economic, religious, and personal. It develops around any base from which a world view springs. All cosmologies are provincial. This is why a precise pattern of organization is impossible. This is also the cause of most tensions and controversy. Provincialism is at the root of all nationalist-internationalist power-bloc controversy. In the West Communism-capitalism struggles reveal this, for both systems are Western and provincial. The agonizing East-West problems rise out of a larger provincialism, but there are others almost as old: Latin-German, romantic-realist, aesthetic-utilitarian, poetic-pragmatic, Ying-yang, mountain-lowland, town-gown. All these are provincialisms, and all conflicts of view are the result of partial views, for the fundamental power to categorize at all contains also the temptation to provincialize, to mistake the part for the whole.

What bubbles we blow! I have felt German provincialism in Argentina and Texas, Russian prejudice in Paraguay, Shinto ancestor worship in the Daughters of the American Revolution, mountain isolationism in a city apartment house, white supremacy on Christian foreign-mission boards, feudalism in the churches, Confucianism at the University of Chicago, Hitler's Nordic man in the Cumberland Mountains, the Ku Klux Klan in little Baptist churches, Yankee supremacy expressed by American-Chinese, Hindu determinism in a Reformed theologian, Communist-like economic determinism in meetings of bank directors, Catholic authoritarianism in congregational churches, Fascism among schoolboard members and university trustees, German racism in American pulpits, medieval superstition in modern hospitals, cannibalism in business, and pre-Copernican angelology in Sunday schools. How many bars there are on our padded cells, for our provincialisms will not stay home. They roam around.

III

Modern man is as he is by virtue of his institutions. These are frames, cells he has constructed or inherited to hold his valuables. Sir Winston Churchill says this succinctly in the sentence: "We shape our dwellings, and afterward our dwellings shape us."

Mankind, as a whole, does not wish truly to be free. He wishes protection from freedom. Order is more desirable than freedom. We join ourselves to groups and institutions for protection from freedom. We want things labeled so that ideas and forces do not slip around and jar us too much. We crave order, especially social order. We want the edges of our lives clearly marked, with clean breaks. Most of our clubs, committees, schools, churches, lodges, states, and nations are defenses against disturbance. We lean on them, says Gordon Allport, to keep from leaning on ourselves.

All institutional loyalties are value judgments. Institutionalism becomes a structure native to prejudice precisely because the institution exists to mark the edges of a valuable. It limits value. Institutionalism by its very nature elevates the part above the whole. This is why prejudiced people do so well in churches. The craving for security pushes them into the isolated cell of the institution from which sanctuary the part may be preserved and the present can be protected. This is the ethical agony of Christendom, and it is more dangerous than the atomistic materialism of Democritus.

Primarily, these institutional structures exert their power in three great areas: economics, politics, and religion. All of these lend themselves to abuse because of the emotional level upon which choices are made and values are determined. All are structures of power.

Racism, per se, is not a separate structure of prejudice. No organic connection can be shown between the treatment of a minority race group in Southern America and a majority race group in South Africa. Rather, racism is the result of provincialism multiplied by institutionalism. Racism rises out of institutionalism always. For example, all four hundred of the organizations now chartered in America to do business against or in behalf of racism rise out of or in opposition to the institutional base of Saxon supremacy. The five principles of our racism exist to protect economic, religious, and personal institutions of value. These principles, as expressed by Joseph Arthur Gobineau, are all designed to serve one institutional end—Saxon supremacy. White (Teutonic) culture is superior; other races can never equal this; ancestor reverence preserves racial purity; nature (God) and prosperity require some to be hewers of wood and drawers of water; decay accompanies any violation of this ordinand by mixture of the races.

17

So powerful is this cleavage emotionally that not even the ten-minute tumultuous ovation given the grizzled and saintly Benjamin Mays at Evanston can erase the horror of his closing word: "I can have your Ph.D., your Bible, and your God; but there is no way I can belong!"

Nor is politics really less an emotional arena than racism. Here appears a time-honored institutionalism with real values involved and whose stylized vocabulary, techniques of enlistment, and end in view are all frankly oriented for an emotional appeal. In a thousand speeches any political year one can hear "new-deal communist confiscatory taxation, Washington is a rat's nest of Bolsheviks, the trouble all stems from the Talmudic philosophy of Europe—send money and help, send me to Washington."

As long as I can remember I shall hear the slap of the stern word of the lawyer Joseph Welch to Senator Joe McCarthy during the hearings in Washington. "I cannot fight with you, sir—you are a man without a conscience." Emotion had run riot and no truth could be made plain. Here appears a fundamental structure of prejudice, here is clearly a natural arena for prejudice. Here go up new bars for our padded cells, for emotionally arrived at commitments keep men limiting their values to the world in which their party loyalty is registered.

Who does not know the pressure that arises from organized institutional religion? Here, more than any place I have lived, prejudice is at home. Ministers, especially, become victims, sell their consciences, and become defenders of a culture in the name of Jehovah God. False beacons throw twisted substitutes for light across the barren landscape of our lives: Korans, Bibles, and Upanishads; muzzeins, priests, and bishops; Father Divine, Joseph Smith, and Daddy Grace. Hapless symbols of our shallow emotional desire to escape life are thrust up for our adulation: Norman Vincent Peale, and Oral Roberts, and Billy Graham. Few escape the resulting abominations like: "white, gentile, protestant America"; "chosen people"; "Gott mitt uns"; "Cross and flag"; "God's country." The Huguenot expulsion occurs all over again with major denominations pushing their fairest, brightest, and best sons into other communions in order to preserve their provincial isolation.

In all the religious torment both the valuable and the personal are swallowed up. A man may live eighty years and never learn who he is or what is truly valuable. Religion has furnished not a gateway to an eternal

18

glory, but another set of bars for the padded cell; bars forged of the steel of the age-old error, that of substituting means for end, of giving intrinsic value to instrumental values. This is why many men, like Lincoln, have refused to give their names and lives to the formal institutions of religion that form such seedbeds for prejudice.

Religion, politics, and economics are facets, along with racism, of our common wish to eternalize values in the institutions we inherit and build. Most often the value enshrined at the first is lost in the layers of shell built round for protection. The cup of freedom becomes a chalice of Paris green—to drink it is to imbibe the rigors of stiff and rigid death to freedom. The institution becomes a padded cell. This is our ethical heartbreak. We deny by our own sacred limitations the invasion of the truth that cannot live constricted and, like St. Augustine, find ourselves trapped in the birdlime of our own nests.

IV

Kierkegaard tells of a peasant who came cleanly shaven to the capital city to sell his firewood. So much did he have to sell, and such a price did he receive, that he was able to buy himself his very first shoes and a pair of long stockings with enough left over for a glorious drunk. As he was trying in his drunken state to find his way home he fell asleep in the middle of the highroad. Later a wagon came along and the driver, not wishing to get down, shouted, "Get up, or I'll drive over your legs!" Aroused at last, the still drunken peasant looked at his legs, and since by reason of the new shoes and stockings he did not recognize himself, he cried, "Drive on! They are not my legs!"

This is the essence of individualism. This is the sin of the world. This is the closest structure of prejudice, for it limits the personal to the self alone. This, ultimately, is the solipsism no philosopher will confess, for this is insanity; this is a padded cell.

The individual is always proprietor, never guest. The game is always "one-eyed cat," each man for himself, no consciousness of team. Individualism reaches its end this side of any social good, and though cleverly disguised as democracy, local autonomy, rights of the individual, or the American way, it is still a form of the moral indifferentism of Thrasymachus in Plato's dialogues.

All moral virtues are disguised forms of self-seeking. Any real indi-

19

vidualist knows this and will not be a fool. Business is business! Might makes right! If you can, do! Do not let anyone do to you what you would do to them! Never run the risk of having been a fool!

When it's over? "Yes, yes, I see it all," says Unamuno. "An enormous social activity, a mighty civilization, a profuseness of art, of industry, of morality, and afterwards, when we have filled the world with industrial marvels, with great factories, with roads, museums, and libraries, we shall fall exhausted at the foot of it all, and it will subsist—for whom? Was man made for [this] or was [this] made for man?"

Individualism, rampant, is the sin, the Promethean sin, the Luciferian sin, of trying to make finite infinite, of seeking to become God. It is fundamental to the structure of our new padded cells from which life will "go right."

The world is made for consciousness, for each consciousness. Consciousness demands communion, but not in the isolation of the padded cells we have built. The metaphysical error—materialism, the epistemological error—provincialism, the ethical madness—institutionalism, and the theological heresy—individualism form four sets of bars and pads in which we confine ourselves. We look out at our limited reality, our foreshortened horizons of community, our emasculated values, and our distortions of personality, and this is why the great phrase of the Hungarian revolt was "the twenty-fifth hour," the hour beyond the last hour. Gabriel Marcel knows, too, that if ours is to be an era like the Hungarian hour, only a padded cell for such an insane culture can give security.

We know a better way, however, we Christians who have been given the moral command to put our own churches, houses, and sacred values under judgment. We suspect that for our sin already done there is no forgiveness that preserves our lives. We know the times demand a desperate sortie. This, however, with Kierkegaard, is our gospel and our understanding of Christianity, *a desperate sortie into the unknown.*

We know, too, that fundamental to the sortie, this new adventure of faith, there is demanded a better grasp of reality than materialism can afford us; a deeper view of community than our provincialism allows; a higher scale of value than uncriticized and unreconstructed institutionalism admits; and a nobler concern for personality than individualism can permit.

20

Underneath it all, we are not without light. The sages and seers have sung of this thing. Luther speaks of the "hail and snow of books" that appear on the subject of our communion. We have light, but lack courage. We have knowledge, but lack the will.

From some nobler source must come the will to tear away these bars to our padded cell:

> Knowledge we ask not—knowledge Thou hast lent,
> But, Lord, the will—there lies our bitter need,
> Give us to build above the deep intent
> The deed, the deed.[1]

[1] John Drinkwater, "A Prayer," from *Poems (1908-1919)*. Used by permission of Samuel French Ltd.

Part One

MATERIALISM

prejudgment of reality

All prejudice is expressed by means of a process of false categorization. All categories, when falsely or too narrowly drawn, become breeding places for new prejudice. Too narrow a view of anything results in prejudiced thinking and action. Any view of anything that is based on less than the facts available is a partial, a provincial, a prejudiced, view. This applies even to that category of philosophical inquiry which addresses itself to questions concerning the real. Metaphysical views, whether idealistic or materialistic, can be, and are, prejudiced views too.

Any view of anything which attempts to compress the whole is a reductionism. This reductionism may represent a true induction of meaning from a larger whole, or, it may be a false simplification of a more complex whole. If it does not truly reduce the whole to its essence it is false reductionism. Any reductionism which has parts left over is a false limitation of reality and is a ground for prejudice. Prejudice thrives in both materialistic and nonmaterialistic cultures, and all prejudice rests on a faulty reductionism. Currently our culture knows more of the

23

prejudices innate in materialism than those of idealism; however, neither of these systems is through with us.

When materialism is through with its analyses it has parts left lying all over the yard. It is like the boy who first dissembles the coaster brake on his bicycle. The whole is less than the sum of its parts, and he never finds a place for all the artifacts left over. Materialism does not truly reduce reality to stuff. There are parts left over; the sum of which is the extent of the prejudice involved in materialism. The prejudices implicit in idealism must wait for delineation another day.

Pressed to its simplest statement materialism is that view of reality which reduces everything in the world to matter. Include all matter in a common pile and nothing will be left over. The world is an assortment of stuff and nothing more. All that is human is physiological. The universe is entirely composed of atoms of matter in motion and in relation (energism). All that is mind and whatever consciousness may be can be reduced to component physical (i.e. chemical) elements. The human is a mode of relation of chemicals, and therefore the universe can be understood by physical science with no spare parts and nothing is left over. That is, the assortment of chemicals in relation which is the scientist can ask the universe "who are you" and get a chemical answer.

I asked my psychiatrist friend, "When are you going to forsake psychiatry and go back to the practice of medicine?"

"In about five years," he said, "when we know the chemical answer to schizophrenia, paranoia, depression, and epilepsy." The frightening thing to all idealists is that he may likely do just this, for it begins to appear that mental states are the effects of chemicals in relation too. The internist knows this and becomes a classic detective in his quest for a chemical answer. The science of the future is biochemistry, and its base is in materialism.

Here in materialism all changes are predictable and determined. The causal series is closed and purposeless. No thought—not even a chemical one—of supernatural agency can be tolerated, and mechanism, determinism, and natural law fit everywhere. "The world, according to this new picture, is purposeless, senseless, meaningless. Nature is nothing but matter in motion. The motions of matter are governed, not by any purpose, but by blind forces and laws." [1]

This is a stark and primitive form of materialism. It has its own priests who have seen to the development of much more highly sophisticated forms. Materialism is now a cosmology and therefore an ontology. Its chemical relations have evolved scientists who are philosophers and can ontologize—a curious chemical reaction. There is the highly developed medical materialism. There is scientific materialism set in opposition to dualistic vitalism. There is the historical (dialectical) materialism which sees the main determinants of social development in economic and class relations and which makes history the effect of the growling hunger pangs of the downtrodden. There is more; over and beyond all these there is the highly sophisticated modern materialism which has abandoned the ultranarrow views of classic materialists and now displays around its venerable materialistic beams and cornerstones enough of the foliage and shrubbery of other world views to make the place habitable by modern man after two world wars and a century of solid revolution.

The modern materialist believes he has arrived at an effective working optimism. He knows that science can cope with all basic human problems through its knowledge of the interrelatedness of things. Any agnosticism or skepticism with respect to the powers of science is frowned upon. He is content that all mental processes should be explainable by reference to neural patterns; he knows that all movement is psychobiological. The only approach to an understanding of mind is through scientific study of behavior. Man's current ethical and moral situation is understood as the unnecessary lag of the socioeconomic organization behind the industrial-scientific level of efficiency.

In time, with the meeting of man's basic needs and securities, man will use his leisure and his abundance to arrive at illimitable potentialities. This "high" humanism removes entirely any need for any sort of supernatural perspective. Man can and will stand on his own two feet, reaching his full stature and station. He needs no other measure of human value, policy, and goodness than his own needs and desires, capacities and strengths. He therefore has no regard for any authoritarian sets of morals, and the modern materialist rejects any reliance on or

[1] W. T. Stace, "Man Against Darkness," *Atlantic Monthly* (September, 1948), p. 54.

appeal to any supposed source of knowledge or experience which is above or outside nature as he knows it.

Materialism, a theory of reality, originally and legitimately a world view, a system of metaphysics within the broad confines of naturalism, is now a complex spilling across all philosophical divisions except possibly aesthetics. It is at once a metaphysic, an epistemology, and an ethic. As an ethic it has its contributions to make to humanistic naturalism, scientific humanism, and pragmatic naturalistic humanism. As an epistemology its tracks appear in both pragmatism and positivism. It has its cousins among the metaphysical systems of dialectical materialism and critical naturalism. Logic accepts its ground rules from the dicta of materialism, and who can deny that in so far as mass and size are important even practical aesthetics knows materialism as a source.

In a book by C. E. M. Joad it is claimed that materialism has declined due to the weakening of its scientific backing, and that neither science nor philosophy continues exclusively materialistic.[2] With this judgment one need not quarrel. He could only wish it were more openly obvious, for materialism wears many new garments, remains as a structure for widely diverse systems, approaches a religion in power among the half-learned, and provides an emotional base for the most evangelistic expression of metaphysical principles the modern world is likely to see.

It is to this vast realm of the practical expressions of materialism that we must turn to see more clearly the nature of a world view which is a basic structure for prejudice. For prejudice is expressed most clearly in a prejudgment of the real—materialism.

[2] *Guide to Philosophy* (New York: Dover Publications, Inc.), pp. 527 ff.

Chapter I

Practical Materialism

In its broad base philosophical materialism is a theory of reality, a world view, a system of metaphysics belonging to the family of naturalism. Negatively, it stands opposed to all idealism and all metaphysical dualism. If this were all it is materialism could have stayed in the textbooks and histories of philosophy, but materialism is far more. It has the effect of an evangelistic faith. It has become a cultural mentality evident everywhere, including the most religious areas of life.

That is to say, materialism is a world shaper, for as A. N. Whitehead has said, "the mentality of an epoch springs from the view of the world which is, in fact, dominant in the educated sections of the communities in question." [1] Because materialism is a world view and a dominant one, because it escapes textbooks and histories and remains a current, throbbing, evangelistic motif in today's world, because it can be joined like any other religion, materialism is eligible to provide a frame or form within which a limited or prejudiced view of reality can provide a base

[1] From *Science and the Modern World* by Alfred North Whitehead. Copyright 1925 by The Macmillan Company, copyright renewed 1953, and used with their permission.

27

for prejudiced life and living. Because it can provide an emotional base for value judgments and definitions of province and boundary, and because it can provide a description of persons, it can serve as a structure of prejudice. Only if materialism could provide a true base for reality could it escape this charge. Because its base in reality is partial its results are prejudicial.

That materialism is a world view and a dominant one needs only brief demonstration. Materialism appeals in the first place because most men are occupied most of the time with physical things.[2] Man's preoccupation with matter occurs for the same reason that the shoemaker is preoccupied with leather. His life is built around physical things. The stuff of which much of his life is made is matter. Materialism further appeals because it is simple. There is no simpler explanation of life and reality. In practical materialism we see the life one lives as a result of his acceptance of the ultimate in reductionism. The materialist, in this practical sense, is one who lives as if the most obvious were the most real. Life has been stripped of most of its questions and of all its freedom and responsibility. This is a great appeal.

Many of those who have found in materialism a base for life and living have become positively evangelistic about their insights. They throw out wide arms to include all whose work or living puts them within the areas claimed by practical materialists. Thus, that which began as a view of the world becomes a religion, a politics, a social program, and a faith.

Champions of materialism name among their number all scientists and so-called intellectuals, all labor leaders, the so-called intelligent minority, those who believe human nature is constantly changing for the better, those whom they call "socially conscious," those who are scientific thinkers—i.e., not emotional or prejudiced, those who believe in the guarantee of economic security by the state, those who have committed themselves to a materialistic concept of history, those who adhere to scientific fact above religious faith, and those who reject all the supernatural. In short, practical materialists are said to include all humanists, humanitarians, freethinkers, deists, dissenters, nonconformists, doubters, and agnostics. Further, practical materialists include those

[2] Harold Titus, *Living Issues in Philosophy* (2nd ed.; New York: American Book Company, 1953), p. 238.

who deny the possibility of life after death, those who oppose the religious training of children, those who believe in compulsory education, and those who consider criminality a disease. Materialists are said to believe that all war is economically caused and that war is never necessary, though revolt sometimes is. Materialists have been said to be those who deny any divine right to rulers, who believe in a civilian government, not a military one, who support the United Nations, who favor a rulership by socialistic groups, who are internationalists, who believe in the merit system, and who are aiders of labor. That is to say, materialists are now those who refuse to exploit human beings, who believe in human above property rights, who support public utilities, public monetary credit, public enterprise, public ownership of natural resources; and who believe that democracy will not suffer under socialism.[3]

On the other hand, the enemies of materialism are "supporters of idealism." They are the supernatural interventionists whose economic security depends on the ability of religious organizations to collect money by promises of supernatural aid and a future life of happiness. Other enemies are all capitalistic owners and employers; the uneducated majority; the farmers, farm workers, and country people in general; the rich who believe an ignorant class is necessary to provide cheap labor; those who incite dissension among races; those who believe a master race is part of a caste system; those who pretend to believe that human nature will always remain the same; those who believe in the *status quo*; those who lack social responsibility; and those who lack faith in socialized medicine. Other enemies of materialism are emotional or prejudiced thinkers rather than scientific thinkers; those who are believers in faith, belief, and intuition. They are the lunatic fringe. They claim a theological concept of history.

Enemies of materialism usually appear among the aged, the grossly ignorant, and those who believe that any catastrophe is God-caused. The opponents of materialism believe in an anthropomorphic God; they believe in rewards and punishments; their pie is in the sky; they are fundamentalists. Enemies of materialism also believe that religion can

[3] The list in part is that of Charles Sherlock Seely, *Philosophy and the Ideological Conflict*, an analysis of idealism and materialism and the influence of these philosophies on the over-all world struggle between capitalism and socialism. (New York, Philosophical Library, 1953), 319 pp.

29

be combined with politics, economics, and socialism. They believe that religious property ought to be tax-free and that public schools can teach religion. They are parochialists; their criminal code rests on the "eye for an eye." They believe wars to be necessary and revolutions desirable; they subscribe to a divine right for rulers and believe in the dictatorship of small groups. They are militarists, anti-United Nations, isolationists, and believe in the political spoils system. They are generally political and professional people; they value money more than ethics; they oppose labor unions and leaders; they help others by helping themselves; they value property rights above human rights; they believe in the private ownership of utilities, the private control of credit and money, private enterprise, the private ownership of resources; and they believe that the only competent economic system is democracy.[4]

It could well be objected that the compilation of such lists constitutes no real evidence of the existence of an emotional and religious evaluation of life based upon some sort of philosophical materialism. Yet, it is claimed here that this is evidence of such and, furthermore, is good evidence. That a materialist of some repute would openly and avowedly claim to be able to find in his base in materialism a platform upon which such a varied list of emotional subjects and objects could be opposed is good evidence; that he could find a reputable publisher for his list is still better evidence; and that there is, in fact, a way of life which approaches a religious faith which actually does include the groups of people he mentions is about all the evidence one would need to supply. When a metaphysical view of reality can attract to itself adherents on any emotional base it is already far more than a metaphysical view. When it has gone so far as to draw lines of inclusion and exclusion that sound like the interdictions and anathemas of one of the general councils of the church it is far more than a textbook view of existence and has come to approach the significance of a religious faith.

Other evidence for the weight and significance of such a religion is not lacking. Life in any college dormitory, in any atomic development center, around any set of scientific laboratories, in the seminars and discussion rooms of any department of philosophy, wherever modern young people gather and discuss, in the beer halls and taverns, even in the church

[4] This list also comes from Seely, op. cit.

30

discussion halls, reveals further evidence of materialism as a base for practical living.

One of the most telling evidences for the existence of a cult life among materialists appeared in the humanistic British periodical *New Statesman*, wherein competitors matched wits at naming new humanist heresies:

"*Clerastianism:* That heresy which accepts the supremacy of the clergy in family affairs. Members of the sect submit their infants to ceremonial head-wetting while placing the tongue in a ritual position in the cheek, precede their nuptial rites by ancient formulae to which they make mental reservations and bury their ancestors only after a ceremony which they believe will insure respectability, if not immortality.

One Wee Prayer-ism: The shocking heresy that, in moments of acute stress and danger, one wee prayer is permissible. This may be attributed, later, to behaviouristic reflex responses.

Antidisestablishmentarianism: The belief that the established church should be preserved as a bulwark against religious enthusiasm.

Diabolarianism: The belief that while it may now be confidently asserted that there is no God it is not yet safe to say the same about the Devil.

Somewhere-Elsers: Those who, despite their humanist indoctrination, cannot help thinking that, although there can be no "heaven" for them to be in, their dead exist somehow-else, somewhere-else.[5]

Such a religion also has a text:

Idealism is an historical episode, and it will end when the class struggle ends, that is, it will end when there is no longer a need for defending material inequality. . . . Society must be arranged so that it will not produce ignorant and superstitious people. . . . [This] will be done when society abandons idealism and accepts materialism.[6]

It is contended that when a metaphysical view has become a platform for life which is able to attract adherents on an emotional base, able to define its creed and therefore its heresies, able to accumulate texts for preaching against its arch enemies; when it indulges in diatribes against those enemies, listing and identifying them as such, it has al-

[5] Cited in *Time* (March 28, 1955), p. 65. Used by permission of *Time* and The Statesman & Nation Publishing Company.
[6] Seely, op. cit., p. 87 f.

ready become not only a new mentality, but also a faith of vast dimensions and of terrific potential. It now remains to demonstrate how such a faith expresses itself in the culture of the Western world.

Frontierism

Most any person now in his middle years in America grew up on the old notion that the frontier always moved west. This is now known to have about as much validity as the new psuedoscientific notion that a drunk always faces toward the east. Nevertheless, and in spite of frontiers in India and Russia that move eastward, from where we were the movement was westward. It began in Bulgaria and along the Danube—or a thousand years earlier in Asia when the Visigoths came out. It proceeded across Europe, leaped across oceans and seas, and began again on our east coast, thence westward across Allegheny and Mississippi to bring us at last to the escarpment of the Rockies, "across the wide Missouri."

This is where most of us came in. Except for those who preceded us around "the Horn," and whose descendants now commute eastward to the new frontiers at Reno and Las Vegas, the movement was westward. It was a flamboyant, colorful, masculine orgy of expansion involving horses, herds, guns, Indians, barbed wire, drouth, wagons, buffalo, beaver hides, and wampum. It furnished enough characters for a million books, enough plots to make at least five morality plays an evening for a hundred years of television, enough vigilante hangings to depopulate the West, and enough barkeeps, cutthroats, rustlers, female fortune hunters, and refugee Englishmen to repopulate it. Throughout this frontier orgy enough slogans were coined to cover this period of our history quite thoroughly in idealism and to obscure very effectively the reality that underneath all the color, pageantry, poetry, and slogans frontierism was everywhere a materialism.

The frontier movement was serious business. Frederick Jackson Turner gave it the quality of a determinism.[7] De Tocqueville saw common elements in the frontiers of Russia and America and claimed that "each of them seems to be marked out by the will of heaven to sway the destinies of half the globe." In his monumental *America as a*

---

[7] His classic essay for the American Historical Association entitled "The Significance of the Frontier in American History" is published in a volume of essays, *The Frontier in American History* (New York, 1920).

Civilization, Max Lerner notices this and comments on De Tocqueville's notion that the United States of America and Russia would one day be "the polarizing forces of the world." [8] Although different in nature and in extent, that which marks both Russians and Americans is "a continuing arc of energy" which proceeds from a frontier materialism. Many seem to have seen, but do not say, that American freedom had at least a leg-up on materialism and derived some of its energy from the desire to manipulate, to control, to manage, and to own which freedom permits. This, fundamentally, is a materialism. A key work for frontierism and, said Lerner, itself a major extension of the theory of Frederick Jackson Turner, and a work which did receive and will receive continued wide acclaim, is that of Walter Prescott Webb, the distinguished American historian (Cambridge and the University of Texas).[9] Stirred by insights into this swirling ethnic movement as a genetic force in America Dr. Webb has built a widely influential academic career on his "frontier" thesis. The force that produced frontier institutions was primarily a materialistic force, however. The great qualities of independence, self-reliance, endurance, initiative, alertness, inventiveness, and shrewdness are precisely those qualities that are demanded for survival in a frontier—i.e., materialistic—age. Lerner, who goes beyond frontierism to make a triad of forces in the explanation of the American genesis, cites industrialism, democracy, and capitalism all of which have some sort of materialistic base along with frontierism.[10]

Frontierism is a materialism. It is not a movement of idealists in spite of its famous mottos. "Fifty-four forty or fight"; "Asia for Asiatics"— these and all other slogans of expansion rest on material forces and material desires for exploitation. Whether eastward-moving or westward-moving, frontierism appears to have a materialistic base. While there is some basis for Whitehead's characterization of the Reformation as "a domestic affair of the European races," the Reformation also was a frontierism based on a new materialism among other things, and

[8] New York: Simon and Schuster, Inc., 1957.
[9] *The Great Frontier* (Boston: Houghton Mifflin Company, 1952). The literature of Frontierism extends: Lerner cites Henry Nash Smith, *Virgin Land: The American West as Symbol and Myth* (Cambridge, Mass.: Harvard University Press, 1950). He lists also Ray Allen Billington's *Westward Expansion* (New York: The Macmillan Company, 1949) and Bernard De Voto's famous *Across the Wide Missouri* (Boston: Houghton Mifflin Company, 1947) and his *The Year of Decision* (Boston: Little, Brown & Company, 1943).
[10] *Op. cit.*, p. 39.

derived much of its carrying strength from the new mines, hard money, and trade expansion that accompanied westward movements.[11] Whether with the rise of the mining Fuggers in Germany, the trades in Florence, or the new frontiers of business and mining in Siberia and Alaska, frontierism is materialistic. Only the exhaustion of land and resources stops it, and then it begins the trading process again as "business," with all the material immoralities that can grow out of this. Materialism is a mentality that descends upon and undergirds from beneath all frontier situations.

Industrialism

Industrialism is fundamentally a materialism, too. The testimony of a spate of modern writers to the effect that industrialism has turned the corner, that it is no longer a devouring nemesis, that modern man has learned to live with it, is impressive. While the modern record of industrialism in America is one of high humaneness and concern for the welfare of workers, it still can be maintained that industrialism is basically a materialism and is another evidence of the extent of materialism as a mentality in modern life.

There is much to be said about the humaneness and the high record of concern for human welfare that is characteristic of modern industrialism. It is quite natural that industrialism would have a general concern not to destroy its customers. The humaneness which Lerner saw in the Lowell factories in the early 1800's was lost and covered up by the exploitation of the masses that resulted from the 1837 panic, the reaction to war and its aftermath, and the burgeoning demands for production in the latter part of the 1800's and the first part of the 1900's. That exploitation has diminished in the general prosperity of the times. Industrialism, according to some, was never as evil as painted by its detractors of the nineteenth century or it would never have allowed the modern birth rate of Europe and America to be achieved. That is, if industrialism were as bad as painted more of us would have died or would never have come to be. In general the slogans of industry speak of development, progress, and improvement. The old saw about how many household slaves it would have taken to do the work of the number

[11] Webb had to begin in pre-Reformation central Europe to understand the forces that made the American West.

of electrical appliances in the modern home is well known. In its advertisements, the speeches of its executives, the themes of the meetings of its annual associations, and in its general idealistic façade, the tenor and life of modern American industrialism approaches that of a highly idealistic religion. It spends millions annually on improving the condition of its workers. It air-conditions; it provides lint catchers and filters; it provides life guards and railings; it speaks of retirement plans, model villages, and company hospitals. It has Kodak development rooms, chessboards, and low-cost movies for its workmen. Industrialism is proud of its families and advertises its pride. Electronically controlled cranes bear the molten metal in ladles along floors where the straining Poles, Italians, and Irish once agonized. One man on a gang saw can do the work of eighty men twenty years ago. One man behind an electronic control panel can pick up huge logs, slam them into horizontal position, and slice them up for further trimming as if they were of the consistency of cheese. One can walk a mile and a half alongside the same machine in sanitary, air-conditioned, almost noiseless comfort, watching wood turned to chips, then to mush, then to paper, and rolled, stamped, and marked for shipment all in one operation. The foreman tells you of his shares of stock in a great paper company; the sweeper whispers of an automatic raise to come at the end of the month; even the debris is carried out by electronically controlled streams of air and automatically lifted hoppers. Workmen now have annual leave, sick leave, holiday leave, and indoor toilet facilities. Industrialism, as a whole, is concerned to preserve the great American way, the American family, the American educational system, and American prosperity. Underneath it all, however, it is a materialism.

Industrialism, by and large, is a driving way to get at more raw stuff. It masticates, swallows, digests, and spews out. It debarks, slices, trims, drives, resaws, and sells. It digs, bleaches, spreads out, dissolves, and redistributes. It takes gas from holes in the ground in Louisiana, compresses it in tanks on wheels, converts the gas into a solid in Tennessee, and manufactures door knobs in New York. Industrialism is based on the desire to get at more raw stuff faster, more abundantly, more efficiently, and more attractively. It maintains its laboratories, its demonstration centers, its technical schools and workrooms, and its drawing boards primarily to get at more stuff. True, it aims to get all this material for its customers, and just as truly, it aims to make a profit in the process. This is justifiable. It cannot be successfully denied, however, that at bottom there is a materialistic mentality which lives in the realm of industrialism.

In eating this stuff on which it thrives, industrialism becomes carnivore and still eats men, too. In the long winter nights when I used to feed coke and steel into the devouring fires of the banks of furnaces, I lived in an atmosphere in which men told tales of when this finger or that hand went in the shears; when this man or that was caught between the cars; or when a slithering roll of red-hot steel jumped the tracks and wrapped around a Negro workman. During the midnight supper there would sometimes be the tale of some man who fell in the liquor pit at the next plant where chestnut logs were converted into tanning acid and chips for paper. Industrialism is carnivore and likes its meat, still. In early boyhood it was something of a wonder to me to feel the sockets of missing fingers that industrialism had eaten. When my uncle came to visit us, we had always to investigate his thumb stubs, left from the pounding of the hammers. The bent backs of men we knew was evidence enough to us that industrialism likes its meat. I used to sit on a barrel and feed slabs of steel into the crunching shears and was always cautioned to remember that shears eat steel and men. Industrialism is a materialism and cannot care too much for the flesh that serves it.

Industrialism grows out of man's work in a world of machines. Its concern must be with capacity production. It lives for incessant output to meet a contrived incessant demand. It requires the mechanical co-ordination of human beings to serve its open maw. Industrialism feeds on two markets. It searches for new fields in which to distribute its products, and it seeks to promote waste in old fields so that new products can be produced to take the place of the old. In the process, as Arnold Toynbee remarks, "the potter has become slave to his clay." [12]

It is quite true, as the classical writers have claimed, that the Renaissance and Reformation would have been stillborn, if not crushed, had not the capitalists of the day supported materialism under idealistic banners. It is just as materialistically true, however, that a society in which consumption has to be artificially stimulated by advertising and by notions of premature antiquation of products in order to keep pro-

[12] A Study of History (New York: Oxford University Press, 1948), Vol. I, Introduction.

duction going is a society that is founded on trash and waste, and this is what it is to be materialistic. Such a picture produces what Dorothy Sayers called "an appalling squirrel cage of economic confusion."

Industrialism has sought to ride many horses, but its chief steed, its stand-by and basic principle, is its materialism, for without the matter which its materialism so highly regards no industrialism could exist. The practical mentality of materialism cannot be wholly covered up, fumigated, or even embalmed by the idealistic slogans of advertising, industrial improvement leagues, chambers of commerce, and business enterprises. Nor can the idealistic claims to humaneness and the improvement of matters generally quite obscure this base in practical materialism.

Scientism

The overestimation of the reliability of scientific results rests on a sheer materialism. This is a third area in which the mentality of materialism has become a general feature of our times. The average student, beginning at about the sixth-grade level, is so exposed to the materialism of modern scientism that if he has any aptitude for techniques and any gift for equations he can be so diverted from the whole of humanitarian concerns that he is already a provincial and confirmed materialist before he finishes with his high-school education. Indeed, I have met first-year men in universities who already have finished with any concern for the whole of philosophy, literature, art, and religion. Such men can be convinced that they are put here to manipulate material values in a material world, and they are seeking only technical know-how. How refreshing it is to hear one of the greatest of modern philosophers of science speak to this issue:

The overestimation of the reliability of scientific results is not restricted to the philosopher; it has become a general feature of modern times, that is, of the period dating from the time of Galileo to our day, in which period falls the creation of modern science. The belief that science has the answer to all questions—that if somebody is in need of technical information, or is ill, or is troubled by some psychological problem, he merely has to ask the scientist in order to obtain an answer—is so wide-spread that science has taken over a social function which originally was satisfied by religion: the function of offering ultimate security. The belief in science has replaced, in large measure, the belief in God. Even where religion was regarded as compatible with science, it was modified by the mentality of the believer in scientific truth. The period of Enlightenment, into which Kant's lifework falls, did not abandon religion; but it transformed religion into a creed of reason, it made God a mathematical scientist who knew everything because he had a perfect insight into the laws of reason. No wonder the mathematical scientist appeared as a sort of little god, whose teachings had to be accepted as exempt from doubt. All the dangers of theology, its dogmatism and its control of thought through the guaranty of certainty, reappear in a philosophy that regards science as infallible.[13]

All this is within the metaphysical; it is the creation of new gods of reality that are composed of matter and stuff. Out of this five-hundred years of life and work in a world of machinery and scientism we have learned to expect things to go right. We now expect this same scientific effective energetic output from our livers and lights that we once could get occasionally from gadgets. Surgeons must perform successfully like automatons. Friends must respond at once like closing switches on a circuit. Ideas follow from automatic emotional reactions. Marriage and family relations are automatic, scientific, and mechanical. Salesmen follow pseudoscientific principles and exist only for output. Recreation is measured on dials and charts. Profits are guaranteed. Sons and daughters are mechanical toys. God is a successful scientific mechanic and what is worse mechanics are gods. The great high priest, the service man, is, like God, on duty twenty-four hours a day and only God can help him if he is in television, automobile mechanics, or air-conditioning and is not available. The distinctively human is not only swallowed in the distinctively mechanical, it is also swallowed in the pseudoscientific. Even our toys and games for our children reflect this materialism of pseudoscientism, and out of our little erector sets we build ourselves a mechanomorphic, scientific God, whose metier, source, and function rest in and proceed from that matter with which he is concerned. For such a metaphysic even Protagoras is an advance, for he, at least, saw "man as the measure of things" and not vice versa.

[13] Hans Reichenbach, *The Rise of Scientific Philosophy* (Berkeley, Calif.: University of California Press, 1951), pp. 43 ff. Used by permission.

Religious Materialism

Here the whole heart-bending contradiction between the claims of religion—to be preoccupied with a reality beyond and including this present time and its values—and the actual life of religious institutions—demonstrating an altogether frantic necessity for preoccupation with the stuff of this present world—forces us to admit that the phrase "religious materialism" represents an actual way of being religious and materialistic at once. It is not a contradiction in terms. Religionists are materialists, which is much worse than its opposite, for materialists are entitled to be religious about their grandly prejudiced limitation of reality.

The tragic reductionism of religion to a materialism does not mean that high religion has no dealings with this present world at all. This would be the opposite reductionism implicit in subjective idealism—even solipsism. All religious views have to live with stuff—matter of our existence. Religious materialism means simply that religionists are caught in the stuff they are called to master and include in a larger whole. Called to have dominion, we have been dominated by the stuff we were sent to use. *Deus machina regit.*

No single area of modern life reveals the invasion of the mentality of materialism as organized religion reveals this. Riding the crest of a multimillion-dollar annual income in the United States, American churches have become possessed by the working philosophy and techniques of a particularly vicious kind of materialism—that of exuberant, expansionist, frontier capitalism in all of its brassy and overbearing traits. In the main, the polity, goals, techniques, and operations of major American denominations are about seventy years behind the economic community. In the operational life of the churches we are in the Jay Gould era of exuberant swashbuckling railroadism, with all of its pirating of human values. What is more, we have an inexhaustible land grant to sell off as bait for new settlers who will make their own financial contribution to the material coffers of the churches whose uncanny skill in handling this world's goods still has produced no known method of transferring the goods to any better world.

The expansion of headquarters buildings cannot keep pace with the addition of new bureaus and offices for services available. The creation of new foundations for the storing of vested funds, the stock-piling of donated farms, ranches, motels, banks, hotels, radio and television stations, bus depots, tobacco stock, railroad stock, livestock, oil stock, utilities stock, and stadium bonds makes every major church in America participant and active partner in every major economic enterprise and every economic crime in the total structure of economic life.

The new multistory headquarters buildings, properly dispersed geographically to avoid making too tall a stack and to attract better regional support, demand a proper regard for business efficiency in operation. In every detail the modern church draws its pattern for operation after the business community. If, in the fourth century, the Roman Church was becoming a model of the *modus vivendi* of the decadent Roman Empire, the twentieth-century denominational centers are as good a model of the *modus vivendi* of American capitalism as can be had.

Witness the wholesale reorganization of stodgy bureaus and boards now to be streamlined and modernized according to the bulbous reports of business efficiency survey firms. The new Rome is the business way; the new church reflects its Roman model; the new book is an efficient organization manual; the new priest is an efficiency engineer; the new Pontifex Maximus is the presiding secretary or bishop, whose chummy relationship with big banking is as vital as his sales ability. Madison Avenue and the public relations and advertising moguls are at least as evident in the public life of American denominations as they are in the liquor business. We act as if the divine smile were pasted on us, and we had no future to worry about. The kingdom of God is the sum total of the effective operation of a central headquarters, and God is an American chairman of the board of an international banking house with branch offices in every community of an expanding economy featuring the creation of thirty-thousand new outlets every five years.

I sat in hot academic regalia to hear an eager engineer do a commencement address entitled "Be An Executive for Christ" for a class of young priests. I heard the professional representative of a fine new approach to trebling one's church income claim, "We will simply brain-wash them for the Lord." I know a substantial gift for a denominational project which hinged on the successful completion of 3,500 baptisms of fresh converts, which commendable acceleration of an already exuberant zeal doubtless filled every horse trough in the territory. What is more incredible still, I know a $7,200 auditor for the Tennessee Valley Authority who resigned to take a $2,700 income as a circuit pastor and who now must rear his three children on the edge of penury, but does this with a great gladness for he is "serving the Lord"! Most of us are better paid.

This hodgepodge invasion of the mentality of materialism is no new thing. The institutions of religion have always faced the agonizing prospect that the incarnation of spiritual values into temporal frames would go all the way and become demonized. All spiritual ideals run the risk of becoming their opposite. This is the implied threat to any incarnation.

The modern scene reflects six current manifestations under which heads all of our religious materialism can be expressed:

1. *An invalid transfer of biological concepts to practical theology.* The survival of the fittest applies to the techniques and programs of religion. Ideas that survive are best and are true. Whatever grows numerically is *vox Dei.* The real test of spiritual validity lies in whether or not a given scheme of work produces growth. The processes of growth are like biological growth. If one can lay hand on the principles that produce expansion they are divine, effective, and universal. "Whatever works in Louisville will work in Tokyo," I heard a mission speaker say. An Argentine missionary, crowded alongside me in the balcony, muttered an indignant "My God! Is he serious?" This preoccupation with growth and its techniques represents an easy assumption of "automatic progress" based on a misunderstanding of biological evolution, falsely transferred and erroneously translated at that.

2. *An invalid use of and reliance on the techniques of pragmatic, scientific, laboratory enterprise.* If it "works" it is divinely inspired. If it can be organized for results with masses of people it is judged to be properly based in truth. "By their fruits ye shall know them" is a reference to statistical fruit. The worth of an enterprise is based on its product.

3. *An invasion of the notions of a behavioristic psychology,* long out of date in good psychological circles, but now at some sort of peak in religious manners and mores. It reflects itself especially in the emphases on training, the technique for producing certain action as indices of religious maturity. Issues are not confronted; rather, actions are performed! One attends, regularly, on time, and brings his Bible. One con-

41

tributes, regularly, reads his lesson, and does not cheat at cards. To be religious is to act in certain ways. One "stays for preaching" and does not dance. This it is to be religious.

4. *An economic determinism in spiritual affairs* which rivals both Communism and capitalism in their reliance on the material. It is almost literally true that a major recession or a wild stock market could close up religious shops around the world. "If this gets out it will cost us a million dollars," an official said when the orthodoxy of one of his departmental representatives was seriously questioned.

5. *The growing edge of enterprise must be contained in a developing bureaucracy—the housing of materialistic organizational patterns.* This approaches a dictatorship by pragmaticrat. The success of the venture rests on a promotional-financial wizardry that deals with matter for the same reason that scientism is concerned with matter. That is to say, its work is with stuff because its interest is with stuff. Sometimes the bureaucratic expert even resigns, borrows capital, and opens a rival enterprise to get in on the rising market.

6. Summarily, it all rests on the *colossal error involved in transvaluation: the exchange of ends and means.* This permits the adoption of the materialistic techniques of mass enterprise. Church groups open their own banking business. They make loans to weak and creditless churches at high interest rates, since they are using borrowed funds. Because of the risk they extract a principal gift of an additional five per cent to avoid the charge of usury. Here the methods best known to secondhand automobile dealers, small loan companies, and pawn shops are transferred, blessed, and appropriated for use at high levels of church operation. The result is a resolution of the saved-secular conflict which issues from the wrong end of the corridor. The secular was supposed to go home with saved folk to get saved, not vice versa.

Enough, lest I seem to lose my mildness and fall into bitterness. The subject is materialism in its religious moments. At least we did not mean to be materialists and have kept our idealistic slogans. Besides, some catastrophe or another will surely come along to save us from the total worship of Mammon, history being what it is and all that. Meanwhile, there is a bright young man here who gives great promise of being able to coin bright new slogans for our stewardship campaigns. Have we an opening for him?

The young Cicero, it is said, learned by heart at school the Twelve Tables of the Roman Law. If, as T. R. Glover says, "the first things you learn may shape your mind forever . . ." then: "Consider this Roman education; no Greek drama; no Greek philosophy; no Greek art; (or very little), hardly any books; no science, no mathematics; next to nothing to train the imagination but Law, Law, Law—whenever a Roman thought seriously he must think along legal lines!" [14]

The young man we will take for our slogan maker—consider his education. In the spirit of that frontierism—televised and real, that industrialism, that scientism, and that religion he will have had next to nothing to shape his views of reality except matter, matter, matter—whenever he thinks and coins his slogans he must think along material lines.

[14] *The Ancient World* (Baltimore, Md.: Penguin Books, Inc., 1945), p. 198.

Limitations of Materialism

Materialism is a cosmology, a world view, a way of looking at reality. There are other cosmologies, other ways of considering the real. According to Whitehead, "the various human interests which suggest cosmologies are science, aesthetics, ethics, and religion. In every age each of these topics suggests a view of the world." [1] Perhaps the prejudgments of materialism will appear best against some insights from other possible world views.

In Science and Aesthetics

The continuation of materialistic philosophy and its proliferant development in the modern era, including its creation of its own ethic and moral philosophy, would have been impossible without the four-hundred-year rise of modern science. The concerns, the techniques, and the field of operation for modern science have had an irresistible attraction for materialistic thought. So powerful has been the attraction of science for materialistic philosophy that there has appeared no stronger apparent

[1] Op. cit., p. viii.

affinity in modern form than the relationship of materialism and science. Materialism as a metaphysic, however, is patently less than science as a world view. "Materialist philosophy has been attracted to physical science, not because of any natural affinity between the two, but because [materialists] have seen in it [science] the best buttress to naturalism and an anti-clerical moral philosophy." [2] That is to say, materialistic philosophy has used the scientific enterprise as the best bed within which the naturalistic moral philosophy of materialism could be arrived at. Materialism has wished to do more than define reality. It wishes to prescribe an ethic as well. It has assumed the prejudiced position of resentment of supernaturalism and religious abstractions. In fleeing both, by the route of reductionism, materialism has run headlong into the error Whitehead has called "the fallacy of misplaced concreteness." Materialism, in its reduction of terms, has thought to rid us of our unsanitary metaphysical notions, but the child still comes to some sort of manhood with all his transcendental longings incorrigibly active.

Materialism cannot offer a wholistic and clear-cut theory of the universe by refusing, as it does, to take into account other possible means of arriving at a world view. Any means which assumes the status of an end is of itself prejudiced by its innate limitations. Materialism simply cannot see all that is there before it, much less explain the whole. The concerns of science are larger than materialism permits or can explain. Science has its problems, and they are not all a matter of mere matter. Ideas worry her too. Against the backdrop of the scientific inquiry materialism is seen to be limited, partial, a reductionism, and a means of sustaining a previously arrived at value system in terms of its own moral philosophy. This may explain in part the bitterness with which materialists have rejected the claims of all idealism.

I cannot discover that materialism knows anything about or has anything to say to any of the theories of the experience of beauty. If so, it would doubtless be a quote from positivism to the effect that a question which has no measurable answer is not a valid question; hence materialism has no questions to ask about beauty.

Any view of life is prejudiced by its rejection of power which appears outside itself. Materialism would reject the aesthetic power, color and

[2] John H. Randall and Justus Buchler, *Philosophy: An Introduction* (New York: Barnes & Noble, Inc., 1942), p. 182.

45

movement which are ultramaterial in other spheres than those served by its own laboratory, pragmatic, scale-of-weight techniques. Materialism has no understanding of that kind of beauty and power being generated, for example, in the Mexican, Negroid, and Asiatic cultures.[3] Empirical science has been characterized as indifferent to goodness and beauty—that is, to ethics and aesthetics—which renders it amoral, even cynical. It follows that science "has thus become an instrumentality ready to serve any master, God or Mammon, and any purpose, whether socially beneficial or disastrous, constructive or destructive."[4] If, as Pitirim Sorokin believes, science has no proper moral content, certainly that matter with which science is concerned can have no appreciation of beauty, contrast, color, and movement, all of which rise out of concern with and involvement within culture. Hence, that materialism which is an attempt to construct a view of reality out of the stuff with which science deals can have even less to do with any of these. Its only notions of beauty are based on size.

Canon B. H. Streeter asked whether quality as well as quantity is not of the essence of reality.[5] Sorokin has insisted that quality does belong and then goes on to describe that "disease of colossality" which afflicts a materialistic culture when it cannot rely on its quality. Such a culture must always resort to a quantitative appeal. Sorokin claimed this to be our problem in America:

We construct the tallest buildings, and boast that they are the best precisely because they are the biggest. We maintain huge choruses and orchestras—the bigger the better. A book sold en masse is regarded as a masterpiece; a play enjoying the longest run is accepted as the best. Our motion pictures are conceived on a vast scale. . . . The same is true of our sculptures and monuments, our World's Fairs and Radio Cities. The bulk of our daily newspaper often exceeds the life output of many an eminent thinker. A person enjoying the biggest income, a college with the largest enrollment, a crooner or radio artist with the biggest public, . . . a preacher or professor having the largest audience, a research project entailing the largest cost . . . becomes for this very reason the greatest or best. . . . We brag

[3] See F. S. C. Northrop, *The Meeting of East and West* (New York: The Macmillan Company, 1952).
[4] Pitirim Sorokin, *The Crisis of Our Age* (New York: E. P. Dutton & Company, 1941), pp. 124-25. Used by permission.
[5] *Reality* (London: Macmillan and Company, 1929), p. xi.

of . . . the largest number of books published or pictures produced; the largest number of museums, churches, plays. . . . This, again, is the reason for our pride in mass art education, musical education, and adult education.[6]

This gauging of the aesthetic by the material and the statistical is but a variant, said Sorokin, of the famous boast, "England has only two universities, France has four; but in Ohio alone we have thirty-seven colleges." [7]

All of this is simply to say that the stuff of the aesthetic and the stuff of the material are in different realms. The stuff of the material exists only as raw matter for the use of those in the realm of the aesthetic. While it is quite true that beauty may reside in the eyes of the beholder the only function of the material seems to be to provide something for the hand of the beholder to use.

Materialism simply does not tell the whole story. This is why materialism can fairly be called "an over simplification of half truths." This is why the charge can be made that materialism is inconsistent in that it covertly makes law a third category to go alongside matter and motion. It values simplicity of explanation above adequacy of explanation, and hence its reductionist techniques; it is partial; it is guilty of the reductive fallacy because it simply will not see that though the physical must always be the base, the physical cannot itself exhaust reality. This is why it seems so very artificial for materialism to try to use language that refers to ethical situations. Materialism ought, if consistent, to deny value situations altogether, but it does not. The result is a kind of ethicoreligious cosmology of materialism. This is an illegitimacy, and to it we must come.

Materialism denies many things that are fundamental to many. It is an arrived-at hypothesis which is carrying the burden of a superstructure of attitudes toward the values of religion, institutions, and other world views which was built before the basement was dug. It is a design to seem to produce certain limitations of reality that were arrived at out of reaction to already existing beauty and value. This is partly demonstrated in the fact that materialism itself now produces an epistemology, ethic, and aesthetic. While claiming to desire only immediate facts of

[6] Sorokin, op cit., pp. 70-71.
[7] Ibid.

experience it has to endow matter with self-consciousness in order to get its facts of experience properly noted by self-conscious observers. It cannot properly account for the existence of the observer. Canon Streeter archly inquired about this human-matter-observer—this epiphe-nomenon—this functionless shadow with the curious "impotency" of thinking, knowing, self-consciousness.[8] It is odd, said he, that the universe of Automaton should give birth to little automata alive enough to know that they are but an illusion! If theism is anthropomorphism, materialism is mechanomorphism. It requires an attempt to fashion the infinite in the image of a machine, and the construct is valid. Is the universe one gigantic accident consequent upon an infinite succession of happy flukes?[9] Materialism is a mode of thinking necessary to an arrived-at view of ethical and religious systems. Its covers are too short for the bed. It is not a mode of being, for the new concept of matter—mass as energy—gives materialism trouble. It now has no place to focus. If, as Bertrand Russell said, electrons and protons are "logical fictions," then the *humana* at least must stand for an element in reality that can compose theories about electrons and protons.[10]

Perhaps Arthur S. Eddington is right in calling the division between the material and the spiritual superficial.[11] Perhaps the cleavage is better described as lying between the metrical and the nonmetrical. This makes room for two fundamental constructs which seem necessary to our in-vestigation of reality: science and religion. Science gives an approxima-tion of ultimate reality; religion has a picture to suggest, too. In the autobiography of Robert A. Milliken this is succinctly put: "human well-being and all human progress rest at bottom upon two pillars, the collapse of which will bring down the whole structure . . . the *spirit* of religion (faith), and the *spirit* of science (knowledge)."

It is in facing the apparent necessity for making some sort of judg-ment about the validity of religious claims that materialism denies itself by constructing a set of ethical-religious world views of its own. These world views are previously arrived at, with the base of metaphysi-cal materialism inserted later to support the views of ethics and religion

[8] *Op. cit.*, p. 7.
[9] *Ibid.*, p. 10.
[10] *What I Believe* (London: Frederick Muller, Ltd., 1937), p. 17.
[11] "The Domain of Physical Science," *Science, Religion, and Reality*, ed. Joseph Need-ham (New York: George Braziller, Inc., 1955), pp. 189-218.

that were arrived at on the basis of a misunderstanding of science and an emotional rejection of the truly bad in religious and ethical systems. Materialism seems to be the only possible base for the views of value and communion that men who are materialists seem determined to hold. Interestingly enough, they seem emotionally, prejudicially determined to hold them, for few, if any, know much about current theological and ethical positions, preferring to react as if all religious thought were accomplished before Copernicus.[12] Meantime, look at the ethicoreligious views of materialism. They offer prime evidence of being emotional ways of prejudiced thinking, a reaction to the demand for certainty in scientism, and they demonstrate again that the base of all culture is religious, for even materialism has to provide a theology.

As Ethical and Religious World View

Here one can take his choice of three world views, although that choice has likely been determined for the materialist by a chemical condition in the liver and lights of this human epiphenomenon which chooses. "The stars, she whispers, blindly run," and so do the molecules of the human body; therefore no real choice remains. One simply has to accept that frame of mind imposed on him by his glands.

Negative Naturalism

If a man is lean and spare, cold-headed, and a good calculator, if he is inclined to be precise, logical, unemotional, and clear, he will be a *negative naturalist, a pessimistic positivist:*

Man is an accident in a world that is foreign to him; he is abortively, purposelessly produced by processes over which he has no capacity to be responsible. He is a victim destined universally for suffering and death. His only power over these is a farce—for he can only dope one and embalm the other after he has postponed the inevitable as long as he can by the counteraction of chemicals. Meanwhile, be a man! Be brave! Sursum corda! Chaos is king! Join the fellowship of the en-

---

[12] See an illustration of this in Bernard Meland's editorial correspondence in *The Christian Century*. Meland comments on Julian Huxley's statement at Chicago that "religions are destined to disappear." This is a naïveté and an isolationism, says Meland, and rests on Huxley's position of thirty years ago, and on his ignorance of philosophical-theological thought of the last twenty-five years. *The Christian Century* (December 9, 1959), LXXVI, No. 49, 1429 ff.

lightened who expect nothing of life that is not already happening in the chemicomechanical concatenation of molecules which has organized itself to house one's own existence.

Positive Humanism

If a man is inclined to be expansive and generous, if his chemical make-up has shaped an individual who is co-operative, social, healthy, good-humored, a poet, and a good fellow, he will be numbered among the *happy humanists, the positive positivists:*

"Every day, in every way" he is devoted to progress. Man is his own master, his own only hope, and there is more in the old boy yet to come out of the processes of evolution. The sun has just begun to rise, and given another day or two in our laboratory shrines, we will build our own *paradisio;* meanwhile those of us who form the fertilizer for the glory to come may rejoice in our day by anticipation. For via democratic individualism, collectivistic autocracy, or some improvement in social-ism which gets rid of greed, we are going to evolve into something the most bombastic hedonism finds hard to describe. This religion is very ignorant about history, but is a great believer in miracles.

Optimistic Secularism: A Folk Religion

Finally, for the uninitiate, the unenlightened masses who happen to be "on stage"; for all modern men of good gland and high spirit; for culture, progress, and peace and men who are devoted to the same and will join a hundred secular churches, lodges, and clubs to prove it; there is the only real rival our culture has produced to challenge the Christian faith. Growing out of happy humanism, materialism offers a way of life, a mode of thought, which has developed a full-blown religious con-struction. It is undoubtedly the most powerful single factor in American culture. It is a *Volkeskirche of egoistic hedonism;* it is our truly estab-lished church—the American state church—optimistic secularism—practical materialism.

This state religion organizes, ordains, and sends missionaries to Europe. It is a cult, a philosophy, a theology, and an ethic. It has shrines, a trinity, an eschatology, and bishops. It sports cathedrals, liturgy, vest-ments, and has *curiae* to judge orthodoxy—and more, it even has a local hell in most communities to which it consigns the unrepentant and

50

unco-operative prophets like Thorstein Veblen and country preachers who see its egoistic and hedonistic base. The great American faith begins in an ethical frame—hedonism.

Its ethic is fairly represented in the quest for happiness. The Horatio Alger novel of the early twentieth century was its *Pilgrim's Progress*. Its hero is the lad who once picked cotton and now owns the mill. Success is always worthy, but in the absence of genuine success any simulated success which can be appropriated by means of multiple tail-lights, swelled fenders, split-level suburban housing, club membership, public service and a foreign-made "second" car is an acceptable substitute. Its fundamental values are power, influence, and publicity which will come automatically to men of industry, moderate sobriety, and thrift. Any violation of industry, sobriety, and shrewdness may produce failure such as that represented by a lady wearing an $1,800 fur piece, and living in a $50,000 house, who confesses to her neighbor that because her husband is neither industrious, sober, nor shrewd she simply does not know where she will find the money for hamburger meat to serve at dinner, and her unpaid maid has quit besides!

Underlying the ethical values of practical materialism is a metaphysic. Only to the real high priest, the blood and thunder, hardheaded go-getter who dominates the economic life of a section, is this the metaphysic of materialism. To all others, to the lesser clergy, the deacons, acolytes, ushers, and pew-holders, the metaphysic is idealism. The hymns, prayers, and sermons, the slogans, campaign watchwords, and goals are all idealisms. Only to the truly initiate is the real metaphysic apparent. The masses sing a mass with words like "togetherness," "personality," "universal education," "family life," "the new look," "irresistible you," and "true love." Add the slogans of material security offered by all venders of schemes and policies: "a happy old age," "life begins at fifty-five," "live on easy street from forty," and the material basis of existence shows through more clearly.

As to the aesthetics of practical materialism there can be little deception, for our sense of beauty is plainly preoccupied with mass. From mammary glands to sales of recorded music, from book publishing to sculpture the preoccupation with mass affects our judgment of beauty. While function, form, and silhouette have place in the canons of taste,

51

these reflect levels of sophistication in judgment rather than relief from the materialistic base of aesthetics.

Worship in this cult is no better. There is a holy trinity of scientism, meliorism, and imperialistic economic nationalism. Under the great arching love of Father Progress, the Messiah is a better way, and the Holy Spirit is the scientific method. The theology which produces all this is a hyphenated and distorted naturalistic evolution, based on Laplace, Lyell, Darwin, Spencer, and Huxley. Inverted almost totally from its valid base in biology, this developmentism, this progressiveness, this evolution upward, is used to account for everything. Competition between cobblers is "the struggle for existence." New business forms emerge by "natural selection." Success is the "survival of the fittest," and World War I was nature clearing the earth of its inferior models.

Nature failed us here. The best did not necessarily survive. The sons of British nobility, the French poilu, and the American backwoodsmen died in the same trenches. While, unexplainedly, more than 700,000,000 racially, biologically, and culturally inferior persons did survive. With all their hungers, desires, and ambitions for living well; with all their "transcendental longings incorrigibly active"; nearly a billion survived nature's clearing actions of war, pestilence, and famine. Now new threats, new empires, new status seekers, new hunger marches, press on new power associations, and modern materialism has no salvation to give us except that process of restacking the piles of material in a form more favorable to the classic "have-nots" of the world.

Add to this the eschatology of practical materialism: the dread of the new physics. The threat of "the bomb"—and with our faith in unpolluted water stored in cellar hideouts, canned corn beef, portable radios, and army blankets piled in damp cubbyholes underground, the only way we have to go is up.

This we can do—just as soon as we can orbit a man in space materialism can offer a newer hope. More worlds to conquer have appeared, and the great political agonies of hungry earth men can be diverted and subsumed under the new struggle to decide who owns the moon.

"This tragic round. How dreary to be alive, gentlemen," says MacNeile Dixon, if there is no higher ground, no new position; if, left to our own devices, we can devise no better base than the transfer of our earth agonies to the planetary system, hoping with the acquisition of new frontiers and unlimited real estate to resolve old tensions. This tragic round will have only a larger arena in which to express itself, and who can write that history, once we begin our struggle for survival on a hundred foreign spheres at once.

Practical materialism has no salvation to give us. General Douglas MacArthur, therefore, buried it from the deck of the mighty Missouri in Tokyo Bay. There has been no grander rival to Pericles in modern oratory except Winston Churchill at Dover, or at Fulton, Missouri, but the funeral did not quite come off. Practical materialism survives—and prospers.

The remilitarization of Japan—her vow of peace scuttled in the face of economic threat; the whirling dervish seeking of the 52 per cent of earth's people who live between Karachi, Tokyo, and Colombo; the new aches of Africa and Asia; and the threat to American industry that the maintenance of a hundred thousand unneeded men poses to the steel companies alone—these are apparent in the new technology, this tragic round!

Meanwhile, the most fantastic economic race the world has ever known will divert us. In the Ruhr Valley, the Ohio Valley, and the new might which now emerges from Russia's valleys of Don, Danube, and Volga—in this throbbing, pulsing race for markets and its balm for needy peoples, in its promise of raising the life and living of the world there is hope, but it is a material hope, and is therefore another tragic round. The central problem is still death—and ultimate reality—and our own estrangement from it.

Is there no high ground? Is there no new position? Where can a man go to find a larger provincialism, or a lesser prejudice, or a grander view than that tragic repetitive cycle of prejudiced materialism?

Chapter III

Christian Realism—Via Nova

When materialism preaches (strange anomaly that a sect so satisfied should care for converts) she really preaches:

The Burden of Dumah: down with idealism! All that is not materialism is idealism and is therefore bad. Wash you, make you clean! Put away the evils of your ideals from before mine eyes! Join the intelligentsia and save the world up to the point where the sun refuses to shine or else gets so hot that we might have to move to another planet.

It is by way of damning idealism that the materialist preacher claims that "no thinker can take a position between idealism and materialism."[1] Materialism is to science as idealism is to religion. There are only two streams of philosophical thought; there is no philosophical idea that will not be included in one of these. Idealism and materialism contain all the philosophy in the world; any thinker is one or the other. Both of these systems wish to change things—which evangelistic desire is a

[1] Seely, op. cit., p. 1.

terrible contradiction for materialism—and there is no middle ground, we hear. I will discuss idealism and materialism, he says here, without any reference to ethic, or to what should be.[2]

What if old Lotze was right when he claimed that the ground of metaphysic is ethic?[3] Is there no higher ground than idealism or materialism? Is there no newer position?

Reality and Relation: Total Event

There is another tradition. There is a larger whole to be viewed than the materialist reduction can allow. There is a less prejudiced way of looking for reality than the predetermined refusal to look at anything but matter. There is a view of reality that includes the viewer. As old as philosophy[4] in some senses, it has come into its own only in the twentieth century,[5] but first found its place in reformed theology in America in the eighteenth century.[6]

That Christian theology which has its base in realism has learned that there are many matters, including death, about which we have to be bluntly biological. Because we live in a world of matter and change we cannot moralize, ignore, or make small the problems of disease, decline, destiny, pain, evil, and the threat of nothingness. One cannot, as Neoplatonists seem to do, live as if evil and its power structures do not face us as real matters to be dealt with. Therefore, the Christian realist wishes to do his thinking and his acting in the light of a situation the elements of which he sees. He aims to come to terms with the universe.[7] These matters and this matter we face are real, both in terms of thing in itself and in terms of value judgments which involve persons. "The

[2] Loc. cit.

[3] Metaphysic.

[4] See J. Donald Butler, Four Philosophies and Their Practice in Education and Religion (New York: Harper & Brothers, 1951), pp. 275-392. In a discussion of realism in religion and education Butler finds it necessary to include Aristotle, Aquinas, Descartes, Spinoza, Locke, Kant, and William James in his list of classic philosophers who have "realistic" elements.

[5] C. E. M. Joad, John Macmurray, A. N. Whitehead, Bertrand Russell, G. E. Moore, Santayana, Lloyd Morgan, Samuel G. Alexander, C. D. Broad, and the "six" neorealists Holt, Marvin, Montague, Ralph Barton Perry, Pitkin, Edward G. Spaulding, along with James B. Pratt and John Wild all hold various positions in the varied general field of modern realism. See also Titus, op. cit., pp. 291-310.

[6] John Witherspoon, with him as president in the 1760's, brought to Princeton the so-called common-sense realism of Thomas Reid (d. 1796).

[7] Husserl, Lebenswelt; not just being-in-a-world, but "being in a world that is." This represents an advance over the shadow world of existentialism, said Rudolf Allers, "The Subjective and the Objective," The Review of Metaphysics, XII, No. 4, 48, 520.

thing is real and the idea is the true or false appearance of the thing." [8] We know better than to pretend this to be a new problem, however. We know its ancient lineage and medieval prominence.[9] Since Occam we have had to be conscious of reality in terms of sense impressions. This was the opening of a "modern way." To the theologian realist, these sense impressions indicate a valid picture of a desperate state. We know our contradictions, our plight, our situation, and we know further that our reality is not made by us. We have discovered it and have discovered ourselves to be within it, not outside it.

The vital aspect of realism for the theologian is that it speaks of the vitality and importance of relation within the reality experienced. We find ourselves in a situation we judge to be real, but we also find ourselves capable of originating and responding to relations beyond ourselves. This is the *sine qua non* of our philosophical base. No relation, no reality; no relation—then we are solipsists, and this is impossible, absurd.

This is why modern realists like John Wild appeal to us.[10] This explains the grand renaissance of realism in reformed thought, especially in Reinhold Niebuhr, from whom we have learned. He makes us look at "the situation," and in our knowledge of "relations" open to us we can afford the view, the desperate view. We like the flatness of Edward Spaulding's "the universe is what it is, no matter what men may think about it." [11] It sounds a little like our compeer Paul Scherer claiming that God is God no matter where our silly lives leave him.

The Christian realist likes what he understands of A. N. Whitehead's organismic event. He helps clear out the worst of our idealistic carry-over by showing how disfranchised from reality we are if we mistreat nature:

[8] John Macmurray, The Philosophy of Communism (London: Faber and Faber, Ltd., 1933), pp. 21 ff.

[9] Frederick H. Ginascol, "The Question of Universals and the Problem of Faith and Reason," Philosophical Quarterly (The University of Fife, Scotland). A clear modern treatment of this medieval realism is Ginascol, Mediaeval Origins of Modern Philosophy and Science (Doctoral dissertation, University of Texas, 1952), pp. 278 ff. See Etienne Gilson, History of Christian Philosophy in the Middle Ages (New York: Random House, 1955); and L'esprit de le philosophie Mediaeval (2nd ed., 2 vols.; Paris, 1944); and his more recent work on Duns Scotus (1952). See also Barry, "Christian Philosophy of the Middle Ages," The Journal of the History of Ideas, XX, I (January, 1959), p. 105.

[10] See Introduction to Realistic Philosophy (New York: Harper & Brothers, 1948).

[11] Philosophical Realism.

The philosophic idealism which finds the ultimate meaning of reality in mentality that is fully cognitive . . . has been too much divorced from the scientific outlook. . . . It has swallowed the scientific scheme in its entirety as being the only rendering of the facts of nature, and has then explained it as being an idea in the ultimate mentality. . . . These idealistic schools have conspicuously failed to connect, in any organic fashion, the facts of nature with their idealistic philosophies.[12]

No realist can endure disassociation from that nature wherein his own events transpire. So Whitehead helps us by calling for "a further stage of provisional realism in which the scientific scheme is recast, and founded upon the ultimate concept of organism." [13]

For "it appears . . . that we are *within* a world of colours, sounds, and other sense-objects. . . . We seem to be ourselves elements of this world in the same sense as other things which we perceive," [14] and therefore subjectivism in any form is to be distrusted since the contrary view of nature and ourselves would deny not only the organismic event, but also our naïve experience.

Recognizing that a clash of ideologies is no disaster but an opportunity,[15] Whitehead disposes of old foundations of scientific thought as "unintelligible," and asks, "what is the sense of talking about a mechanical explanation when you do not know what you mean by mechanics?" [16] He demonstrates the potent prejudices of materialists in the charge that they arrived at their unlimited powers of explanation by ignoring everything which refused to come into line.[17] Then, after dealing for realists with both idealism and materialism, he recalls ontological judgments as part of the total event in that they are at least motives for the scientific venture: "Without judgments of value there would have been no science," [18] which prepares us to attempt to state his doctrine of total organismic event on which base his realism rests.

[12] Whitehead, op. cit., p. 64.
[13] Ibid.
[14] Ibid., p. 90.
[15] Ibid., p. 185.
[16] Ibid., p. 18.
[17] Ibid., p. 103.
[18] Ibid., p. 153.

The cognitive subject and the object of his cognition are in a common world on common terms. The "things" seen by the seeing subject are actual objects in a world which is a complex of things. That world transcends but includes our acts of cognition. The things experienced are distinguishable from our knowing. This brings a facing of event as the ultimate unit of natural occurrence. An event has to do with all that there is and in particular with all other events. This interaction with other events is absolutely basic to the doctrine of relation necessary to realism. The word "event" means "a spatio-temporal unity," but the "total-event" discloses "a prehensive unification of model presences of entities beyond itself," which says, too, that the "itself" is included. Total event includes observer-in-event-in-relation, and this materialism cannot allow. Further, while molecules may blindly run—in accordance with general laws—they differ in intrinsic character according to the general organic plans or patterns where they are. Things endure, retain shape, reiterate themselves, have a history and a future—all in a complex of relation including the observer, and realism cannot do without this relation. By this concept of total, organismic, relational events we are convinced that we are within and a part of reality. Which is to say, with Paul, we do not shadowbox. The realist lives with reality. He is in a real situation, involving real contradictions for real values.

There are others than Whitehead from whom the groping realist has learned. Though we are not consistent in what we take from Bergson, for we know his *elan vital* to be something of a compromise with idealism, and are closer to receiving the full impact of the physicochemical constitution of life than we wish to be—we still hope there is this vitalism, separate, *sui generis*, a seed at least of spirit to make a soul,[19] resident in protoplasm, for we still need very much the concept "spirit" in our dealings with life as it is. On the whole, we have profited more from Bergson's creative evolution and its "becoming-ness." This provides a magnificent tour de force when our younger ones quiz us on the earlier chapters of Genesis and allows us to be proper evolutionists and quote Shaw to the effect that properly understood Genesis is sublimely true. Yet Bergson's "becoming God" is something of a trial to us and we suspect him of having cut a back door to the deification of man

[19] See Edmund W. Sinnott, *The Biology of the Spirit* (New York: The Viking Press, 1957).

through a reverse humanism that will cut that great God down to size when it can no longer conceive of him as absolute. Even this kind of relativism has its moments of appeal.

All in all, one has his friends and cousins in the general field of Christian realism; the point being that there is another tradition than either materialism or idealism.

The "true humanism" of Jacques Maritain, with his clear, prophetic claim for an integral and transcendent, even heroic humanism;[20] the grasp of evil, historically and actually, as "gradational evil" which one finds in Radoslav Tsanoff;[21] the new symbolism of Susanne Langer,[22] the Gifford Lectures of Edwyn Bevan,[23] and the Roman Catholic philosopher Gustave Weigel[24] have opened up new vistas of the meaning residing behind the old forms.

On the other hand, the "operational" philosophy of Rapoport,[25] like William James's pragmatism, assumes the presence of intelligence somewhere within or behind matter and therefore insists that things ought to work. While Nietzsche, drawing strength and nourishment not from naturalism or humanism, someone said, but from his opponent, Jesus Christ, has pressed his prophetic consciousness and his value on values into the complex of our search for allies who understand the reality of our relations within a universe that is.

MacNeile Dixon, the prose poet laureate of realism, has been meat day and night for Christian realists: "Holiness is a strong perfume, and a little of it goes a long way in the world: I have never been very clear whether it was compatible with laughter, and I should be very loath to bid an eternal farewell to laughter—how gay and gallant, how amusing so many of the rascals." He has more: the mighty opposites, the ancestral estate, the one and the many—he knows the agonies of the moral realist, and with him one can live.[26]

[20] *True Humanism* (London: Centenary Press, 1938).

[21] *The Nature of Evil* (New York: The Macmillan Company, 1931).

[22] *Philosophy in a New Key* (Cambridge, Mass.: Harvard University Press, 1942).

[23] *Symbolism and Belief* (Boston: Beacon Press, 1957).

[24] "Myth, Symbol, and Analogy," *Religion and Culture: Essays in Honor of Paul Tillich*, ed. Walter Leibrecht (New York: Harper & Brothers, 1959).

[25] *Operational Philosophy* (New York: Harper & Brothers, 1957).

[26] *The Human Situation* (Gifford Lectures, 1935-37, New York: Longmans, Green and Company), p. 14.

The Courage to Be Extra-Rational

Miquel de Unamuno, the Basque, the essence of the Spanish heroic soul, romantic, flamboyant, word stretcher, and quixotic saint, is above all a realist! One can live with him, too; for it is in that real abyss between reason which is skeptical and sterile and faith which is antirational and uncommunicable that Unamuno begins, and he cannot cool down.[27] All stops are always open on his organ. He is the realist par excellence in that he understands that where the tears flow inward the blackness melts.[28] He is the realist with the courage required to be extra-rational; the realist who can put Kant and Luther in the same bed because they belong there, for both abominate Aristotle and reconstruct God; the man who knows faith to be *salto inmortal*, the leap of death that is not death; the romantic-colored realist who suffers from God-ache; the poet-realist who learns that in the presence of the nonrational the rational is impertinent and an upstart; the weeper Unamuno, who knows his weeping is a common weeping;[29] the realist who relates himself to Marcus Aurelius, Augustine, Pascal, Rousseau, Thomson ("City of Dreadful Night"), Leopardi, and Kierkegaard[30]—whom he "discovered" when he learned Danish to read Ibsen. Reason he makes the creature of love, but he knows reason to be a matricide. Therefore, he throws himself in the teeth of reason on the wings of his urge to live and resolves to live such a life of ethical concern that if he is not immortal a great injustice has been done. "If it is nothingness that awaits us, let us make an injustice of it; let us fight against destiny, even though without hope of victory."[31] In coming to this, Unamuno had already nailed to his personal masthead his loved quotation from Senancour's *Obermann:* "Man is perishable. That may be so; but let us perish resisting, and, if it is nothingness that awaits us, do not let us so act that it will be a just fate."[32]

By now it must be obvious that in the transition from philosophical

[27] Salvador de Madariaga, Introductory Essay to Unamuno's *Tragic Sense of Life* (New York: Dover Publications, 1954).

[28] Unamuno, *Niebla.*

[29] *Del Sentimiento Tragico de la Vida*, trans. J. E. Crawford Flitch, *The Tragic Sense of Life* (New York: Dover Publications, 1954), p. 17 *et passim.*

[30] *Ibid.*, p. 18.

[31] *Ibid.*, p. 268.

[32] Letter 90; L'homme est Perissable. Il se pent; mais perissons en resistant, et, si le meant nous reserve, ne faisons pas que ce soit uni justice.

questions to theological assumptions one can lose every shred of realism as a philosophical discipline and may simply include his own cell mates because he loves them. Not so! These men are realists, all of them, for they have this informing principle: they are fascinated by, attracted to, horrified with, life as they know it, and this is the essence of neorealism: *to include the seeker with the object of his quest in this human situation as real.*

Therefore does one spend his nights with Nikolai Berdyaev, and his cousins, Dostoevski, Gogol, Pushkin, the Basils and the Gregorys. This is why one fills a long shelf with Sören Kierkegaard; is grasped by Karl Jaspers' incredible sense of time and is nailed down by Martin Heidigger's being *there.*[33] This is why one reads Sartre and prays for Albert Camus.[34] These men are involved, caught, seized by this human situation, and this is another tradition than that which has produced the set of values and cultures seen in twentieth-century America. If in this interlude he should also reach for an hour with his veteran, warring idealist, W. E. Hocking, or his concept-stripping flagellant, Bertrand Russell, who is to know he has defected? There is another tradition.

Meantime, in one's less agonizing moments of awareness he is grateful for that beautiful Kantian categorical imperative about the sanctity of persons which he finds at the heart of Brightman's personalism, and he is glad that Knudson knew this. In the interludes between his philosophical-theological questing and his ethicial demands for action, he is grateful that at the edge of his own warfare with metaphysical provincialisms there broke like a clap of thunder the recovery of a new and convinced biblical theology.

A Convinced Theology: Incarnational Realism

Since that break-through of a convinced incarnational realism he has reached most frequently of all for his paterfamilias, grand William Temple.

Here, in *Nature, Man and God,* the serene, sacramental sanctity of a thinking and giant saint steals over him, and he revels in a grove of trees, rests, worships, and tries to submit himself to that "commonwealth of value," which Temple knows to be the fellowship of the

[33] *Da-Sein.*
[34] Whose fascinating, hopeful development was cut off as this was written.

saints. It began in Martin Buber's *I and Thou;* it formed a word in Emil Brunner's *Divine-Human Encounter* and demanded a response. Its big chimes boomed in many a horologue with Karl Barth's *Das Wort Gottes,* and then, in the order of encounter, Anders Nygren, Gustaf Aulèn, Baron von Hugel, Reinhold Niebuhr, Richard Niebuhr, Robert Calhoun, P. T. Forsyth, Frederick Denison Maurice, Oscar Cullmann, Paul Tillich, John Baillie, H. R. Mackintosh, Rudolf Otto, Ernst Troeltsch, Adolf Harnack, Reinhold Seeburg, and so to the masters— blessed Luther, gaunt Calvin, and the Augustine we did not know— and Paul. There is another tradition.

Is there a high ground between the provincialisms of materialism and idealism? I think so, but I honestly do not know whether it is just another eclecticism or a new ground of twentieth-century realism, and I do not know what to call it, or myself. I know my debt to those with whom I share it and from whom I got it and it has given me grace and patience to seek release from whatever new perversion and partial grasp of reality it has imposed. It has a base in realism for it begins with observer-in-event-in-relation in this place and in this time between future and past. It takes at least its verbs from Augustine's insight into the place of the mind of the observer-in-event:

> But how comes that future, which as yet is not, to be diminished or wasted away? Or how comes that past, which now is no longer, to be increased? Unless in the mind which acteth all this, there be three things done. *For it expects, it marks attentively, it remembers* (nam et expectat et adtendit et meminit).[35]

1.

nam et expectat

New horizons have broken and are breaking and will break upon the observer in a universe which latecomer humans have but begun to understand, and in the face of this kind of world any closed system is fatal to new knowledge or the advance of any understanding and is therefore a desperate shortsightedness. Christian realism *expects.*

[35] St. Augustine's *Confessions,* Liber XI, ch. xxviii.

2.

et meminit

Out of the memory of the past truth has already been given, or acquired, which men must live by to live for any good at all, and to close the doors on memory of truth is as fatal an error as the rejection of new horizons. *Christian realism remembers.*

3.

et adtendit

That that is to come and that which has come, in expectation and memory, comes alive and remains alive in the experience of this present moment, the moment which has potential for incarnation, the moment for truth, marked attentively in experience (*adtendit*); and in this moment living past and coming truth meet to provide that moving ground of the present existence upon which observer lives in event in relation and from which he seeks by way of expectation and memory the ultimate in experience, communion, understanding, beatitude. *Christian realism attends the present moment.*

These statements involve as much of idealism as is necessary for truth to come from beyond us; as much of idealism as may be necessary to a proper regard for personalism; as much of personalism as is necessary to a valid definition of persons, a vital ethic, and an inclusive metaphysic; which means matter can not be ignored. There is, therefore, involved the awareness of our dependence upon matter to such an extent that no thought can ignore matter, or escape matter, for long—for we have this treasure in earthy and earthen vessels—the ground of incarnation. This means we need as much of pragmatism as is necessary to goad us out of mere superstition, enough of reason to deny all religion except the best, and this realism permits us to live where we are in relation. To live in this present, remembering and expecting, implies as much of existentialism as is necessary to require one to be where he is involvedly, and enough of modern realism to allow "the mind which acteth all this" to be participant in that manifestation of future and past in this present matter and time which is the continuing matrix for incarnation.

This constitutes the ground of my understanding of our present situation. The metaphysic of Christian realism seems to provide the breadth

63

of field within which both idealism and materialism can be questioned as provincial, partial views of reality. The key to an answer is theological realism. But if so, is this just a more inclusive prejudice than idealism or materialism? Or does the prospect that incarnation is reality and that the understanding of Christian incarnation can resolve the contradiction in these imposing and ancient metaphysical systems have no validity? I think this incarnational realism valid. The answer lies in that invasion of matter by the Spirit that makes all matter come alive. This is why someone must deal with that continuing and present Christian event in terms of creation and incarnation.

Part Two

PROVINCIALISM

prejudgment of community

Marius is the horizon-hungry juvenile lead in the Broadway play, *Fanny*. He is defensively accusing as he speaks to his father, old Cesar, barkeep on fisherman's wharf: "You think Marseilles is the center of the earth!" "It is," cries Cesar. "That is north, this is south; that east, this west, I am *here*, the *center!*" "But there are others!" shouts Marius. "*They are off-center*," and Cesar turns, triumphant. This, I think, is provincialism.

A distinction must be made between provincialism and patriotism. One cannot wish for himself another native land, not often. The distinction to be made is simply that distinction that maintains between prejudice and loyalty. Provincialism is to patriotism as prejudice is to loyalty; or, provincialism is to any real and personal community as prejudice is to conviction and high purpose.

Patriotism is of different stuff from provincialism. When Winston Churchill said in the Canadian Parliament, "Look at the Londoners, the Cockneys, look at what they have stood up to! Grim and gay with their

65

cry, 'we can take it.' " [1] Or, "I have seen the King, gay, buoyant, confident, when the stones of Buckingham palace lay newly scattered on its lawns"; [2] or, "When I warned [the French government] that Britain would fight on alone whatever they did, their Generals told their Prime Minister . . . 'in three weeks England will have her neck wrung like a chicken.' Some chicken! Some neck!" [3] This is patriotism, not provincialism. Even when he says, "Russia is a riddle wrapped in a mystery inside an enigma."; [4] this is still patriotism; or, when he says of Lenin, "He alone could have found the way back to the causeway. The Russian people were left floundering in the bog. Their worst misfortune was his birth, their next worst,—his death." [5] All this, even the assault on German motives and morals, is not provincialism, although Churchill can be provincial. This is all tempered by the times and by the position he had taken forty years before:

Cologne Cathedral took 600 years to build . . . sometimes a generation built wrongly, and the next generation had to unbuild, and the next to build again. Still the work went on through the centuries, till at last there stood . . . a mighty monument of beauty and truth to command the admiration and inspire the reverement of mankind. So let it be with the British Commonwealth. [6]

These are the words of a patriot, not a provincial. They represent the seasoned loyalties of a great and committed man.

Even Demosthenes' cry, "Greece above all" is not provincialism. The mutiny of Alexander's Macedonians was not provincialism. It was a fight against the provincialism that forbade them membership in the larger whole of the Greek *homonía* that would change the world. There is a difference between patriotism and provincialism.

---

[1] *Maxims and Reflections* (Boston: Houghton Mifflin Company, 1949), p. 105; from a speech to the Canadian Parliament, December 30, 1941. Used by permission.
[2] *Ibid.*, p. 101; speech at Edinburgh, October 12, 1942.
[3] *Ibid.*, p. 100; Canadian Parliament.
[4] *Ibid.*, p. 55; Address, British Broadcasting System, October 1, 1939.
[5] *Ibid.*, p. 48, *The World Crisis.*
[6] *Ibid.*, p. 92; speech at Dundee, 1908.

Chapter IV

The Nature of Provincialism

The universal sentiment of true provincialism might well be carried in the famous motto of Meynell, "all foreigners are fools." [1] The attempt to arrive at the real base of provincialism is surprisingly involved, however. The effort tends to end in either a cluttered assortment of psychodynamic, sociocultural generalizations or in a pious and pathetic set of oversimplifications. Modern sociological and psychological explanations of provincialism form a hodgepodge of complex and contradictory factors and ideas. Perhaps theology or ethics can furnish a clearer answer. Perhaps some new *Gestalt* of personality will be found to help in this, I do not know. If we could understand ourselves, and group dynamics, would we still end up with an explanation of provincialism in terms of Freud's phrase—"a Narcissism of small differences"? If we could make respectable philosophically the metaphysics of solipsism and then transfer it to ethics in a recognizable calculus would we yet

---

[1] Bergen Evans, *The Natural History of Nonsense* (New York: Alfred A. Knopf, Inc., 1946), p. 247.

have other than a caricature of personal evil to offer as a theological explanation of universal provincialism?

At any rate, the sources of provincialism are complex and varied both in terms of dynamics and in situational social expression. That is to say, many factors produce it, and it takes many forms.

Psychological Sources of Provincialism

Whatever their eventual nature and extent, the sources of provincialism will be discovered to be within, and not outside, one's culture. We are fettered within our culture, and like a bird of prey it hovers over us.[2] Within this cultural bind we are all "bundles of prejudice" as Charles Lamb has said long ago. All provincialisms have their base in prejudice, and De Lawd in *The Green Pastures* murmured, "Even bein' Gawd ain't a bed of roses."

Praejudicium is based on something that has happened to us before. This previous happening provides a basis for decision. This decision becomes the basis for later decisions where "this" is judged to be "that," but the decision is premature. It is kept alive for use over and over by the emotional reaction to that earlier event—smelling a room or a man, some abuse, noise, or pain—and this mostly negative emotionally controlled memory judgment produces uniform judgments in all subsequent similar situations. In other words, said Gordon Allport, prejudice is "being down on something you are not up on."

Without doubt, discriminatory judgments and prejudiced actions are social and personal facts in our everyday life. The very social structure is built on and requires the continuance of judgments. All social structures are marred by bad judgments, prematurely arrived at judgments, and we act on these judgments, even unconsciously. Hence, all social structures feature discriminatory actions. All clubs, churches, and lodges are the effects of discrimination.

There is also the fact of the attitudinal make-up of persons. This personality structure formed by experience in society by the time of the late teen years is everywhere, when left alone, a prejudiced-acting structure of being. As nearly all authorities claim, it requires a multiple approach to explain this.

Of all the theories I have followed through, the psychodynamic theory

---

[2] Carlyle Marney, *Faith in Conflict* (Nashville: Abingdon Press, 1957), Section III.

of prejudice seems most hopeful of bearing real fruit, but it leaves some unanswered questions too. Allport gave the clearest analysis; he knew, however, that the psychodynamic theory needs help from other sources.[3] The elements of such an explanation spill over the borders of any single *Gestalt* of personality and various extra factors have to be accounted for.

Frustration, rebelled against by all living organisms, prods us to seek someone to blame, a scapegoat. This escape is found in our judgments against races, groups, persons, ideas, or values. The craving for power can be satisfied through the process of minimizing the competition. Some innate structure theories explain the interactions of prejudiced personality. The notion of group dynamics built on the demand in us for social entrance is given credence by our urges to belong. This has the wide range from the extreme neurosis of complete mimicry of the group down to the normal but powerful pressures to belong in children's peer groups. Our conflicts and rebellions are subsidized by our conformity to our own domestic frames of value in connection with our own image of ourselves. The need for status is answered by caste and class. The demand for security is spoken to by our institutional attachments. Hence, Allport claimed, there is a strong argument for saying that prejudice is basically a trait of personality. Its severity is determined by the center of gravity of a number of complex personality factors. This prejudice component, taking root, grows as a single unit. If a man is anti-Jewish he is usually anti-Catholic or anti-Protestant. He usually has disregard for any comparable "out-group." [4] This argument is further strengthened by the common observation that scapegoats of widely scattered breeding are so often harnessed together by the unit of prejudice, the person. For example, in a single rambling statement by a troubled woman I have noted twelve scapegoats tied into a single bundle between breaths, all of which existed to keep her from facing her own problems. It is the totality of prejudice that is important. This argues for a general psychodynamic trait of prejudice which may then express itself against half a hundred different ends.

But I still have questions:[5] Who is this eternal character, Cain?

[3] *The Nature of Prejudice* (Reading, Mass.: Addison-Wesley Publishing Company, 1954); unabridged.
[4] *Ibid.*, p. 68.
[5] So does Kyle Haselden in his brilliantly written theological characterization of prejudice as sin. See *The Racial Problem in Christian Perspective* (New York: Harper & Brothers, 1959).

Why do we all have some of this Cain in us? What is this Cain-ly desire for combat that keeps the race killing itself off? Is it more than a prejudice? George Bernard Shaw sees this clearly in *Back to Methuselah*:

CAIN: I want her to create more and more men: aye, and more and more women, that they may in turn create more men. I have imagined a glorious poem of many men, of more men than there are leaves on a thousand trees. I will divide them into two great hosts. One of them I will lead; and the other will be led by the man I fear most and desire to fight and kill most. And each host shall try to kill the other host. Think of that! All those multitudes of men fighting, fighting, killing, killing! The four rivers running with blood! The shouts of triumph! The howls of rage! The curses of despair! The shrieks of torment! That will be life indeed: life lived to the very marrow: burning, overwhelming life. Every man who has not seen it, heard it, felt it, risked it, will feel an humbled fool in the presence of the man who has.

The old master, Shakespeare, does this more subtly. Cain's last line is Shaw's attempt to improve on the last line of a speech before the battle of Agincourt in *King Henry V*. Shaw still has the insight, however, to see that Shakespeare and he and Nietzsche are talking about the same unexplained lust in man, and his Eve knows Nietzsche when she cries to Cain: "Superman! You are no super-man: you are Anti-Man."

What is this "anti-man" craze in us? Is our provincialism in which we gather our "hosts" together for combat a psychologically determined and perverse protection against the suicide of being exposed to ourselves alone? Why, when we have got what we want, do we fight over the things we have won? Is there that trait of the wolf in us too? The horse bands of the Indian guides run wild in the Yukon winter. When wolves combine to pull an old mare or a young colt down, the death of the horse breaks up their combined effort and they fight each other for the strip along the spine, the loins, and the tender organs. Why, too, have we so much in common with the ant? It, alone, of all species of living things, except for man, organizes for combat with his own kind, and not for food. What is this strange fascination for devouring our own kind which only slavery could sublimate, since slavery was more profitable than the cannibalism of our Irish, Danish, and Scottish

70

ancestors of less than eight hundred years ago? Why in the machine age do we continue our cannibalism in more subtle forms just as destructive to persons?

These are but samples of the questions a theory of psychodynamic provincialism does not answer. These are questions some deeper *Gestalt* of personality outside the present anthropological judgments of theology will have to answer.[6] We simply do not know enough about us to give a clear explanation of the sources of our prejudice and our evil. Meanwhile, the loci and foci of our provincialisms are plain enough. I turn to some sociological illustrations of our more obvious provincialisms—those classified by Whitehead as provincialisms of space and time.[7] These we can see.

Sociological Sources of Provincialism

The social matrices of provincialism can be delineated almost ad infinitum, and illustrations are everywhere on the ground like walnuts in a grove after a storm. Competent sociologists list as many as ten sociological situations within which provincialism is especially to be marked. I see three fundamental social breeding and nurturing places for overt provincialism: (1) Any forced situation of broad cultural divergence; (2) any situation marked by pressed and rapid change; and (3) any situation dominated by the general psychological trait of frustration in the presence of the unfamiliar wherein the new baffles men, who then withdraw to the safety of the known.

Situations of Broad Cultural Divergence

Anywhere military occupancy, the joint residency of allies, or economic pressures force a shifting of masses; anywhere so-called melting pots occur; wherever varied groups are pressed in together, temporarily or more permanently, dependently or more equably in the past or in the present; in any situation of cultural variance, you have a social matrix for provincialism. Here the pressures push up nascent provincialism like paste from a tube.

Colonel Purdy, chief of occupation forces on Okinawa in *Teahouse*

---

[6] Haselden, op. cit., states a theological definition of prejudice but must use terms gained from psychology to do it.

[7] Op. cit., Introduction, p. viii.

of the August Moon, is not farfetched. He issues orders for "Orienting the Oriental." He says, "These natives are going to learn democracy if I have to shoot every one of them." He prohibits the learning of Okinawese, "Don't bother with their dialect, we won the war!" He rejoices when at last the fourth-grade school children of the islanders learn the English alphabet down to "M" and can sing "God Bless America." Sakini, the wise one in the same play, learns that pornography is a matter of geography and that Oriental bad manners and Occidental good business are the same.

Under similar pressures, a member of the Iran legislature moved to establish a home base for Iranians in California.[8] A Hungarian claimed that an anti-Semite is one who hates Jews more than is absolutely necessary.[9] The West Indies natives look down on us "Pinks" and hold their noses at the odor of passing Americans. The Koreans have their private and unprintable jokes about the bedroom habits and manners of the Japanese; the living Boer veterans laugh about the back ends of the kilted Scots in retreat at Magersfontein;[10] and later, in South Africa, Gandhi knew that the Hindu was no more than fourth on the list of provincials. Above the Indian who despised the Bantu there was the Jew who despised the Indian, the Afrikaans who looked down on Jew, Hindu, and black man, and the Britisher, who would lord it over all if he could. In America the Creek Indians so feared the Negroes who fled slavery to the cover of the Alabama swamps that they destroyed both mother and child if there were any Creek blood involved on either side with Negroid blood. While the prejudices between groups of hyphenated Americans in Northern cities are matched only by the spirit that maintains between Spanish, Indian, and Negro minorities in the American Southwest.

In such pressure areas as those under military occupancy there occurs the transfer of the prejudices of the dominant occupying group to the subordinate group. For example, on a tour of night clubs and brothels— with proper escort—on a payday Saturday night, on the waterfront in Ashiya I discovered that the usually splendid acceptance of Negroes

[8] Time (January 19, 1945).
[9] Allport, op. cit., p. 4.
[10] Ex Angustam Portam, unpublished memoirs of G. J. Rousseau, b. 1880.

in the military did not extend to such recreational enterprises as drinking and wenching. The Japanese prostitutes, innocent of any racial distinction in their customers, soon learned for business reasons to segregate their activities. Some places quickly became reserved for Negroes only. Though these places were off limits and were strictly patrolled and policed, no power could put them all out of business, or stop this absorption of another culture's prejudices. Once a girl or a place did business with one group, she or it was off limits in a strictly unwritten sense to members of the other group, and to each other.

Sometimes a member of one racial group so absorbs the prejudices of his "host" group that he forgets the virtues of his native stock. I remember being urged by a missionary of Chinese parentage to watch out for the welfare of the handsome son of a wealthy Hong Kong family who was a student at an American university. The Chinese-American was afraid his third-generation Christian protégé might so respond to American mores that he would become a woman chaser and a drunkard. It was another veteran missionary, a Virginian, who reminded the Chinese that his protégé might conceivably go home to Hong Kong no longer Christian and no wiser than when he came over, but that he hardly anticipated he would go back to his father less than the Chinese gentleman he was when he came. He spoke further of the great traditions of chastity and soberness that have characterized Chinese gentlemen for four thousand years. The Chinese had forgotten his own heritage!

Situations of Forced and Rapid Change

Anywhere there occurs a situation of crisis, fear, rapid social development, positive or negative, a social matrix of provincialism is created. The situation may be one of economic boom or recession; it may be ideological, national, or partisan in its determination; it may involve only a rapidly growing minority in a larger situation; it may result from the competition of new forces with old and established patterns, or just the presence of a fear of such a threat. In any situation of rapid social change the fear of the new and unfamiliar speaks out as an easily defined provincialism.

The classic protest of provincialism out of such a social matrix appears in the writings of the founder of Latin Christianity, Florens Tertullianus. In his addresses to the general public, to emperors, and to magistrates, he decries constantly the prejudiced treatment the majority delivers to a fast-rising minority of Christians:

Day after day, indeed, you groan over the increasing number of Christians. Your constant cry is that the state is beset (by us); that Christians are in your fields, in your camps, in your islands. . . . You love to be ignorant of what other men rejoice to have discovered; . . . you now cherish your hatred.[11]

It becomes evident that the crime laid to our charge consists not of any sinful conduct, but lies wholly in our name. . . . No name of a crime stands against us, but only the crime of a name.[12]

"Lucius Titius is a good man, only he is a Christian." "I wonder that so worthy a man as Caius Seius has become a Christian." [13]

I know more than one husband, formerly anxious about their wives' conduct, and unable to bear even mice to creep into their bed-room without a groan of suspicion, who have, upon discovering the cause of their new assiduity, and their unwonted attention to the duties of home, offered the entire loan of their wives to others, disclaimed all jealousy, (and) preferred to be the husbands of she-wolves than of Christian women.[14]

In the same slashing, brilliant style:

You insist on our being the causes of every public calamity or injury. If the Tiber has overflowed its banks, if the Nile has remained in its bed, if the sky has been still, or the earth been in commotion, if death has made its devastations, your cry immediately is, "This is the fault of the Christians." [15]

In the famous *Apologeticus*, the text reads, "*Christianos ad leonem*." Only the *leno*, the brothel-bed, was worse than *leo*, the lion.

As the empire crumpled Christians more and more frequently were "lionized." And how is it that given a slumping cotton economy the rate of Southern lynching of Negroes rose? [16] Is it that prejudice is

[11] "*Ad Nationes*," i, *The Ante-Nicene Fathers*, eds. Alexander Roberts and James Donaldson (New York: Charles Scribner's Sons, 1905), III, 109.
[12] *Ibid.*, p. 111.
[13] *Ibid.*, p. 112.
[14] *Ibid.*, p. 112.
[15] *Ibid.*, viii, p. 117.
[16] A. Mintz, "Lynching and Economic Indices," in the *Journal of Abnormal and Social Psychology* (1946), 41, 154b; cited by Allport, op. cit., p. 221.

THE NATURE OF PROVINCIALISM

prejudice and seeks a scapegoat whether in third-century Rome or twentieth-century Alabama?

In 1947 forest fires in Maine were blamed on the Communists. In 1950 a potato famine in Czechoslovakia was said to have been caused by American potato bugs. The higher the Negro population, says Heer, the heavier the white vote for Strom Thurmond, the Dixiecrat.[17]

The threat of change does things to us. Witness the reaction to the publication of the Revised Standard Version of the Holy Scriptures by the National Council of Churches. The threat to Jesus Christ was so intense during the Scopes trial at Dayton years ago that we thought Clarence Darrow, Charles Darwin, and the Devil were one and the same. When the spire of St. Mary's church fell in at Shrewsbury, the rector preached that it fell because the people of Shrewsbury were planning a memorial to Darwin.[18] Apostles of discord flourish in any situation of threat, crisis, or rapid change. Such apostles are able, in any time of threat, to discredit most anybody. Not many can retain the confident aplomb of an old lady who was roused from her sleep on a careening bus in western Florida. "Aren't you afraid?" queried some neighbor G. I.'s as our bus roared down a narrow road. "Not I," said the little old woman, "thank God I'm saved and I don't give a damn how fast he drives!" But the pressures of threat and change made Mc-Carthyites of many in the same year, who were not so sure of their "salvation."

Situations of One-Culture Dominance

Situations of one culture dominance are particularly productive of provincialism. This dominance may be of any degree up to cultural isolationism. In such situations there is always exploitation and something to be gained by exploit. Might is right; customs of a single lineage dominate; race or cultural interest is powerful by sheer weight of percentage; no cultural pluralisms are desired, understood, or even endured without protest, and ignorance lives as the child of isolation and bigotry.

Here, again, illustrations are legion: Where I grew up we never wore khaki-colored clothing out in the timber lest we be mistaken for revenue agents. No one ever carried his gun into a neighbor's house, and if his

[17] *Caste, Class, and Local Loyalty, as Determining Factors in S.C. Politics* (Unpublished paper, Harvard University); cited by Allport.
[18] Evans, op. cit., p. 195.

dogs failed to bark you always located yourself to the householder by a good loud yell. Mountain isolationism respects its privacy.

Once, on a grand jury, I watched a fellow hillman from hills a thousand miles from mine silently indicting himself for premeditated murder, until I casually remarked that sometimes, in cases like this, a hillman could be released from the code that kept him quiet about his "woman." This released his tongue, and he overcame his prejudice against admitting that an "outsider" had been successful in invading his castle. He would have paid whatever the price to keep from admitting his cuckoldom and the attack on his person with a hoe, in defense against which he had killed.

There are more polished forms of this kind of provincialism. Burge-Lubin, in *Back to Methuselah*, expresses it: "If ever there was a race divinely appointed to take charge of the non-adult races and guide them and train them and keep them out of mischief until they grow up to be capable of adopting our institutions, that race is the English race." This is the paternalism that grows out of situations of cultural dominance. Hear it again: "South America free! and English if possible!" cries Canning in the British Parliament. The Lady Marechale said, during the Revolution, "Depend upon it, Sir; God thinks twice before damning a man of *that* quality!" [19] According to Lin Yutang, the Lady Astor outdoes her: "I would like China and Russia to be in the framework of a new society formed by America and the British Commonwealth, but they would have to get into the 'British way of thinking.' " [20] Such gems, says Lin Yutang, can only be cut in London. In *Candide* one of Voltaire's characters apologizes, "I beg your pardon for wishing to roast your son in public—I took him for a Jew." While in China, in better days, Americans were simply the best of the foreign-devils.[21] Down in Paraguay, much to my discomfiture, I was introduced as "Texanic," but a native relieved me of my embarrassment by saying he had heard of Texas, it was a place in Chile! To the Zuni Indians in New Mexico their mud huts are "Koowi," the center of the earth. A kinsman of the famous Major Littlefield, founder of fortunes and banks in old Texas, told me that at the Major's death they found $50,000 worth

[19] Carlyle, *French Revolution*, p. 12.
[20] *Between Tears and Laughter* (New York: John Day Company, 1943), p. 18.
[21] Cited by Allport, op. cit., p. 4.

of worthless small notes made out for Confederate veterans or their sons, but none made to any other kind of man.

"If," we ask, "the yellow and brown and black peoples are our equals, why didn't they invent iceboxes, and autos, and canned dog food?" [22] "Show me a Catholic," asked my neighbor visiting in Pensacola, and braced himself to stand the awesome sight. Who does not know tales of the great American tourist obnoxing his way through the cultural treasures of older lands?

The classic illustration has already been found by Bergen Evans. He cited the opposition of a subcommittee of the House Military Affairs Committee under its Chairman, Representative Durham of North Carolina, to the distribution of the booklet *Races of Mankind*, by Margaret Mead, on the ground that Adam and Eve were pictured therein with navels. Then Evans commented:

> The Honorable Gentlemen's motives for raising this particular objection can only be surmised . . . assuming that Navel Affairs came under their jurisdiction; but the chances are they were just laying down a smoke screen, for the pamphlet in question . . . prepared by two Columbia professors, contained information that almost any politician would feel it his duty to conceal. It stated that the concept of race is based largely on prejudice, that most of us are of mixed blood, and that nonphysical racial characteristics are probably the product of environment. And, most horribly of all, it chose to illustrate this last assertion from tests given by the U. S. Army in World War I which indicated that the average intelligence of Negroes from some Northern states was higher than the average intelligence of whites from some Southern states.[23]

What, then, after all this, is provincialism?

Provincialism is the loss or absence or distortion of one's critical faculties with respect to one's self or one's environment, whatever its extent.

Provincialism is the inability to be other than subjective; it is an acquired incapacity for objectivization posited on a preoccupation with, a satisfaction with, or at least an uncritical acceptance of one's own values and environs, which issues in a series of false generalizations not

[22] Evans, op. cit., p. 198. Used by permission.
[23] Ibid., p. 9.

subject to change or criticism through the acquisition of new knowledge. It always produces a limitation to the possibility of new community.

Anything judged to be of value, personal, environmental, or ideological, can contribute to provincialism as a means of expression. Everywhere it appears its effect is to limit communion between persons and groups.

Chapter V

Major Manifestations of Provincialism

The distortion of personality due to provincialism is not a local affair. The wavelets from the impact of domestic provincialism spread and pile up in great tidal movements and may be studied as major cultural phenomena. Too precise a scheme of organization for study serves only to demonstrate one's own provincialism. The segments of life thus exposed for study are raw and throbbing with life. They will not lie still on the table. They keep spilling over each other.

Provincialism may be studied from a base that is geographical, political, ideological, or ethnic. Nationalism, for example, could be all four and an institutionalism besides. Communism too fits somewhere in all these brackets. I have, therefore, arbitrarily chosen culture as the general framework within and outside of which some of these provincialisms may be seen for what they are. This opens two vast areas of analysis from the viewpoint of any observer in any culture.

Provincialisms are either intra-cultural or extra-cultural. There follow, presently, some sample runs through each of these two categories.

79

Notice first, however, that so obvious a social fact and provincialism as nationalism refuses to fit as an example of intra-cultural provincialism. This is true precisely because one cannot "get at" any national history as a unit. National histories are never local enough. If, as Arnold Toynbee says, "British national history is not, never has been, and almost certainly never will be an 'intelligible field of study' in isolation; and if that is true of Great Britain, it must surely be true a fortiori of any other national state," [1] then it is not really practicable to study nationalism as intra-cultural provincialism. This is true because nationalism is not just a provincialism. That is, more than an involvement with boundary and community is involved in nationalism. Nationalism is also concerned with values—values derived from varied sources—and this makes nationalism an institution. It will therefore see its delineation later under that heading.

Look at racism. Certainly racism belongs to intra-cultural provincialism because it belongs to all cultures. Racism derives its shape, form, and object, however, from institutionals—values to be preserved enter the picture. Racism, per se, does not cross cultural lines, organically: e.g. I find no organic relation between American and South African racism. The geocultural similarity creates the effect of one prejudice, but the object of prejudice in both cases is institutionally determined and only happens to be the same race group. Racism is an institutionalism like nationalism. Therefore, racism, nationalism, and for similar reasons, religionism will find delineation in this study under institutionalism— the prejudgment of value.

All this is to say that intra-cultural provincialism, to be properly studied, must find a larger medium for its demonstration than nationalism, racism, or religionism, though each is provincial. To be truly intra-cultural a provincialism must run all through a culture regardless of race, national, or religious lines. Such a category would be political, ideological, geographical, and possibly ethnic to be properly called intra-cultural. This demands something bigger for its demonstration than denominational or national or race quarrels, and drives us to consider first, in two opposing forms, the political, ideological, economic expansionism which sharply divides the Western world behind its various and flimsy curtains.

[1] Op. cit., I, 21 ff.

80

Intra-Cultural Provincialism

There are two political, ideological, economic systems in the Western world which intend themselves to expand to the point of maximum dominance. This universalism in effect appears as Western colonialism, two-pronged, competitive, and capable of assuming more than economic proportions. This colonialism, identical in intention and effect, is the prime intra-cultural provincialism of the nineteenth and twentieth centuries. It is a double-headed provincialism:

1. Communism is an intra-cultural affair. It belongs to the West; it cannot be truly Eastern in that it could not have originated in the East.[2] Its roots are Roman-German, materialistic, and Western.

2. Capitalism is an intra-cultural affair. It belongs to the West; it cannot be truly Eastern in that it could not have originated in the East. Its roots are Roman (Italian)-German, materialistic, and Western.

The expansionist tendencies of both forms of property concern in the West are identical and form a common framework for discussion— Western colonialism, an intra-cultural provincialism larger than nationalism, racism, or religionism, for folk of many nations, races, and religions are involved.

Communism

Communism is a materialistic provincialism. It is this because its concern is with stuff and its end is less than the whole. It is patently a provincialism within a provincialism because it does not express, much less exhaust, the spirit of any culture where it has found partial, temporary, or semipermanent rootage. It does not exhaust the Italian spirit. Communism's banners turn dull gray against the background of Milan. It does not express the German spirit which reflects Frederick Barbarossa, Luther, the great god Thor, and a thousand more. Communism never sees the depth of the Orient, for it has no concern for ancestors, form, and the inner worth of trivials, and therefore misses persons, and all the East.

Most of all, strange anomaly, Communism fails to exhaust or even to

---

[2] The East had its forms of trade, property exchange, and value, but they were neither Communist nor capitalistic. An offense involving property value never could demand the forfeit of human life in the Hebrew world, for example. Oriental caste is based on other values than property, though property or its lack certainly accompanies caste.

express the spirit of Russia. It knows nothing of Mother Russia or the Messiah who is to come to Moscow, the Third Rome; it cannot understand Tolstoi's *Piebald Colt*, or Dostoevski's Fyodor Pavlovitch or his Grushenka, and terribly, it cannot comprehend Alyosha, or Dmitri, or even Ivan. Only Smerdyakov is understandable by the laws of Communist biology and heredity. The Communism of Lenin, Stalin, and Khrushchev is at best an illegitimate stain, a bastard bar sinister in the fabric of the most vivid, flamboyant, wildly spiritual, devastatingly God-obsessed, practically and beautifully schizophrenic people of the West. Russia is more Eastern than Italy or even Turkey and is really farther from materialism than any of us. The Russia of literature, art, music, thought, and religion is not Communist Russia. Great Russia whirls, howls, weeps for its sins; begs, writhes, twists for its destiny; marauds, rapes, confesses, extols, and loses its mind with frustrated hope. Russia is Messianic; Russia is Dionysian; Russia is Slavophilic, not materialistic. The dances of Russia are too wild for plebeian Communism, though Communism learned much of its *danse macabre* from the Russian obsession with death—and birth.

Communism is a provincialism within a provincialism. It cannot express even Russia. Charles Malik of Lebanon, product of Eastern Orthodoxy and Western philosophy, Lebanese delegate to the United Nations General Assembly, understands this better than most, and in one of the Assembly's most brilliant addresses sums up Communism's inability to absorb all Russia:

One reason why I sometimes wholeheartedly laugh at specific points in the exposition of a Vishinsky, or a Maniulsky, or a Pavlov, or an Arutiunian is precisely because I see in the imagery used, or the humor resorted to, or the parable or anecdote related, or the deep humanity revealed, or the sheer boundless exuberance, or the childlike inconsistency, or the utter, joyous self-abandon of spirit, certain authentic features of the free Russian soul bursting forth through the drabness of Marxist dialectic, like a volcano erupting the dead crust of the earth.[3]

He asks for a published compendium of nineteenth-century Russian literature—the work of Krylov, Pushkin, Gogol, Turgenev, Chekhov, Dostoevski, Tolstoi, Soloviëv, and Gorki—in order that this inability of Communism might be obvious to the West.

---

[3] Address, United Nations Assembly, pp. 25-29. Used by permission.

To carry his point beyond controversion, Malik then proposes to outline a "phenomenology of the Russian soul." To him, as indeed to any Westerner who reads the readily available paperback volumes of a half-dozen Russian classicists, the tragic sufferings of the Russian soul are obvious. Berdyaev says, "They [Russian writers] are in the throes of religious anguish, they seek salvation . . . they thirst to make expiation, they suffer for the world." Dostoevski's Father Zossima knows this way of redemption. The Russian spirit is permeated with contradiction, contrast, antithesis, even antinomy. To the Russian, things must be wholehearted, robust, full, elemental, or else they are not really Russian. Malik says that "the Russian soul everlastingly itches to make a clean breast of things." She would "take the very process of creation itself into [her] own hands." Russia has to walk "perilously on the brink of the precipice." Pushkin said that there is a deep universalism, an absolute receptivity, a complete identification with every state of man, everywhere. There is also, opposing this, a deep disdain for culture. This nihilism denies and seeks the West. It is affected by the native Russian quest for a better world; a deeply impregnated utopianism which would make the Third Rome Heaven if it could. The thing sought is always "a way of life." Russia does not know the prodigious German power of philosophical abstraction.

Most revealingly, Malik claims, there is the Russian desire for wholeness, completeness, unity. "There is the mystical burning for absorption and reconciliation, a self-projection onto an ultimate universal harmony. The Russian soul at its best is consumed by a mystical flame of the purest type." The Russian rebels against things as they are, he craves to taste things as they ought to be: this makes him prophetic, apocalyptic, eschatological. This genuine religious consciousness is wholly alien to the materialism of Marxism and is the deepest characterization of the Russian soul; so deep that within the speeches of members of the Praesidium one can occasionally find the phrase "God willing." [4]

Even without the provincial thrusts of Communism there would still have been a great Russian problem in today's world:

[4] Irving R. Levine, "This Is Your Enemy," *Argosy* (February, 1959), p. 106; and recall Khrushchev's frequent, casual apparently habitual use of the name God during his 1959 American journey.

Even if the Tsarist regime had not been overthrown, but had itself embarked on a policy of progressive industrialization, today, in the geo-political balance of power, the world would still face a great Russian problem. It is absolutely absurd and stupid to entertain the hope that 250 million Slavs, with their great vitality and culture, with the infinite material resources at their command, and whether or not they are ruled by Communists, can simply be dismissed or ignored by the rest of the world.[5]

The hope of resolution is that the Russian people may recognize by what a vast margin Communism fails to express what Russia has to give and to say. The hope of peace lies in the recognition by Russia that the basic ideology of Communism reveals its nature as a full-blown provincialism, for Communism is a prejudgment of reality, of community, of value, and of persons. The eight major tenets of Communism are its eight major errors and its eight major provincialisms:

Ultimate reality is through and through matter.
The proper attribute of reality is change and strife.
There is no objective and eternal truth.
Only the temporal and immanent exist.
There is no God.
The nature of things is pointed to only within the tradition of Democritus, Lucretius, Fuerbach, and Marx.
Man is perfectible by his own efforts.
The human person is for the sake of society and the state.

In these tenets can be summed up the major metaphysical, epistemological, ethical, and theological provincialisms of history, but the results of the mass operation of these provincialistic principals can and must never be overlooked or underestimated.

No one can fail to admire the magnificent achievements [under Communism] of the Soviet State. It did away with Tsarist autocracy. It has, in thirty years and despite two terrific wars, set one-sixth of the globe, hitherto exceedingly backward, on the path of industrialization. . . . A Soviet representative is never more sincere than when he attacks all forms of social or economic discrimination. There is a passionate attempt at socialism—the Soviet socialist system strives to achieve real equality of opportunity for its

[5] Malik, op. cit., p. 29.

84

citizens—talent, whatever be the status of the individual or family in ques-ion, is recognized and encouraged to realize itself. The peoples of the Soviet Union seem to be straining their utmost to realize a new harmony between their diverse national, racial, and linguistic stocks. In a world bitterly divided by national, racial, and cultural antagonisms, the multi-national, multi-racial, multi-cultural super-state is a novel mode of political organization holding forth great possibilities for the future. The world will always be indebted to the heroic achievements of the Red Army in the recent war. . . .

Undoubtedly these are great achievements. It is only blindness or ig-norance or prejudice or sheer nihilism that fails to recognize them. . . .

But . . . these great things . . . have been achieved at a frightful human and spiritual cost. Need they have been achieved at such a high price? [6]

It is precisely this high price—30,000,000 human lives at least—that reveals the provincial nature of Communistic colonialism. This de-mands a broader view.

Give Communism credit for all its genuine social passion and con-cern with economic justice. List all its enduring and positive achieve-ments. It still is a provincialistic ideal, for it is "materialistic, atheistic, dialectical, relativistic, purely immanent, man-made," and its totali-tarianism is therefore a provincialism. It cannot include the whole of things by virtue of its own self-limitations. Malik concludes from all this that even if end justified means the Communist revolution is not justified.

Furthermore, as seen in the Burma Conferences, when Communism spreads it expands just like any other form of colonialism—just like British imperialism or any imperialism, be it economic, nationalistic, or ideological—the mere fact of colonial aspiration reveals its partialness and therefore its provincialness and essential incompleteness.

Capitalism

The capitalistic system is about 450 years old—little more—and not much that is really new has appeared in capitalism within the last four hundred years. Chain banks, for example, are quite old. Local competition is fairly new. Installment buying is very old; except that the depth and width of its operation is fairly modern.

Modern capitalism succeeded the medieval kind of Communism

* *Ibid.*

85

because it produced results that the medieval system could not produce. The general rise in trade, mining, industry, agriculture, and banking followed hard on the heels of the frontiersmen in an expanding world. The expansion of horizons that marked the late fifteenth century and its climax in the Renaissance can almost make the Reformation appear to be a domestic affair of the European nations, as Whitehead termed it. The history of money and banking in the context of Copernicus, Columbus, Descartes, and Newton would tell a fascinating story.

The capitalistic revolution had, at first, a purely mechanical cause. There was a terrific increase in the production of precious metals. The development of hard money made the storage of wealth possible. Wealth became a truly transferrable commodity. Cartels could happen, combines could form, control could change hands more easily. Kings, nobles, and officials were power men, and the development of government concessionaires and bankers made possible their continuance in power. Public loans were the backbone of ancient capitalism, as now. The lending of money is ancient, but it was a private practice and a temporary expedient. There was, hitherto, no habitual conduct of business on borrowed money. True capitalism uses money as a commodity to be sold as a base for the conduct of business on a more or less permanent borrowing basis.

Two new factors brought about this development to permanent loanings: the new smelting processes in German and Italian mines of the early sixteenth century; and the widespread maintenance of power structures through the use of hired soldiers and expensive new armaments involving the purchase of gunpowder. The loan sources, at first in private houses, and the interest on these war-government loans made banking an international power in a single decade. The three iron balls over a Medici door became a coat of arms for the royal House of the Medici, which family named popes, kings, and queens. The House of Rothschild could signal from England to France to Italy and to Holland more rapidly than the wind.

There came to thirteenth-century Florence double-entry bookkeeping, and clearinghouses for the exchange of paper wealth did volume business at Genoa, Antwerp, and Lisbon. The American Bank of California is only the latest of the great Italian houses; there were others centuries ago using essentially the same techniques. The Guadegni in Florence spoke of loans up to 520,000 florin. The Fuggers, a family of German miners for whom Luther's father worked, had a bank in Augsburg doing business in sums of 4,700,000 gulden ($12-15,000,000.00). During the years 1511-27 they reported an annual profit of 54.5 per cent. Monopolies were sought in everything. From the time of Genseric, the Gauls and Germans had liked Asiatic red pepper. Rott of Augsburg bought 1,600 tons of the stuff, but still had competition and could not corner the market. Mortgage loans have risen in volume steadily from the mid-thirteenth century, when interest was sometimes two thirds of the principal, until the present. The whole New World was, and is, mortgaged to somebody! Interest payments varied from 5 per cent per annum to 5 per cent per month. Government war economy and municipal bonds are still, as in the waning Middle Ages, the backbone of capitalism, and installment loans are just the icing on the cake. Not since 1492 in the New World has there been any kind of real ownership of property other than absentee ownership, and as late as 1930, of every $100 of wealth in the United States more than $80 worth of the ownership was in Northern, banking, control.

Capitalism, like its just as Western enemy, Communism, is a materialistic provincialism. As patently as Communism, capitalism is, in its classical expressions, a provincialism within a provincialism. It neither expresses nor exhausts the spirit of any culture where it has been the dominant economic structure. It has given rise to numberless flamboyant personalities and colorful episodes in terms of the development and exploitation of new fields of natural resources, but it is only means, not informing principal, and cannot explain, much less exhaust, the spirit of all the peoples who have moved against new frontiers. Only if all frontier movements were shown to be wholly materialistic could capitalism explain and contain the Western world.

Like a vivid, horrible joke, the chapter heads in Thorstein Veblen's classic *Theory of the Leisure Class* cut across the safe and comfortable self-appraisals of capitalism's home territory: "Pecuniary Emulation," "Conspicuous Leisure," "Conspicuous Consumption," "Pecuniary Canons of Taste," "Survivals of Prowess," "Devout Observances." Veblen's insights reveal capitalism to be as provincially materialistic as Communism. In fact, one has to struggle and idealize to escape the same

87

sort of economic determinism so blatantly basic in Communism.[7] Only the loudly shouted slogans of Western idealism can veneer, however thinly, and camouflage, however unevenly, the fundamental economic determinism of the materialism that lies at the base of the uncurbed ownership of private property. This wild concern for property, protected by law that can require the life of habitual thieves as payment, is Western and provincial.

Critical literature is replete with great and courageous books about capitalism. The writers were in bad shape, however, if they depended upon a profit economy, for such books seldom pay big royalties. Thorstein Veblen, one of those lean men, "hated by plump flunkies," was an idle and curious man watching bustling citizens beat him at games he refused to play: "football is to physical culture as bull-fighting is to agriculture." In spite of his great books, he failed at various posts and died in a shack near Stanford in 1929. It is really unfortunate that he did not live to know of October, 1929. He might have enjoyed it. The books were these classic critiques of capitalism:[8] Veblen, *Theory of the Leisure Class, Theory of Business Enterprise,* and *Absentee Ownership and Business Enterprise;* Tawney, *The Acquisitive Society* and *Religion and the Rise of Capitalism;* Webb, *The Decay of Capitalist Civilization;* Sombart, *Moderne Capitalismus;* and Small, *Between Eras: From* *Capitalism to Democracy.*

It would be grossly unfair, however, to let such critics of a system state its fundamental principles. For these we turn to the most powerful form of capitalism extant: the American Way of Life. Let the fundamental operational bases of expanding economic enterprise be seen in a clear expression inducted from the whole complex of capitalism's life in the New World. These principles can be fairly stated as follows:

The profit-motivated economy has a fundamental validity when covered by an emphasis on "equality of opportunity."

[7] Even Charles Beard, in his younger days, felt that economic determinism had its merits, though he later repudiated this. Yet, Lerner said his *An Economic Interpretation of the American Constitution* (New York: The Macmillan Company), approached this view and left its mark on other writers. *Op. cit.,* p. 32.

[8] See also Harold Laski, Robert Lynd, C. Wright Mills, Vernon Parrington, Edward Bellamy, and William Dean Howells. Thurman W. Arnold's *Folklore of Capitalism* (New Haven, Conn.: Yale University Press, 1937), was important. Yet Lerner claimed that capitalism was "neither the Plumed Knight nor the Robber Barony it was depicted." *Op. cit.,* p. 33.

The rapid development of natural resources is a moral value, a virtue of the highest order, for the "improvement" of matters generally is an ordinand of God.

The transfer of property control by inheritance is the just way of transfer.

The share of control and ownership of those who contribute labor only is rightly to be limited by those who control capital.

The right of any man to unlimited personal property is a divine right.

The economic determinism implicit in these principles is as obvious as the overt materialism of the whole. The concern with "stuff" is innate. Weber's great social thesis involving Protestantism in the service of these principles, and by which the ethic of social Calvinism turns out to be respectability, frugality, thrift, sobriety, and occasional philanthropy, is not entirely without basis. Protestantism has, in all its institutions, been singularly concerned with the stuff of capitalistic society. The classic picture of Protestant respectability and piety in terms of Grandfather, frock-coated, with gold watch chain, Phi Beta Kappa key, cane, and gloves, passing the First National Bank where he is president, on his way to the First Presbyterian Church where he is ruling elder, is not farfetched. It, perhaps, is exceeded only by S. L. Stealey's description of Baptist piety in terms of "a paid Sunday School worker in a fur coat."

Neither Weber nor his interesting thesis must divert us from the main issue, viz., the main tenets of capitalism do not express the cultural values amidst which they have grown. They are, therefore, partial and limited, more provincial than the culture they inhabit.

This is to say, with Small, that the profit motive is simply not great enough for what is great in man. The best in man is never revealed in his desires for profit. The profit motive is ethically bankrupt. Its bankruptcy is its inability to encompass true value which is personal. It may serve personal value but cannot express it. This motive looks through too narrow a defile—it is a provincialism and cannot see the whole.

Further, the vaunted virtue in the development of natural resources, in practice, becomes the exercise of one's own personal resources for manipulation, control, and monopoly. This is another word for the exploitation of all in behalf of the few. The idea of God's concern over the ownership of property to the point of divine right is a fictitious fraud like the divine right of kings. Yet, this divine right to the pursuit of

89

property is a cornerstone of the Horatio Alger classical kind of American economic system. Algers are everywhere; even helpfully so. Our provincialism appears in our assumption that divine concern with our property rights could have so vicious an effect on human rights. Perhaps the viciousness of crediting Deity with our rights to property control seems overpowerful to one whose earliest memories are of the skinny-legged children of hungry miners who were brawling for ton increases in pay with the absentee owners of holes in the hillsides outside the little soft-coal mining towns of an earlier day.[9]

Now that private ownership is so seldom private, the problems and the provincialisms are of a different hue. Formerly or presently, the effect of political-ideological-economic expansionism has been colonialism. It will be so as long as there are new markets to be built on top of the uncut forests of various kinds and to be dug out of the various kinds of holes in the ground where wealth is hard money and can be stored, transferred, and sold. Whatever the plundering technique, in the minds of those people who are colonized, colonialism is colonialism, capitalist or Communistic. Colonialism, a political, ideological, economic expansionism, is an intra-cultural provincialism with which the West must reckon for its very life until it learns of a larger community.

Extra-Cultural Provincialism

What Westerner can talk intelligently of the East? It is of Western provincialism only that I can speak. Which Westerner can know truly the East? Yet, I have sought to know it. I have read the *New Testament*, *Ramayana*, and *Upanishads*, along with the speeches of Gandhi, the *Koran*, *Tales of Arabian Nights*, and Omar Khayyám; but I still do not know the mind of the East, for the translations were bad, and the idioms were lost. I have read Northrop, Toynbee, and Nolde; I have talked to missionaries, have read the Marshall Plan, a *Burma Diary*, the novels of Pearl Buck, *Terry and the Pirates*, and the sayings of Confucius, but I do not know the East, nor do you. I crawled through the belly of an eighty-foot Buddha, looked at pictures of Tibet, read of the ascent of Mount Everest, sang "The Road to Mandalay," devoured *Kim*. I own a Burmese nutcracker, a Korean papa-san pipe, and a set of

* Disraeli's famous phrase "the two nations" referred to such a wide spread between rich and poor.

camphor wood Happy-gods, but I do not know the East. I know the freight rate from Moji and the smell of Kunsan harbor; I have been to Anyang Li, Yong Dong Po, Cheng-ju, and the thirty-eighth parallel, but I do not know the East. Once I shot Mallard ducks only eight minutes by plane from Shanghai, heard Russian and Chinese on radio, felt the Yellow Sea swell under my feet, and counted scabby little heads in a leprosarium, but it is of Western provincialism only that a Westerner can speak.

I know some facts about the East, however. I know that if you fly from Karachi, Pakistan, to Tokyo, Japan, to Colombo, Ceylon, and back to Karachi you have flown over less than one fifth of the earth's surface but have passed over 52 per cent of its people. They writhe, twist, scheme, plan, compete, ache, die, and multiply, seeking a full belly just once before they die. I know that the Western Saxon white man is less than one sixth of the earth's populace and will soon be less than one twentieth of its people and has no continuing corner on any room whatsoever. I know that India is very proud of the second-greatest steel mill in the world, and that any race of men, in time, will come up in the world if it wills it. I know that in my adult lifetime more than 700,000,000 people have gotten a new political independence, that their surge toward newer independences continues and will not recede.[10]

The New East

Two trends have dominated the postwar years.[11] There is a great new surge toward social and economic equality inside the bounds of sections like the United States, South Africa, Asia, and Russia. There is a grand new insistence on the equality of rights and opportunity between nations. The new world which we timidly enter is a single world. The styles, colors, fabrics, weavings, materials, architecture, art forms, and music of the East have appeared across counters, in Broadway theaters, on mass communications media, and in the color magazines, salons, and schools of the West. Philosophy, literature, political ideas, mores, and values will follow—in other ways they have already preceded. "For the first time in history," says F. S. C. Northrop, "East and West are

[10] See O. Frederick Nolde, paper, World Council of Churches Assembly, Evanston.
[11] See a paper by Dag Hammarskjold, World Council of Churches Assembly, Evanston.

in a single world movement, as much Oriental as Occidental in character." [12] A man can be carried from West to East so rapidly that his bowels, liver, and lights cannot adjust to the change in time for a fortnight, and the trip from East to West is even faster because of tail winds over the Pacific.

The East now sees our missionary paternalism as the ego-ridden generosity of a *noveau-riche* younger child—for the East remembers where the West got its fundamental ideas. The East has reminded us of our debt to our Grandmother Asia. The Eastern world knows that all our science—mathematics, astronomy, navigation, medicine, agriculture, and industry; all our philosophy; all our religion; and all our politics had Eastern origins.[13] The East is no longer willing merely to respond to the political, economic, military, and religious gifts of her own grandchild. The older relative still has some lessons to teach us, lessons in tradition, culture, and politeness which will certainly alter our own cultural ideals and economic-political programs.[14] The East rejoices in her new day, and it is a day of trouble for the West. We call her Modern Asia now, and this means, said Malik at Evanston:

> Asia and Africa are rising. They desire the full enjoyment of their natural rights. The Asian and African will is taken into account in world councils today more than ever before. You are not only dealing with the vast majority of the human race and with incalculable natural resources: you are dealing with ancient cultures proud of their achievements, jealous for their spiritual values, and becoming increasingly conscious not only of their latent inner strength but of *how much the West has owed them*.[15]

This Modern Asia, this new Asia-Africa, means that Asiatics and Africans have learned from our returned science and technology that nature is a realm of discoverable law by obedience to which they can profit. Asia now knows, said Hocking, that the social changes her future prosperity demands can be made to occur through human effort. Social change in Asia-Africa no longer must come through inherited, traditional, divine patterns of slow social process. Asia has learned from us that she may

[12] Op. cit., p. 4.
[13] Marney, op. cit., pp. 98-99.
[14] Northrop, op. cit., pp. 1-14.
[15] *Asia and Africa Ask Searching Questions*, speech, Second Assembly of the World Council of Churches (August 18, 1954). Used by permission.

move swiftly. Further, Asia now rejoices in her recent discovery that the nation, and pride in the nation, can be swift, sharp, modern instruments with which these social changes can be effected. It all means that "the Orient has not lost the eyesight by which it discovers the weak places in our armour and so recovers its own sources of power." [16]

Of these vast changes that swirl and stir, the West has remained mostly ignorant, though prophets have spoken. This is our common provincialism. The symptoms of this provincialism of Westerners—the East has her own—are even more frightening than the disease itself. This provincialism does things to us.

Symptoms of Western Provincialism

The typical Western group, European or American, has almost no notion of the extent of Western dependence upon Eastern ideas. No family, tribe, nation or culture which loses touch with its sources, which forgets its ancient heritage, which is cut loose by the lapse of memory from its origins can ever be anything but ignorantly provincial in this regard. This is the crime of the abomination of history; this is the isolationism that lives on estrangement. It is the cardinal sin of lust for life at the expense of one's sources. This is Oedipus Rex, who sleeps with his mother and does not know. This is the provincialism that breeds incest—especially when the source is raped by its grandchild.

Prime evidence of Western provincialism is our preoccupation with the effectiveness of our own standards, tools, and techniques. The provincial man is always convinced of the innate superiority of his own weapons. If we are crass enough to think our own power politics on a world scale will solve anything, we are provincial. "If," said Lin Yutang, "we are naive enough to think that all we need to do is to transfer the standards of Europe to Asia and impose the white man's power politics on a world scale, we shall have the whole world, instead of Europe, as an arena of periodic bloodshed and slaughter." [17] The West, further, in its provincialism, has so overrated its technological achievements in plumbing, refrigeration, incubation, and cosmetics that it simply cannot understand why the East will not scrap all her own traditional, indigenous, familial, communal values in order to have our flush-bowls, iceboxes,

[16] W. E. Hocking, The Coming World Civilization (New York: Harper & Brothers, 1956), passim.
[17] Op. cit., p. 22.

contraceptives, and electric razors. It is utterly provincial to think that Asiatic concepts of the individual, family, law, and government will ever be so Westernized as to be gauged by our standards and norms. Whatever culture is achieved will take its uniformity and power from an intercultural order. The West is obligated to help make this an orderly achievement, and it will likely feature as many Burmese teak tables and exotic fruits and dances in Chicago as it will display American trousers, cheap jewelry, and pornographic literature in Bangkok. A small Dominican professor at San Marcos University in Lima once shamed me no end with the accusation that our exports and our calling to help the world did not match up. Coca-Cola cannot be expected to replace the milk of human kindness so thirsted for in Asiatic villages.

Another symptom of provincialism appears in the way we Westerners assume the presence of all badness on the opposite side of things. More subtly still, the way we assume the understanding by Easterners, or Russians, of this "goodness of motive" that we feel characterizes us wholly. Only the most provincial of views would see all goodness as American and all badness as Russian. No particular people can ever be considered as permanent enemy of the right or of the truth.[18] All badness can never get on one side of an argument. True goodness would be ours only if we were wholly white, and so many of our deeds are gray, or red! No national boundary, much less a hemispheric one, can ever demarcate between good and bad, freedom and slavery. No single side is ever black or white. All of us are gray hued, and Asia has reason to fear the grayness of our motives. She has even more cause to withdraw before the energy and vigor with which we have pressed our ways and blessings upon her. She has real reason to resent the high-handed deprecation of her timidly offered tools and patterns; our calm acceptance of her nationalism as being so weak and pressureless that it could never constitute a threat to us.

Most keenly provincialism speaks by its rejection of criticism. Bertrand Russell in *Sceptical Essays* shows how swiftly we make criminals out of those who tell the truth in wartime. It is no less criminal to ignore the critique of nations we as yet do not fear. This is to tell the Asiatic to hush; this is to deny him his place at table; this is to stop

---

[18] To this point Bertrand Russell and F. S. C. Northrop speak more pointedly than most any of the modern Christian prophets.

his voice in world affairs; to fail to take him seriously is provincially criminal. Worse, the refusal to hear his curses is to refuse to take him as a person and is to get in the way of his freedom to *become!* It is a criminal abortion to cut off his growing powers of criticism and judgment, for this is his road to freedom and life. He may also see in us something he needs, but, said Malik: "It is a mockery of man, of truth, and of God, if after much suffering a man sees in freedom more light and still he cannot open the window to let it in." [19]

[19] Speech at second assembly of World Council of Churches.

Chapter VI

Escape from Provincialism

There is no escape from provincialism that is not based squarely upon a valid doctrine of community. I am attempting such a doctrine with a kind of prose poem.

A Doctrine of Community

Satan was trembling with anticipation as he took Jesus "along side himself" to an "exceeding high mountain" and showed him all kingdoms of the earth, all politicoeconomic divisions, all the realms of the earth, all frames within which men obey, all institutions that hold men together, all the informing, controlling, subduing, motivating, confining funnels through which men's hopes pour. All countries are here; all nations, alliances, empires; all races, tribes, and continental solidarities; all churches, lodges, governments, and congresses; all orders, all categories, all professions, and "the glory of them." Everything that ties men together is here, all that makes them one, united; all their kinships and commonalties; all their ties of race, creed, color, and line; all their potentials and their common destinies; all their prejudices and their

96

common hatreds; all their inheritances and their resources; all their subject millions in people and wealth; all their fertility, reproductiveness, magnificence, and extent—"all these I will go on giving thee."

They glitter and writhe before him there on the mountain, sparkling and twisting, bound in their sheer tinsel and stark captivity; all the uniting principals of earth in one mighty act—delivered by the one who owned them to the one who came to free them! This has a deeper meaning than we have ever dreamed.

Satan did not offer the Christ power. Satan did not offer him authority. Satan did not offer empire. We miss this if we say that Satan offered earthly dominion. We miss it if we say the gift was kingship. We miss if we call it honor. We miss with any earthly pomp. The meaning lies far, far below these levels. Satan offered the one thing mankind most wants, his heart's desire above all others, the one thing he expects from all religions, the thing he demands, seeks to buy, aches to own, the one great boon man wants with all his soul. What is more, he offered the one thing God wants too, the desire of God that made the incarnation, the great wish from God that would endure the absence of the Son, the great agony of God's heart that is greater than the cross of his Son.

So, there on the mountaintop, Satan offered the incarnate Son the one thing both God and man had eternally desired. He offered *community*; he offered unity, oneness, unitedness. All the conquerors, the Timours and Genghis Khans, all the Charlemagnes, Caesars, Hannibals, Napoleons, riding in their clouds of dust that rise to the moon from their swirling hordes of sabre-thrusting demons, thrust up on earth's beaches by the tides of conquest—all have sought only to unite mankind. All the political philosophies, the Nazisms and Communisms, the socialistic Fascisms, the internationalisms and alliances—all have sought only to combine us. All the great super-churches; all who claimed to know God's desires, the Romanisms and Parseeisms, the Hinduisms and Pantheisms; all missionary enterprises; all economic and cultural concerns; all spiritual, personal, ecumenical, imperial, hemispheric solidarities—all of them have sought only to make us all one!

All the towers of Babel—from the first in Babylon to the current one in New York—have sought to make men unite.

"Thou dost know," Satan said to him that dread day, "even God,

97

thy Father, wants his children one, all mankind has desired it! Save mankind his agony of striving for community. Meet his universal craving. Unite him in one ultra-grand, unanimous, harmonious ant-heap. Give him a center pole to surround; give him a God he can see; give mankind someone to guard his conscience here on earth! Take this cup and in it mingle the blood streams of all the earth into one grand family of earthbound men.

"Give at once everything man seeks on earth. Do it! Put all political, economic, personal, and spiritual loyalties of mankind into one bag— and thus give both God and man their long desire!"

Satan knew there on the mountaintop that community is determined by the acceptance of a common cultural hinge. When Messiah cried, "Upage Satanos," "go down, Adversary," he rejected an inadequate cultural hinge. He rejected, said Dostoevski, the hinges of mystery, miracle, and authority. He did not reject community—this Messiah came to create—he rather rejected the inadequate cultural hinges that have made all the cultural communities of earth what they are. His rejection is the claim that any intercultural community must swing on a stronger cultural hinge. This points the way of escape from any provincialism.

Escape, then, lies always in the direction of a stronger cultural hinge, a more valid reference point, a higher principle of organization—that is to say, ultimately, escape from provincialism lies in the direction of ultimate community. The rejection by Jesus was his rejection of the lesser hinge; he refused the lesser god. (All cultures swing on the hinge of value that is their god.) He held out for a higher center of reference.

One escapes the limitations of his provincialism only as he finds higher value reference points around which new community is created. He builds "more stately mansions" though each contains a newer provincialism to be escaped.

In a brilliant series of lectures for the Hazen Foundation, Blake Smith characterized our own culture by its hinges. He claimed that our culture actually swings upon our faith in temporal experience. The goal of our culture can be reached with satisfactory temporal experience. The spirit that characterizes our culture is the spirit of devotion to group solidarity and prosperity. This is not an advance over individualism. It is just that in the group our weak hinges become respectable.

No culture known to history has ever more sorely needed to escape

98

its provincialism than ours. The only escape in view requires a higher and better hinge, a more valid reference point, a grander community than temporal experience can provide.

What, again, is provincialism? Provincialism is the loss, absence, or distortion of one's critical faculties with respect to self and environment. Provincialism is the inability to be "other minded" by reason of one's own preoccupation with and his uncritical acceptance of his own. Provincialism is an attitude of mind which issues in a series of false generalizations not subject to change or criticism on the basis of new experience. Provincialism is that distorted prejudgment of community which destroys the prospects of communion. It is the determined choice of the smaller world, a reductionism, an exclusivism, and ultimately an isolationism. It is the rejection of the other, all others that are truly "other." At bottom, it is a solipsism, which is philosophically untenable, unthinkable—but who has to think in his provincialism? It may appear in an international, religious, racistic, cultural, or personal mold, but at bottom it is always the same: a prejudgment of community in favor of the smaller world. On its vast scale which we have seen, provincialism is intra- and extra-cultural. In its deepest form provincialism is intra- and inter-personal. It is always the same, however: it is the predisposition to choose the lesser, closer world. There is a sense in which this predisposition is our oldest and most powerful enemy.

All escapes from provincialism lie in the same direction—toward community, and time is not the healer; time heals nothing. Time gets everything and does nothing for us. "Whatever man earns, nature eventually collects." [1] Time is not the healer, for, said Whitehead, man can be provincial in time as well as in space. It is not more time we need; we find escape through new experience. The cry for more time is the cry against new experience, for new experience creates the painful possibility of an enlargement of one's capacity for new relationships. The expansion of community is a painful thing when the culture hinges are rusted by provincialism. It is a tearing thing to have one's cultural hinges opened.

The Technique of Release

The nature of a culture is predictable on the basis of its value reference points. Any escape from the lesser to the greater would, therefore, re-

[1] A. C. Reid, *Man and Christ* (Durham, N. C.: Duke University Press, 1954), p. 51.

quire an expansion of one's concept of the valuable. One escapes the limitations of his provincialism only as he finds higher value reference points around which new community is created. *The basic means to this end is new experience, and the effect of new experience may be educative, but experience must be educative in a redemptive sense and must result in the reference of conscience to a higher community before experience can be said to be educative in the sense that it is a means to true release from provincialism.*

The experience that breeds familiarity may also breed blasé worldliness, which is compassionless, professional, and quite as provincial as any other localism. By the same token, education per se bears no true release unless its value reference points provide the prospect of redemption from lesser value judgments. I see no release from provincialism in any emphasis on group or function that reduces the personal center of value. This requires a further conversation. What is required of education as a technique of release from provincialism?

Education As Release

All thought and capacity for thinking rest on man's ability to generalize. He can see that *this* is *that* and arrive at general impressions. He associates, then categorizes. Just as all thought rests on categorization, so all wrong thinking begins in wrong generalization. Prejudice is the emotion-controlled type of wrong thinking and acting that results from false generalization. It is the basic requirement of education that its character be such as will guard us from all types of false categorization. True education is never parochial in any sense of that word. There is no Lutheran *mathematique*, nor is there a Baptist biology. If Catholic theology is pre-Copernican, and if fundamentalism's view of scripture is pre-Kantian, so much the worse for both.

The problem is more general than this. By and large we are ridden, in educational circles, with the "curse of departmentalization." [2] Bad departmentalization is a powerful form of false categorization from which nothing but a prejudiced view of community can follow. Bad science begets bad metaphysics even in grammar school, says Whitehead, then voices his complaint that we teach algebra, from which nothing follows;

[2] See Frankfurter's introduction to Whitehead, *The Aims of Education* (New York: The Macmillan Company, 1929), pp. 18 ff.

geometry, from which nothing follows; and so with history, language, and literature, with nothing following.[3] This produces the curse of closed systems, scrappy information, paragraph picking, and general generalizations for avoiding the difficult. The net result is provincialism in time and space. For example, the highest-ranking liberal-arts graduate of a large university in twenty years approached me to discuss his ulcers. I discovered that the only philosopher he had read was John Dewey. When I suggested that some of the problems he and Dewey faced were also faced by Otto, Bergson, Whitehead, Russell, and even Reichenbach, he wanted to know their copyright dates—as if the last word had been said!

Is it possible that education can arrive at categories that will permit mature precision and not its prevalent opposite? Is it too much to ask of education that some synthesis occur on the basis of a recognition of the interdependence of the branches of study? Must educational processes result in the smothering of even the beginnings of a broad metaphysical inquiry by an overregard for exactness? Can education bring it to pass that personality will no longer be swallowed up in bad sociology without also increasing that overt individualism which makes fascistic the groups we can never totally forsake? Can education make community happen in terms of persons in communion?

The peculiar task of Christian education is the leading into expanding life of the "new creation." Can Christian education acquire and pass on an understanding of our mutual dependence in terms of the departmentalizations that so provincialize us? Is Christian education too parochial to provide a base in both culture and technical knowledge? Can there be mature precision, which means absence of distortion? Can the institutions of Christian education hold together under the pressures generated by ferment and tension between the mighty opposites without which no learning truly happens? Can Christian education endure the stress of putting its learners in strut, tort, and tension with their most personal and intimate values and provincialisms? Dare we go under judgment? Can judgment be developed that realizes the variousness of things and that permits a not-too-timorous synthesis from which the continued provincialism of analysis can be moderated? If so, we have an approach to "reverence for life," for the wholeness of things in pres-

[3] *Ibid.*, pp. 18 ff.

ent, past, and future; and more, we have the base for a higher sense of value within which our redemption from provincialism begins.

My relation to education is primarily that of a frustrated but veteran suitor for I have sought her longer than many. I am still in love with her, however, and still carry the illusion that her pursuit ought to involve a progression from one wonder to another. I can join in cursing fervently the dullard who destroys wonder. In one of his introductions, C. D. Broad agrees with Kant that almost everyone is interested in these questions, though the interest can be killed "by a boring enough presentation of the subject." If my pursuit of learning has been so much a flight from boredom that I have failed more hours than many teachers teach, I have at least learned the truth of the dictum: "classical scholars, scientists, headmasters are alike ignoramuses." Indeed in *Doctor Ignorantia* Nicolas of Cusa claimed the beginning of wisdom lies at that point where one knows himself to be an ignoramus, while another saint of mine has discovered that "the world is made interesting by a delightful ignorance of important truths."

I know now that education involves putting some things together, and scraps of information have nothing to contribute to it. "A merely well-informed man is the most useless bore on God's earth." I know now that a fatal disconnectedness kills the vitality of modern programs of study. The average graduate transcript reads like an unalphabetized table of contents "which a deity might run over in his mind while he was thinking of creating a world, and had not yet determined how to put it together." I am familiar, too, with that *tedium vitae* which William James said is peculiar to reflecting men, and with the nightmare of pessimism common to men who ask too many questions and assume too little responsibility for demonstrating answers. Life in such a barren sputnik is more awful than life in Limbo. Nor, on the other hand, can education ever be the process of packing folded answers into a suitcase for some journey.

This is to say that all of us who seek education for ourselves and others are committed to the life of tension. Unless we understand, accept, and use these tensions we will go on squeezing through the educational factories men and women, "who can act skillfully but cannot think, who are trained, but not civilized, people who are deaf and blind in the arts, and because of their ignorance of history know nothing of the values of tradition and who exist in the present alone with no sense of continuity." [4] The primary condition of education is a situation of tension. The educational effort that does not put its people in tension with their past and their values and their environs is no true educational technique. It is technique that belongs to a training school, not to the university. Thoreau is close to this when he asks: "Why should we be in such desperate haste to succeed and in such desperate enterprises? If a man does not keep pace with his companions, perhaps it is because he hears a different drummer. Let him step to the music which he hears, however measured or far away." [5]

The goal of education is to hear a different drummer, but this is for both pupil and teacher a situation of tension and incitement. The beating of drums creates tension always; to hear the drummer is to wish to march, and is an incitement. But here is the point: the pupils go away bearing their tensions with them. Yet the tensions stay in the educational institution too, in the teacher, where they belong, with the incitement!

"Education," said Whitehead, "must essentially be a setting in order of a ferment already stirring in the mind; you cannot educate mind in vacuo." [6] Which is to say that tension is prerequisite to the educational situation, and the tensions are everywhere. Their name is Legion: knowledge and ignorance, freedom and responsibility, curriculum and person; unity and fragmentation, synthesis and analysis, parochialism and universalism, individual and community, town and gown, means and end, the one and the many, faith and knowledge, gnosticism and personalism, romanticism and realism. The educator lives in a world of mighty opposites. He has a dichotomous calling and must live between the tensions in suspension.

This situation of tension has its problems, and three of these, in any discussion of educational technique for release from provincialism, must be faced.

1. *Authority and Freedom: the problem of responsibility.* "Every encounter, whether friendly or hostile, whether benevolent or indifferent, is in some way, unconsciously or consciously, a struggle of power with

[4] William S. Carlson, *School and Society,* Vol. 81 (January 8, 1955); cited by Drake, article, *AAUP Bulletin,* Vol. 42, No. 4 (1956).
[5] *Walden,* p. 290.
[6] *The Aims of Education,* p. 30.

power." [7] Civilization is power, even if for the sake of human dignity men sometimes give it their backs. Organization is power, and if we aim to blow the world to pieces, as Menen claimed in the Ramayana, "that will still call for a greater organization than history has ever seen."

Education involves encounter, which is a situation of power which demands organization, and this is authority. Charles Malik misunderstands us when he says that in the West the university and the church are free. All universities and all churches are proprietary institutions. The question is never whether or not an educational institution is proprietary, the question is whether or not it is a university. It may transcend the structures that give it life, if so it is a university. It may wholly serve these structures. In this event you have a training school, not a university.

Education happens in the tension that maintains between the obligations of the institution which educates and the demands of the persons who seek and teach. This means that we can never live wholly free— there is no free place within the institutions of education. Terms like "free institution" are contradictory terms. There is no such thing as a free institution. The word "institution" means an absence of total freedom, for by the word the borders are nailed down.

The educational institution is tied by a thousand threads. Pressures are exerted to make it the guardian of traditions, and the threads hold it bound, like Gulliver, to the myth-system that sustains it. The university reflects "the value impregnated beliefs and notions that men live by and for." [8] Such institutions change slowly. They cannot and do not repent, recant, or confess. This is beyond their power, for corporations and committees do not have this grace. They simply press their weight and their values and are not capable of being wholly free. Kant puts it in this pharase, "Caesar non est supra grammaticus," Caesar is not above structures. Not even the emperor can go beyond the grammar of the language he must speak. The institution is tied by a thousand threads, and so Heinrich Heine used to claim that at Göttingen beadles were chosen each year to guard against the smuggling of any new ideas into the university.

[7] Paul Tillich, Love, Power, and Justice (New York: Oxford University Press, 1954), p. 87.
[8] Mark, article, AAUP Bulletin, Vol. 42, No. 4 (1956).

Can the educative institutions transcend the society within which they operate and become means of release from provincialism? I answer with an equivocating "Yes, sometimes." Great educational institutions do sometimes transcend the authority to which they are responsible. This is what we mean by a "university of the first class," but I wish to add quickly that no educative institution ever rises above its culture, and therefore its provincialisms, except in terms of its teachers. These are men who live in the tension between authority and freedom on the side of responsibleness. They accept a base of operation within an institution, but in their quest for escape from their own self-incurred tutelage they subject that base to the baptism of all the new light and all the new room they can find. Kant makes this mandatory for even clergymen, much less for professors! [9]

Most of us have learned much from men who have found institutions as shackles on their limbs—Spinoza, Locke, Hume, Marx, Nietzsche, Heine, Dostoevski—and in this country, Thoreau, Emerson, Veblen, and Peirce found the institutional life one difficult to be borne. I am not sure that Thomas Carlyle or Edward Gibbon could have taught long in a modern university—nor for that matter could Kierkegaard or Luther have found a comfortable place. I could read the list for the rest of the day of men who have lived with the dichotomy of this calling. Among them, high on the roster, I would place the names of those released men who first snatched my mind from its torpor and lit my candle day and night these twenty years. Can educative institutions transcend the society in which they operate? Sometimes—on the backs of men who are enlightened and empowered to live in the tension.

Teachers change things! Teachers become means in the educative process of release from provincialism. John Dewey seems to contradict himself here. Although he claims that a scholar has as much chance of changing his culture as a baby word has of remaining in the family vocabulary, Dewey still tries to change his culture. The fact remains, baby words do stay in our vocabularies and teachers do change things— and people.

There are built-in risks, however. Teachers too seldom know who they really are, and many are preoccupied with safety. Professors have their problems of tenure, but so do others. When any man has for years

---

[9] *Critique of Practical Reason*, Beck edition, p. 288.

maintained some sort of intellectual and spiritual tension in an unpopular theological, ethical, and even personal climate, when he is subject to the whims of a thousand trustees every time he climbs his pulpit to speak, tenure ceases to be a matter of urgent concern. Let us forget our preoccupation with the womb that is not there any more and teach. There are occupational hazards, there are built-in risks in our dichotomous calling. The goal of education is release from provincialism.

2. *Function and Existence: the question of means and end.* To define education in terms of a primary concern for function is to miss the real end of education. If I wished, however, a thoroughly descriptive list of functions I should look no further than that furnished by Frank C. Wegener. Man's basic functions are: intellectual, moral, spiritual, social, economic, political, physical, domestic, esthetic, recreational.[10] Yet, add these functions all together and you have still a list, not a man. No matter how tempting the arrangement for discussion, nor how convenient for purposes of curriculum planning, this is still piecemeal business, though powerful and influential business in today's educational world. This creates a tension, for there is another approach to release from provincialism.

Education must be considered in its relation to man's existence and the potentials of his existence. Certainly this involves his functions, but not as the end in view. The end is in man. Here, I have come to believe, even Dewey has been misunderstood. Wegener's critique of "Reconstructionism" suggests that we look to a philosophy of education which has faith in the educability of man through his rational powers to rise above "the limitations of an imperfect environment" (provincialism).[11] This, in my judgment, puts the emphasis where it belongs, but the tension between function and existence lies underneath to absorb the strength of the educative release from provincialism. It is so easy to major on function; it is so difficult to convert the ignorance of a boy within the field of his limitations into the powers of a man with less limitations.

Whitehead saw this tension as having the primary form of a radical inconsistency. We are committed, on the one hand, to scientific realism

---

[10] "The Ten Basic Functions of Man," *School and Society*, Vol. 80, No. 2038 (July 24, 1954).
[11] "The 'Ontology' of Reconstructionism," *Educational Theory*, Vol. II, No. 1 (1952).

—at base a mechanism requiring us to use mechanomorphisms. In our beliefs about ourselves, however, we are sure we are self-determining organisms and use anthropomorphisms to explain ourselves and to describe our God. "This radical inconsistency at the basis of modern thought accounts for much that is half-hearted and wavering in our civilization." [12] Man simply cannot be both functional and existential as ends. One must be end, and man is either by existential means a function or by functional means he approaches his potential as existence.

There are finished forms of functionalism around for observation. Any world where "the cathedral and the capitol, the museum and the concert chamber, the library and the university are the façade," but where the shambles are "in the rear" is a world that knows something of emphasis on function as an end.[13] Will Durant claims that so far as mere function is concerned man has ace competitors and "some day, perhaps, these chattering quadrupeds, these ingratiating centipedes, these insinuating bacilli, will devour man and all his works, and free the planet from this marauding biped, these mysterious and unnatural weapons, these careless feet!" [14] Aubrey Menen, however, in delightful humor, in the Ramayana saw the world of mere functionalism best. His hero took his morals from the best moralists and his politics from the most experienced politicians. As a result he was "ruined, exiled, and disinherited." In his world, the world of complete functionalism, when public dismay is at its height, you execute a general, and this always restores public confidence. The over-all goal is "bright shining faces, all in our places," and everyone knows his place, his caste, and his duties. All the impulses of the human spirit are regimented so that compassion becomes almsgiving, courage becomes military service, religion is a drill, and independent thinking is bad manners. But something is left out. This is the essence of provincialism.

The new person is more important than the new techniques. We cannot do without persons as an end, and a functional preoccupation leads to far too narrow a view: "These two billion persons are only one generation of countless generations of the tide of humanity ending, wave after wave, on the breakers of death. Then, what is a person? Is

[12] *Science and the Modern World*, p. 77.
[13] *Our Oriental Heritage* (New York: Simon and Schuster, Inc., 1935), p. 7.
[14] From *Our Oriental Heritage*. Copyright 1935 by Will Durant. By permission of Simon and Schuster, Inc.

he only a momentary, conscious, organic incident?" Is he "Like snow upon the desert's dusty face, lighting a little hour or two—is gone"? [15] If this person is to be so important to us, education must, says Northrop, "concern itself not merely with applied science and literature and art and practical matters but also with man's basic beliefs concerning the nature of himself and his universe." [16]

We must grant the validity of functional concerns. How else can we get at man except through his functions? Samuel Butler knows this in *The Way of All Flesh* but he begins with existence not with function. Yet he gives proper place to both by recognizing how intimately life is dependent upon a function—the power of accommodation. Life is the power of accommodation. If we fail to accommodate, we are stupid; fail flagrantly, we are mad; suspend the power, we sleep; give it up, and we are dead. "A life will be successful or not, according as the power of accommodation is equal to or unequal to this strain of fusing and adjusting internal and external changes." [17] Northrop calls for a resolution of the tension in education between function and existence; "the true relation between intuitive, esthetic, and religious feeling and scientific doctrine is one of mutual supplementation." [18] Franklyn, in Bernard Shaw's *Back to Methuselah* predicts: "Unless this withered thing religion, and this dry thing science, come alive again in our hands, alive and intensely interesting, we may just as well go out and dig the garden until it is time to dig our graves."

At Evanston, Charles Malik, professor of philosophy at Beirut's American University, spoke brilliantly to this tension in the West:

Thousands of Asian and African students come every year to western centers of learning where they are practically never required to go through and participate in the great banquet of being which is liberal education. They go back proficient in this or that technique, but with hardly any knowledge of the deepest things the western world really has to offer, and with even less critical appreciation of the deepest values of their own culture.

His magnificent plea for the East becomes a paean of highest exis-

[15] Reid, op. cit., p. 16.
[16] Op. cit., p. 101.
[17] Cited by Karl A. Menninger, *The Human Mind* (New York: Alfred A. Knopf, Inc., 1945), p. 19.
[18] Op. cit., p. 64.

tential principals of education for all mankind. "The aim should not be to propagandize this mind or to win it to a particular cause, whether political or religious. If the intention is to indoctrinate it with a view to using it even if for the best of causes, it will rebel."

The East, and the West, need:

History, literature, philosophy, theoretical excellence, refinement of sensibility, creative art, the issues of life and death, the art of debate and discussion, the appreciation of quality and the excellence of being, the whole range of the humanities wherein the mind can enjoy, in freedom, the wonderful ecstasy of vision wherein man becomes himself and therefore tragically understands his essential limitations—is there any doubt that the way of peace and truth is to cultivate these things in and for Asia and Africa? [19]

All this, for the educator, is a way of synthesis between function and existence. What is required is not the questionable freedom of being— this is sheer existence, the kind that ends in that abyss for which pessimism and despair are mild terms. What is required rather is the freedom of *becoming*. This is demanded in educators and for pupils. This is the synthesis of function and existence.

Somehow it does not seem strange to me that it is Bertrand Russell, whose comprehension of function goes beyond us all, who sees that the one great task of education is to bring every young man to his great renunciation. It brings him to that point where he comes to understand that the world does not serve him and he must therefore renounce those personal goods, so dependent upon function but so obliterative of existence. The man who resolves that tension for himself and in his students is an educator and is in the process of releasing men from provincialism.

3. *Provincialism and Wholeness: the matter of the many and the one.* Here we come to the crux of the matter of educational responsibility in release from provincialism. Especially in the field of education persons can be provincial in time as well as in space. A man may be so preoccupied with so narrow a base in science, esthetics, ethics, or religion that he loses the other three. He may be so limited in his view of persons that he commits the sin of particularity—with knowledge as an end to the exclusion of other values. This is the problem of insularity.

[19] Speech at second assembly of the World Council of Churches.

This provincialism is illustrative of the romantic-realist tension which affects education and educators as well as regions. Others, as mentioned, are the provincial tensions that maintain between gnosticism and personalism, analytic method and the goal of synthesis. It reserves its greatest damage for the tensions between wholeness and fragmentation, between an adequate cosmology and the gross departmentalization in educational circles which approaches the "fallacy of misplaced concreteness" in the attempt to put a whole life into too narrow a mold.

Archbishop William Temple has claimed that the chief characteristic of the modern period has been departmentalization.[20] Machiavelli proclaimed the independence of politics. The Reformation declared the independence of religion. Francis Bacon, and others, declared the independence of science; David Hume, and others, the independence of knowledge; Adam Smith, the independence of property; but it has remained for modern man to make education independent of life and nearly everything in it. This fragmentation, this attempted compartmentalization, this longed-for disconnectedness continues. No one learns to live, and the miserable people are shunted off to church as if a sermon would help!

At least the Middle Ages had a central theme, however badly based the faith, but now Humpty Dumpty has had his fall and lies thoroughly fragmented into schools, plans, courses, sections, divisions, departments, fields, majors, electives, and totally insular factions. The celebrated critic-at-large, Frank Dobie, has claimed that a man can take over three hundred courses in "education" and still not have an education.

Who will pull *curriculi-curricula* together again? He is an educator. I submit that no one else in today's world can even attempt it. This is why we are so involved with the university. The only escape from these provincialisms involves processes of education; the technique is educative.

This brings up the almost hopeless attempt to state in a few words what is required of education and of educators in what must be the most thrillingly possible and hopelessly involved task modern culture could demand of its wise ones.[21]

[20] *Nature, Man, and God* (London: Macmillan and Company, Ltd., 1951), p. 76.
[21] My obligation to Whitehead is obvious.

The educator who would educate must recognize the awful damage created by false categorization and therefore forswear all parochialism. He will work to escape the bad departmentalization responsible for so much prejudice between specialists, seeking to put all he teaches in its most inclusive context. He will seek to teach nothing "from which nothing follows" because he is aware of the interconnectedness of things. He avoids closed systems, scrappy information, paragraph picking, and those general generalizations which serve as crutches for the avoidance of the difficult. He will seek categories that permit mature precision and not its prevalent opposite. His syntheses will result from an awareness of the inner dependence of other branches of study. He will fan back to life the metaphysical inquiry native to all grammar-school children before it is swallowed up in bad scientism with its out-of-date and deceitful emphasis on exactness. He will protect personality from the overt individualism which makes even the groups we cannot forsake fascistic, but he will do this by seeking to create community between persons, not with false structures of bad sociology. He will recognize the tensions as his friends, without which education cannot happen, and he will seek to learn anew with each of his students the great skill of how to put enough tension on the line to pull a youngster toward release without breaking the line or letting it fall slack.

He knows his work is gradually done. It moves forward in spurts and he watches for "the moment." He knows his work is redemptive release for the student and is universally sacrificial for himself. He begins to taste within himself the creative release of new values, for something comes to live that had no life before. He begins to live a life of redemptive education, and new community opens because he is constantly discovering and centering on higher levels of value. Exciting old words he had forgotten—words like curiosity, hunger, reverence, work—come alive in his students again and one day he knows that he is, with Socrates and Albertus Magnus, a teacher, too. He is saved from pride at all this, however, by the knowledge of the relativity of his own release from that provincial disposition which cannot recognize its limitations. To him, now, his own limitations have become an incitement to conduct which puts its own creativeness to work in any neighborhood and he comes to love and respect the calling of educator so highly that he has a holy optimism that even trustees can be taught and is not averse to trying.

At least, I hope he can be this, all this, without pride. If so, he has a chance to release someone from provincialism, and if so, he is an educated saint. If not, may the dean, who may or may not be himself above pride, assign him to read every day the last page of Swift's description of the Yahoos in "*Voyage to the Houyhnhnms.*"

My reconcilement to the Yahoo-kind in general might not be so difficult, if they would be content with those vices and follies only which nature had entitled them to. I am not in the least provoked at the sight of a lawyer, a pickpocket, a colonel, a fool, a lord, a gamester, a politician, a whoremaster, a physician . . . a traitor, or the like; this is all according to the due course of things: but when I behold a lump of deformity and diseases both in body and mind, smitten with pride, it immediately breaks all the measures of my patience; neither shall I be ever able to comprehend how such an animal and such a vice could tally together.

What is required of education? Again, an understanding of our interdependence, not, as Frankfurter has said, by way of the cross-sterilization of the social sciences. It is required that we shall find a base in both culture and expert knowledge which will enable us to overcome the fatal disconnection of subjects. Whitehead insists that we must throw a few ideas into every combination possible. This is the cultivation of the art of the use of knowledge. He asks also for an approach to precision in learning that does not cut off romantic inquiry for the prospect of valid generalization. He asks that we make the pupils see the forest by means of the trees and this is a kind of synthesis. He begs for the fruition in an expanding order of the ferment previously created. It is not enough to stir. Sometimes we must resolve as well and this requires a realization of life's variousness.

Further, the educative technique of escape from provincialism is required to offer a foundation for reverence, by which Whitehead seems to mean the perception that this present holds within itself a complete totality of existence backward and forward. In this present all that has come to be exists and all that is to be exists at least in miniature. Augustine himself seems to have provided the backdrop for this view of time beginning in Book Eleven of his great *Confessions.* The Old

112

Testament prophets understood this. For them the God of Abraham, Isaac, and Jacob was their own God and the God of the future. For them all that had come in the past was alive in the present and bore its impress and its predictions of the future. In its approach to release from provincialism, education has incumbent upon it the task of providing an awareness of the structures that have made the present what it is and that predict what the future shall be. To ignore or miss this is to commit a crime—the abomination of history, of which so many students in modern times are guilty. To have done this is also to miss, with terrible potentiality, the prospect of continuance.

The end result of this approach is the creation of a sense of values. Aristotle talked of this with his doctrine of levels. Whitehead, too, in *The Aims of Education*, said:

> The ultimate motive power, alive in science, in morality, and in religion, is the sense of value, the sense of importance. It takes the various forms of wonder, of curiosity, of worship, of tumultuous desire for merging personality in something beyond itself. This sense of value imposes on life incredible labours, and apart from it life sinks back into the passivity of its lower types.[22]

It is the lack of this kind of education that produces provincialism to begin with. It is the long continued process involved in this kind of education that effects our redemption. But before we discuss the redemptive aspect of the educational technique for release from provincialism notice that the East-West crisis could respond best of all to a proper educative technique.

Restoration of Heritage

Charles Malik once more is convincing: "The possibilities of liberal education and humane culture strike me as not having been touched, so far as Asia and Africa are concerned." He charges that the importance of a liberal education, the cultivation of intellectual virtue for its own sake for Asia and Africa, is not understood by Christians in the West. We have been too involved, he says, with political, economic, social, cultural, and scientific problems. Upon these our attention has focused, and we have missed the importance of liberal education. The hope of Asia, Africa, and the West, and the resolution of our tensions, is some-

[22] P. 51.

how involved with the revival and cultivation of the tremendous intellectual values in the local traditions of the East and in the authentic traditions of the West.

The revival of Avicenna and Averroes alone in the Middle East will produce an intellectual revolution in one generation. The responsible publication of the world's greatest classics in the major local vernaculars will produce an intellectual revolution in less than two generations. A concentrated and sustained attack upon the problems of language so as to close the gap between the language of higher thought and the language of daily life will produce in time a considerable economy in the wasteful spiritual agony that creative thinkers in the East usually undergo.[28]

During the fifteen years since the close of the great war, and especially since the close of the war in Korea, I have come to know several hundred students from Asian countries, and even a few from Africa. They come to and they go from the major university centers of the West without too much opportunity to understand the great proficiencies and virtues of the West. They come here as Muslims, Hindus, Shintoists, Eastern Orthodox, and as products of mission schools. They come here as people educated in their own culture. They have keen minds and bright futures. Many come from homes of wealth in their native land. They are Chinese, Japanese, Indian, Jordanese, Arab, Egyptian, Lebanese, and some I have known bore the tribal markings of their primitive surroundings where childhood was an eked-out existence. They leave us as petroleum engineers, chemical engineers, physicians, physicists, and technicians, but they do not often go home as envoys for the Western world. They go back with technique, but with hardly any knowledge of the things that have made the West the West. They feel the inside of our churches; they see the inside of a home or two; they form their opinions of Western morality, Western values, and Western goals. They have their opinions of American women. They contrast the surface conditions of both cultures. *Most of them decide that the only meaning worth retaining is the deeper meaning of the culture from which they came.*

It will not be until education does something about the combination of great ideas, many of which originated in the East, something about creating a base both in culture and expert knowledge, something about

---

[28] Speech at second Assembly of World Council of Churches.

114

the fruition in an expanding order of a ferment previously created, something about a realization of life's variousness and the foundation of reverence and the creation of a sense of value, even in the West, for even Eastern students, that the real value of these transmigrations of students will begin to appear.

Meanwhile, Eastern countries have many desperately lonely creative men. They have received almost no love and understanding, and very little encouragement. Their relationships with each other are almost non-existent. They depend for stimulation upon their own surroundings and have little intimate communion. Each of them, therefore, becomes a focal point for rebellion in his lonesomeness. The aim of education has never been to propagandize these minds or to win them to a particular point of view, not when true education is in the picture. Only when East and West can come together on the highest intellectual plane in terms of virtue, freedom, and equality will we be able to know all those other than ourselves as ends in themselves. In this concession and progression on our part we and they will become peers in a world that is a common world.

The technique of education does not require curricular discussion at this point. Both East and West need everything—literature, philosophy, history, art, theology, technics, but this is not all. There must be also room for debate and discussion. There must be room for the creation of the appreciation of quality and excellence. There must be room for the whole gamut of the humanities wherein the mind can enjoy the prospect of the ecstatic vision wherein man becomes himself and comes at last to understand his finiteness but comes also to find his brother in the same situation. Is there any room, Malik once asked, to doubt that this is the way of peace and truth for Asia and Africa, and for the West?

Education as Redemption

By all this it must be obvious that when we speak of an educative technique we are speaking of redemptive education. Without the redemptive aspect of the educative approach education itself is immoral. There is a redemptive effect in Christian education without which the process of education is not only not Christian, it is not even education and is immoral. Nor is this to say that education is a means to redemption—rather, it is to say that there is redemption for education, corporately and personally. Persons effected by such a redemption produce a redemptive effect as educators. The redemptive effect of the educative technique is release from provincialism.

This is first a gradational redemption because the release is gradational.[24] I am not wholly released from my provincialisms, not totally and not yet. When I am released from my current limitations, in what new and more subtle provincialism will I find myself? I may escape from my nationalism, but even hemispheric solidarity would be a provincialism. When I have triumphed over all and so approach the limits of finitude that there is nothing left for me but to become a rival to God so free am I from localism, I still am involved in the ultimate of provincialism, my selfhood! The release is gradual, even gradational, and so is the redemption. At no single level of education can a man feel himself to be truly educated, all of which is to say that at no single level of redemption has redemption yet been made complete. I am still threatened by more highly refined provincialisms, even when I have escaped the lesser.

This redemption, this redemptive educative technique, has also a universal meaning—the recognition of the possibility of the existence of other and higher value judgments than our own. In the framework of release from provincialism there is no room for exclusiveness; there are no closed circles of redemptive eligibility. Only on the basis of this kind of universal and redemptive approach can education bear its gifts for a great sharing between East and West. We have a desperate need to hear; we need to hear each other; we need each other, which need refuses to allow the dwindling, the shriveling, of the universal.

At this point, Christianity, which is involved in both redemption and community, has a genuine universal to offer. Could it be doubted that this universal is wrapped up in that saying which Hocking called the most impressive coming out of the experience of the early church? "Behold, I stand at the door, and knock: if any man hear my voice, and open the door, I will come into him, and will sup with him, and he with me." This is an unbound and unlimited universal, pervasive of the world and of all history and this alone presupposes redemption. One cannot follow this kind of Christ into provincialism, for his "if any man"

[24] See Tsanoff, op. cit., pp. 364-401.

116

calls in the opposite direction to a larger community.[25] This, we say, is the genuine universal of the Christian faith and of education where it is education. This is the universal that has preceded all approaches from West to East and from East to West ahead of modern Christian enterprises of so-called mission. This is the universal understanding of the essence of the symbol of the Christ which precedes us in any redemptive approach to community. Hence, we have to mean not only gradational and universal education, we have to mean sacrificial redemption. This is the meaning of tension and cross. The cross is an extra-cultural symbol too, which requires its local applicableness. It rises up out of all the world's fissures, out of all of life's contradictions and demands, and requires the death of all our ego-ridden notions of cultural superiority, the release of all our white-men's burdens, and all our pride of largess. Some are more ready to receive this than others, but it cannot be denied that this gradational, universal, sacrificial, redemptive education issues actually in the creative release of new values. New values literally rise out of the collapse of old systems. Something comes to life that had no life before in the death of the institutional, denominational, provincial structures that must give way to the coming of new life. A culture finds a new community opening before it because a higher level of value has been centered, and the means of finding this is redemptive education. The curse of closed systems, with all pedantry and deliberate delimitation of community, is lost in an educative approach to our cultural limits based on the interdependence of knowledge, the variousness of tensions, the new ferment, the wonder, the curiosity, and the hungers of reverence. The knowledge of the relative nature of our release in the face of our great need for universal release, the knowledge of the partial release that can be made whole only by sacrificial creative redemption issues in that disposition of mind which accepts any cultural limitation as an incitement to education which puts this creativeness to work in any neighborhood.

The Higher Community

This can happen on earth only in the light of one's consciousness of belonging to a higher community. Christians know this community as the kingdom of God and say that the source and ground of Christian

[25] Hocking, op. cit., Study IV, pp. 64-136.

117

ethics is here. On earth they know their own church as the reflection of that great Church which also lives as the channel and means of God's work in history and which, too, rises and lives in the kingdom of God. The awful sadness, the conviction for sin, the curse of that provincialism that throttles a man is in part the reflection of his awareness that his church does not yet know to whom it belongs, nor where its only source rises, so he longs for the kingdom of God and rebels against the confinement of his provincialism and stands with his chest against the fence wanting freedom to seek this beatitude of universal love on his own.

Why does he stay where he is? How can one stay within a framework he has already discovered to be provisional and provincial? By what processes of compromise and death does a man remain a member of a limited communion when with all his soul he longs for membership in the larger frame?

He knows, first, that any escape that will come to him will provide release only to another, perhaps larger, but limited pasture. He knows any escape is therefore abortive, temporary, and provisional. Should he abandon wholly the frame within which life first found him, he knows that his escape from this immediate delimitation of community will only subject him to newer, more subtle, and even more vicious provincialisms. That is to say, he knows the relative nature of any release and finds in even this a consciousness of kinship with all those men of other confessions, creeds, and nations who stand pressed against their fences, too. He stays where he is because he learns that there is no place to go. He feels the agony of confinement native to finitude and, therefore, joins the human race, where he is.

He can stay where he is, second, because he knows that there are values and potentials trapped within the lower form, his own community. He is aware of submerged worthwhileness, of hidden possibilities that must not be forgotten or destroyed. He sticks around to be used in the saving of the salt. He will not go outside and throw rocks from a larger pasture. He knows there are values hidden here that are worth his life to preserve and in spite of his despair, he has come to love the place.

Third, he senses, then comes to know, the presence of other climbers on the wall, other travelers on the road. He stays because he is drawn to them by the common agony and delight of the seeking and finding.

118

A new church happens for him. Communion comes in a touch of the hand, a flick of the eye, and frequently, on this road, a confession of the heart late at night. There is constituted for him a most holy, most secret, most intimate personal church. In its light and strength and communion he lives his life, knowing he belongs simultaneously to these and to this and that this fellowship with other climbers exists only because there is a climb to be made.

All this is to say that a man can stay in a framework he knows to be provisional and provincial because he knows all the time that he belongs to a higher community. To this higher community both his institutional framework and his "fellowship of other climbers" belong and exist as a reflection. In this awareness of belonging always to the higher he finds ability to live. More, he feels the call of the higher community to come and to stay. He does both, he comes and he stays, knowing all the time that this kind of call will split him. He knows all this and comes to know that this is what it means to live on a cross, for the cross means here the tension that maintains between the higher good and the local potential. Yet, on every day's journey he feels the invasion of the higher into the lower community in that penetration of love that will not leave us as we are and gives us friends for our journey.

Fog and mist hang heavily in the dense, firred forest of the Brazos where it breaks out of its torturous canyon thousands of feet below the Brazos peaks. Climbing from its bed to the crest of the peaks is a thirty-mile agony over razor sharp ledges, torturous turns, dizzy cascades—the work of days, if indeed one could pack enough provender to make it. But there is a long slide of shale and heavy rock, rising sheer to a saddle a thousand feet below the summit of the peaks. If one has the heart, the lungs, and the will, he can start in the forest darkness wrapped in its perpetual shroud and climb as daylight descends the walls—up, up past timber line, agonizingly, heartbreakingly, until at noon he breaks out in good light, and by midafternoon he can crest the Brazos peaks in sunlight that reveals every torturing twist of the excruciating canyons that make northern New Mexico a land of marvelous beauty and wild delight. From the top of the Brazos you can see everything; you can see it all, heaving from your hours of aching climb—but you know all the time that there are higher mountains!

119

Part Three

INSTITUTIONALISM

prejudgment of value

In *Spiritual Exercises* Ignatius Loyola gives some rules for thinking with the Church. His thirteenth rule reads: "To make sure of being right in all things, we ought always to hold by the principle that the white that I see I would believe to be black, if the Hierarchical Church were so to rule it." [1] This is institutionalism in a religious mold.

A matter of hours before our flight left for Tokyo two of the most distinguished ministers on the West Coast had their invitations to participate in a ten-week preaching mission revoked. They were under investigation of a Senate Committee at the instigation of some dissident groups in Oregon and California. The charges were pacifism and the support of certain tenant land reform programs. The effect of the unjustified charges was to brand them more or less permanently as "enemies of the state." This is institutionalism in a nationalistic mold.

Back in 1945, the then Senator from Mississippi, Mr. Bilbo, had correspondence with a Mrs. Apilado, a Negro teacher in Chicago. Ac-

---

[1] Joseph Rickaby, *The Spiritual Exercises of St. Ignatius Loyola*, (2nd ed.; London: Burns, Oates & Washbourne, 1936), p. 223.

121

cording to Bergen Evans, he advised her to get a job as a charwoman, "since evidently you did not try to learn anything until maturity, because you know it is a biological fact that a Negro skull, where the parts of it are connected by sutures ossifies by the time a Negro reaches maturity and they become unable to take in information." [2] This is institutionalism in a racist mold.

[2] *Op. cit.*, p. 206 ff.

Chapter VII

The Nature of Institutionalism

Institutionalism is the effect of the placing of inordinate value upon those frames, standards, ideas, or forms in which human history has congealed. Human history is the record of human ways of doing, thinking, and feeling. Some of these ways of doing, thinking, and feeling we wish to preserve because of our judgment of their value. The process of preserving these ways of doing, thinking, and feeling creates institutions.

Institutionalism is the creation of or the acceptance of previously created vehicles to hold one's valuables, accompanied by a subsequent veneration of the vehicle above its contents and by its veneration above the contents of other vehicles as well.

To make it short the institution is the lodging place of value; it is the repository built to contain a value judgment. Most value judgments are affected by prejudiced judgment. This means that from the beginning the institution and the prejudice rest in the same bed.

Institutionalism and Prejudice

Indeed, the prejudice stands with the relationship of a creative cause in the making of the institution. This is to say that in the fundamental structure of things, institutions and prejudice find themselves together for "prejudice is more than an incident in our lives; it is lock stitched into the very fabric of personality." [1] It cannot be extracted. To change a prejudice the whole pattern of life has to be altered. This means that the institutions our prejudiced judgments have built resist, just as personality resists, the death of prejudice. The dynamics of the prejudice that lives in institutions are the same as the dynamics of the prejudice that lives in personality.

In general, Allport shows, prejudiced people simply do not like freedom, especially freedom from institutions. It is impossible to predict the consequences of freedom. To act on one's own initiative allows too much indefiniteness, disorderliness, and opportunity for change. The prejudiced person resists change and this preserves institutions. It is simpler and easier to live in a bounded set of orders where people, things, and ideas can be labeled and where the sets do not shift around. "To avoid such slipperiness the prejudiced person looks for hierarchy in society. Power arrangements are definite, something he can understand and count on." [2]

The person with character-conditioned prejudices likes order, especially social order, and this forces him to live his life in a world of institutions. He likes clean breaks and clearly marked institutions, and he joins them. He likes the safety and the definiteness that these memberships provide. The clubs, the committees, the schools, the churches, the lodges, the state, the nation, become defenses against disturbance which he dreads. He leans on these institutions in order that he might not have to rely upon his own resources. Prejudiced people give more devotion to institutions than unprejudiced people, according to Allport's research. The most viciously prejudiced people are the most fanatically loyal members of churches, lodges, and similar institutions.

Among prejudiced people this prejudgment of value appears as a fanatical loyalty or a just as fanatical opposition to various symbols of the values one wishes to defend, to preserve, or fears. These symbols, usually verbal, appear in the conversation and daily lives of all peoples.

---

[1] From Gordon W. Allport, *The Nature of Prejudice*, 1954, Addison-Wesley, Reading, Mass. p. 400.
[2] *Ibid.*, p. 406.

Symbols of Institutionalism

In a broad mountain valley I was privileged to come to young manhood. I can recall the conversations I overheard as a boy around the stores and mills, at lunch hour on the ditch gangs and the construction jobs, at the church, the school, and wherever my elders gathered to talk. In general, we supported William Jennings Bryan against Clarence Darrow over at Dayton, Henry Ford, who was paying $5 a day in Detroit—if one could just get there, Congressman J. Will Taylor, the American Legion, the First National Bank, Charles A. Lindbergh, baptism by immersion, the Republican party, the Junior Order of United American Mechanics, the Anglo-Saxon race, the competency of the individual, the Fourth of July parade, Mother's Day, the Volunteer State, the abortive attempt of certain east Tennesseans to kidnap the Kaiser near the close of World War I, and the Tennessee Central Railway. These loyalties even spilled over, in boyhood, to include the brand names of items used at our house and the firms from which they were bought. For example, our clothing came largely from T. L. Cates or Sears & Roebuck; we used Orient flour, Arm & Hammer baking soda, P. & G. soap for laundry, Octagon soap for overalls, and Palmolive soap for ourselves. The *Knoxville News Sentinel* was our newspaper, and the Baptist church furnished our worship and religious education. If, on afternoons at play, we occasionally wandered into some playmate's home and discovered that instead of the brands we used that they ordered from Larkin, or used some other flour, baking powder, or soap, or went to a different kind of church, we walked a little softly, as if among foreigners. At least there was a little feeling of insecurity at being among folk who lived differently.

Usually we were able to agree on our villain institutions. With negative emphasis one could hear in a group of talking men words against Herbert Hoover, Father Coughlin, chain banks, chain stores, the Catholic church, the Huns, Seventh Day Adventists, Federal agents, and some school teachers. On the other hand, we had a uniform and high regard for a certain sheriff, the Tennessee Valley Authority, a certain funeral home whose ambulance drivers we admired, certain baseball teams, coaches, and at least three local citizens who remained tremendous institutions in our eyes. We had little truck with foreigners, but the two Jewish families in the county were warmly received and,

125

so far as I remember, made to be very much at home. A little later on we learned other symbols of antipathy or affection and could speak of Martin Dies, Burton K. Wheeler, or Gerald Smith. We talked about Socialists, the Soviet armies, the Zionists, Felix Frankfurter, Negroes, and Eleanor Roosevelt, with various degrees of like or dislike.

It is interesting, in this connection, that we were always violently patriotic. Our categories were usually irrationally connected and constituted. For example, we excused our dislike for all Jews by expressing our affection for the one or two Jewish people that we knew and did not recognize, in general, that our affinity for certain national institutions existed precisely because there was irrational hostility toward nations whose evil attributes we had exaggerated or overgeneralized. We did not know, then, that most of our reformers were more prejudiced than those they were trying to reform. We blindly refenced our divisions by making exceptions for every attractive Jew, foreigner, or Yankee that we met, which permitted us to maintain our prejudices in spite of mounting contradictory evidence. We were unaware that the very act of affirming our "American way of life" led us to the brink of desperate prejudice.

This is not true of one mountain valley alone; this is true of every center of population of any size, or of no size, on the face of the earth. What are the sources of this kind of institutionalism?

Some Psychological Sources of Institutionalism

The question as to why men always give themselves to institutions is part of a larger question with which we are dealing here, viz., why do men always go too far in giving themselves to institutions?

Not until some clearer *Gestalt* of human personality is advanced will we likely be able to come forward with a clearer picture of why prejudiced people are prejudiced with respect to institutions. We simply know now that prejudiced people do give themselves to the support of institutional values and that this seems to arise out of a reliance on, if not a demand for, unity, order, authority, mystery, and power. Various psychologists use various phrases in explaining this phenomenon.[3] We testify simply that this is a fundamental structure of prejudice because everywhere prejudiced people exist there is the concomitant of an institutional com-

[3] Allport, of course, is widely used. See also Arnold M. Rose, "The Roots of Prejudice," *The Race Question in Modern Science* (New York: UNESCO, 1956), 215-43.

mitment in some form or another. Institutions per se do not cause this; institutions house it. It would exist if there were no values around which institutions could be built. The homing place of all our prejudices, however, appears most clearly in connection with some value that we wish to defend, preserve, or reduce.

There is among men in general a tendency to emphasize externals. This is seen in every religion and in every historical movement of men. Jesus of Nazareth, Spinoza, Nietzsche, and Goethe all commented on this emphasis on externals. William Stern says that personality develops in "convergence with the environment." Out of man's general tendency to externalism in convergence with a common environment, certain general dispositions seem to help determine institutions:

Aristotle noted man's disposition to community including its concomitants, unity, and order. There is in man a gregariousness which, under the influence of this tendency to externals, causes man to erect a unified ordered community displaying hierarchical rank, order, and form.

Bertrand Russell speaks of our more or less general disposition toward authority; that there is within us an innate desire for authority both in the sense of control and of standard. Under the influence of our tendency to externalism this expresses itself as the external authority of race, nation, society, and church.

Fëdor Dostoevski knows best our disposition to mystery and miracle. There is in man a desire for the mysterious and the miraculous as a demonstration of the validity of his belief in his gods. Under the discoloration from his tendency to externalism, this thirst for mystery and miracle issues in the systems that make sacred values sacred.

Nietzsche has no doubt that there is a disposition to power: there is in man a "will to power" which when expressed within the frame of predisposed externalism has the result of thrusting institutions into competition with each other and culminates in the claim of some to jurisdiction over all others as religiopolitical super-states.

There are major expressions of institutionalism in all times. By institutionalism, in this connection, we mean that overweening emphasis on various instrumental values on the part of peoples so committed to their preservation or annihilation that some institution is given the value of an end in itself. Among these major expressions of institutionalism in our time are racism, nationalism, and the institutions of religion.

127

Chapter VIII

Major Forms of Institutionalism

Racism

Race, says Ashley Montague, is a mischievous and retardative term. It is a new concept; for most of human history prejudice has had little to do with race.[1] The concept of race is recent, scarcely a century old, says Karl Barth. Benjamin Marais questioned fourteen leading European theologians on the scriptural sources of race prejudice; apparently there are none. Race and racism are modern problems.[2] Bergen Evans asks, "How did the word race acquire such sinister force?" On its first appearance, in the sixteenth century, it was harmless enough.[3] It signified the children of a common parent or, by extension, a whole generation. Then the zoologists took the word to describe local varieties of animals

[1] Michel Leiris, "Race and Culture," *The Race Question in Modern Science*, pp. 118-19.
[2] Benjamin Mays, report at the Evanston meeting of the World Council of Churches, No. 5A. See also No. 8A, a report by Marais; Everett Tilson, *Segregation and the Bible* (Nashville: Abingdon Press, 1958); Haselden, op. cit.; Juan Comas, "Racial Myths," Otto Klineberg, "Race and Psychology," G. M. Morant, "The Significance of Racial Differences," *The Race Question in Modern Science*, pp. 11-50, 55-71, 285-322; and *The Race Concept*, a result of a UNESCO inquiry, 1951.
[3] Comas, op. cit., 13. "There was no true racial prejudice before the fifteenth century."

belonging to the same species. This was a usage maintained until it began to be apparent that man also was an animal. Mays adds that

it was not, in fact, until the seventeenth century that the outlines of the modern race problem began to emerge . . . it was when Western imperialism began to explore and exploit the colored peoples of Africa, Asia, and America that the beginning of segregation and discrimination based on color and race was initiated. It was then that color was associated with "inferiority," and white with "superiority." [4]

As Invalid Category

This racism is a false concept. "There is no evidence for the existence of so-called 'pure' races." [5] Race is not a valid category of prejudice, in itself, but is a derivative. It is a product of provincialism—prejudgment of community—and institutionalism—prejudgment of value—multiplied by each other. That is to say, community concerns and institutional values become involved with each other and the object of discrimination becomes a falsely conceived racial group.[6] Toynbee claims that the so-called racial explanation of differences in human performance and achievement is either an ineptitude or a fraud.[7] Gunnar Myrdal rules out race as inappropriate in scientific inquiry, "since it had biological and genetic connotations which are incorrect in this context and which are particularly dangerous as they run parallel to widely spread false racial beliefs." [8] Toynbee again points out that man is so nearly one that within the genus homo there are no differences of physical race which have the sexual effect of making cross-union sterile.[9]

Racism cannot serve as an illustration of a fundamental structure of prejudice. It is not this; it is the combination of our limited notions of community multiplied in effect by our prejudgments of value. Eco-

---

[4] Mays, op. cit. See Kenneth Little, "Race and Society," *The Race Question in Modern Science*, pp. 165-209. "A very close connexion between racial myths and national and imperial ambitions." P. 210.

[5] *The Race Concept*, op. cit., p. 15; from the official UNESCO statement, containing comments of world leading anthropologists.

[6] Little, op. cit., p. 175, "race relations are, in effect, a function of a certain type of social and economic system."

[7] Toynbee, op. cit., I, 245.

[8] *An American Dilemma* (New York: Harper & Brothers, 1944), p. 669.

[9] See also L. C. Dunn and Theodosius Dobzhansky, *Heredity, Race and Society* (New York: New American Library, 1945).

nomics, aesthetics, religion, and the family all have their role to play in our notions as to what is truly valuable. These notions of the valuable are sharply limited by our provincialism and our institutionalism; hence a construct like racism, a combination of provincialism and institutionalism, can appear. It is not in any valid way a separate category, for race as a personality determinative or a biological or anthropological construct simply does not exist.[10]

Modern anthropology knows nothing of any racio-psychic characteristics.[11] Modern sociology knows no intra-cultural tie up of prejudice, for prejudice is everywhere a product of provincialism times institutionalism.

There is no organic connection, I repeat, between race prejudice in South Africa and in Alabama. Modern biology knows no organic justification for this; there is only an invalid stereotyping which refuses to see men as individuals and prefers to keep them in nice safe categories. Most important, competent biblical theology knows that race is strictly a modern concept, biologically, sociologically, and theologically false.

Bergen Evans has called race the most dramatic illustration of our "vulgar errors." John Stuart Mill pointed out, in that area where racism first really began to be a power, that it was a product of the deliberate avoidance of thought. "Of all the vulgar modes of escaping from the consideration of social and moral influences on the human mind, the most vulgar is that of attributing the diversities of conduct and character to inherent natural differences." This powerful myth of race remains, however, and is called by some the greatest single obstacle to world peace today.[12] It exists in many forms. There are other than black-white differences. Race prejudice, as race prejudice, exists between and among many different kinds of people. Who can deny, however, that its focal point has been reached and its most vicious expression represented in

[10] See Leiris, op. cit., pp. 119-21, "the origins of race prejudice are economic and social." Also p. 96. See also Mays, "all so-called races are variable population," The Race Concept, p. 17.
[11] "No serious student of race admits or uses such an idea." Dunn, The Race Concept, p. 79.
[12] "At present . . . the term 'race' has only one rational use in anthropology, namely to apply to the whole human race as distinct from other species." L. S. Penrose, The Race Concept, p. 24. Klineberg, op. cit., p. 75, "There is no indication that some races are biologically inferior to others," and p. 84, "The scientist knows of no relation between race and psychology."

that expectation of the white one sixth of mankind that they shall continue to receive the co-operation of the nonwhite five sixths of the whole race of man in maintaining the economic and social dominance of the lesser portion.

The only tools for maintaining such a cultural and social superiority are force or fraud, or both—and this is the definition of war. There is no world order possible within the limitations of our ideas of minority superiority which is not to be maintained as an order by means of war. It is a false construct.[13] For nearly eight hundred years there have been only temporary delays in what appears to be an almost incessant movement in the direction of the competency and worth of the individual, any individual. It is ridiculous to assume that any set of old ideas, even the construct of isolationism as seen in the American South, can be powerful enough to delay for long this movement.

If the South in 1860 would have looked at the world, it would have seen that history had passed it by. Chattel slavery had been abolished almost throughout the western world. The South was already but a tiny island of slavery in a rising sea of freedom of sorts. Its inundation was inevitable.

Today the South finds itself in the same position. Again history has passed it by, this time in reference to educational practice. No where else in the western world, which is one community, with the exception of parts of Africa, is there such discrimination as the South has used and continues to use in many places. Again it is an island in a rising sea and its inundation is again inevitable. The highest authority in the land has spoken, and like it or not, the South must eventually accept the decision, however deliberate its speed. The South tried to escape the inevitable once, and has suffered for it ever since. It cannot afford to make the same mistake twice. It cannot afford to be diverted by a cause already lost.[14]

An impossible race view rests on the simple belief that one can make valid and definite correlations between physical features and spiritual, mental, or innate capacities like intelligence and character. This is to say, one rests his treatment of people on the basis of a simple belief that

[13] Little, op. cit., p. 165, "It is history rather than race which is the main factor in producing the difference between the cultures and cultural attainment of the world's populations."

[14] Walter Prescott Webb, "'Economic Progress of the South, 1930-1950," address to Southern Historical Association, Houston, Texas, November 7, 1957. Used by permission.

white men have certain gifts and black men have certain liabilities. Toynbee points out that this notion of a correlation between physical race and psychical race is really an attempt to explain one unknown quantity in terms of another.[15] Dunn and Dobzhansky claim that racism consists in the belief that spiritual and mental traits are properties of "the blood." [16] We speak of the blood of our ancestors, the blood of the Saxon, our English blood, our white blood, our mountain blood, as if the blood itself were thought to transmit within its molecules the plasms, the very essence, of personality traits. This primitive notion has had and continues to have devastating weight. This "blood" capacity for transmitting traits applies even to Deity, for there are those willing to say that the cardinal truth of Christianity is that *"the blood of God was in the veins of Jesus' body"*! [17]

As Fallacy of Misplaced Concreteness

At this point in the discussion something must be brought forward about social Darwinism.[18] This calm, gracious, and tremendous man, Charles Darwin, this contributor to Christian missions, has been made the author of a theory of hate and inhumanity by those who have misunderstood his misunderstanders. During the decades immediately following the publication of Darwin's work biologists were almost wholly preoccupied with their studies in the field of biological evolution. They did not, perhaps they could not, look far beyond the immediate confines of their science, but there were plenty around to do this looking for them. They were nonscientific, eager-minded men, and seizing upon any tool available, they produced a strange mixture of false biology and political notions which we now refer to as social Darwinism.

Biology to Sociology

Chief among these misusers of the work of Darwin was Herbert Spencer, who, particularly in his *Synthetic Philosophy* and in other works in ethics, set the stage for an abortive misconstruction of Darwin's work.[19] Simply put, the belief of Spencer was that the cardinal notions

[15] *Op. cit.,* I, 209.

[16] *Op. cit.* See also Comas, *op. cit.,* pp. 17-24.

[17] *Soul Winner's New Testament,* 1959 Revised Edition, made especially for The Clift Brannon Evangelistic Association, by National Bible Press, Phil., p. 28.

[18] "It is unfair to level at Darwin . . . the reproach that he promoted this hateful and inhuman theory." Comas, *op. cit.,* p. 15.

[19] Claude Levi-Strauss says that Spencer's social-evolutionism antedates the work of

in biology are transferable to the moral realm and to the realm of human living. That is to say, Spencer was quite sure that evolution was a cosmic principal of unity. He believed that there is a world energy, a power, but we cannot discover the nature of this ultimate reality. Life, then, is the "continuous adjustment of internal relations to external relations." The natural laws of this evolutionary process lead toward good harmony. Man is not to interfere. He is to trust in nature. The biological changes that work in man are headed in the direction of the elimination of evil. The goal toward which we automatically are moving is one of happiness and progress. The state must not interfere, and society must not interrupt, for if nature is not interrupted she will cast off the weak and the strongest will reproduce their kind. The cardinal doctrine of this notion of synthetic philosophy is that throughout the history of the universe there has been and must always be a progress "from an indefinite, incoherent homogeneity to a definite, differentiated, coherent heterogeneity." [20] Therefore we are to leave nature alone. The whole world is to leave nature alone. We are to "leave them alone and they'll come home, wagging their tails behind them." This emphasis on power, nature, development, and adaptation is lifted from a biological frame and thrust precisely within a moral frame. This is a naturalistic ethic, this is the ethic of evolution. In its extreme form, what is is right, or better said, "might makes right." It means that the explanation of the higher, later, or more complex form is always in terms of the lower, earlier, or simpler. The direction is toward progress. Nature's laws determine our behavior. Resident forces explain conduct: the appeal is made to facts of nature as the ethic of domination. What is natural is right. The standard of goodness evolves, process is at work in nature, the good is achieved by natural selection. The fittest will survive. Nature with its conflicts results in man's destiny which is to be achieved through his struggle for power. Virtue is strength and might, or obedience to strength and might. There is one virtue for the strong and another morality for the weak.

In this invalid transfer of ideas from biology to sociology is illustrated

Darwin; that Spencer worked his scheme out not having seen Darwin's *Origin of Species*. Contemporary, simultaneous, or even more in identical climate as to origin, Spencer's work has been the basis for later so-called social-Darwinism. See Levi-Strauss, "Race and History," *The Race Question in Modern Science*, pp. 123-59.

[20] Herbert Spencer, *First Principles of a New System of Philosophy* (London, 1860-62); revised (New York, 1872).

most effectively Whitehead's "fallacy of misplaced concreteness." It comes out with the notion that the ideas that survive are true. Practical results are the sole tests of truth. Whatever succeeds is the voice of God and the real test of any validity is how well such an idea works in organization. Notice its easy assumption of automatic progress. Notice its exchange of ends and means. Notice an economic determinism that applies even to spiritual matters, and notice its instinctualism, its evolutionary progressivism, and remember that the main work of the last forty years in ethics has been to destroy and render invalid this kind of evolutionary automatic progress, this misplacement of biology from its natural sphere to the sphere of morals and thought.[21]

By Spencer's notion of the survival of the fittest, which applied even to shoemakers working in competition, war becomes a process by which nature replaces the biologically inferior. Spencer was followed by others. Francis Galton, the nephew of Darwin, and Joseph Arthur Gobineau, with his monumental work, *Essay on the Differences in Races.*[22] This was enough, enough to establish a philosophical base for all of the principles that a false racism would ever need. Add to this, however, a misunderstanding of Nietzsche, and his Superman became the biologically fittest to survive; thus the transfer from biological misunderstanding to sociological error was complete.

Any modern biologist must declare the complete uniqueness of every human individual. This uniqueness which exists biologically must be recognized in personal, psychological, and political terms, if one speaks in terms of a valid ethic or even of democracy.[23] Meanwhile, Dunn and Dobzhansky have commented, "It is bad biology as well as dangerous deceit to say that man is nothing but an ape with a few extra tricks." [24] Even if an ape, each man is unique, "every human individual differs from all others."

---

[21] See Hastings Rashdall, *The Theory of Good and Evil* (2nd ed.; New York: Oxford University Press, 1924), vol. 2, book 3, chapt. 4, pp. 356-413. See also Windelband, *The History of Philosophy*, trans. Tufts (New York: The Macmillan Company, 1956), pp. 630-69.

[22] Published in French in three volumes, 1853, Volume One translated into English. Count de Gobineau was antedated by Count Henri de Boulleinvillers, 1658-1722.

[23] Roger J. Williams, *Free and Unequal: The Biological Basis of Individual Liberty* (Austin, Tex.: University of Texas Press, 1953). See also Dobzhansky, *The Race Concept*, op. cit., p. 73.

[24] Op. cit., p. 67.

Theology to Biology

The end result of this development of a misunderstanding of Darwinian evolution appeared as a shift from theological thinking to biological thinking. Already, especially in this country, there was plenty of theological support, in the absence of any biology at all, for the kind of life the South had found it economically profitable to live. In the South there was a definite attempt to preserve the doctrine of equality. This was a creedal, theological, political idea, and one intended for whites. George Kelsey has shown the origins of the slavery motif in the sense that it did become, from a beginning in bond service for a limited term, a claim to permanent ownership.[25] This civil institution of continued slavery and inequality for blacks was so economically profitable that the ante-bellum South found in addition to its theological supports a new biological doctrine of inequality which it subsequently was to give an additional theological base.[26] For example, the sons of Ham were judged to be within the will of God when they occupied an inferior status. The race doctrine of biological inequality was a convenient addition, and its conclusion that the Negro was inferior was a natural for all the unsophisticated whites who permeated the culture of the South.[27] After the days of reconstruction, biology and ethnology were used to supplant theology and history in making castes justifiable. Myrdal claims that even the Negroes' friends have assumed that there were great biological, sociological, and psychical differences between the races.[28]

There is a continuing need for race prejudice in our country to provide for us a defense against the accusations of our most cherished ideal, our national creed of equality. Even Senators sense this, and one at least gave a considerable portion of his famous grandly prejudiced speech on segregation to a claim that school facilities in Texas were truly equal.

The end result then in this shift back and forth between theological and biological thinking is as follows: It was an accursed day that ever

[25] "The Ethico-Cultural Revolution in American Race Relations," *Religion in Life*, xxvi, No. 3 (Summer, 1957), pp. 335-44.

[26] Comas, *op. cit.*, pp. 14-15.

[27] "The declaration that all men are created equal was a fine one and remains so, even though and in the best sense because it is untrue in the biological sphere." Comas, *The Race Concept*, p. 19. See also Comas, "Racial Myths."

[28] *Op. cit.*, p. 90.

we theologized and falsely biologized our great discrepancy in our creed of equality. About 120 years ago this fundamental contradiction between our tenet, all men are equal, and our common practice, some white men are equal, began to speak to our consciences. The thing just did not look right. Even though we brought hundreds of slaves into our churches and called them "our people," it still did not look right. Yet slavery, for the "new South," was so vital an economic institution, and prosperity was so obviously God's design for us, that it had to be right. There had to be an explanation and there was.

In the mid-1800's we could not yet call biology to our rescue, for she was barely a science. In the South, theology was queen of the sciences, for astronomy and geology could not replace her without the help of biology, and Darwin had not yet written. Without Darwin to call on, we went a notch higher and used God.[29] Theology would explain this contradiction—and it did, until biology came to bolster the spots where theology sagged at the seams.

God did this thing. He made races; he intended races; and we violate his will if we try to unmake anything he has made. He makes some peoples superior and some inferior. Some are sons of Ham, "drawers of water" and "hewers of wood." Let us not tamper with God's decree. Though such reasoning seeped through the seams of our consciences here and there, the theology did it. This theological argument still survives a hundred years later to form the bulwark of the Dutch Reformed gasps at preserving economic superiority by means of apartheid in South Africa. They are preaching our 1845 theology, as we shall presently see.

Meanwhile Darwin came through, and modern biology was no longer work for naturalists and bird watchers. It became a science. Under the twistings of Spencer and Huxley, Darwin, poor Darwin, was made to make claims he never dreamed. Malthus and Mendel and Darwin, what crimes were committed in their names! A word that once referred to families of flowers now began to be used in a new sense. Race came to mean a difference in color pigmentation of human skin, and other differences. Gobineau expanded them; Houston Chamberlain copied Gobineau; Nietzsche used his own ideas to build Superman; Hitler wrote

[29] Paul B. Barringer, *The Natural Bent* (Chapel Hill, University of North Carolina, 1949). Here a famed pioneer in medical education in the South gives from memory some of the interpretations of cultured Presbyterian divines he heard in his boyhood, circa 1855-1860.

them into *Mein Kampf*, but worst of all, in the Southern United States, we used a butchered biology to bolster a biased theology that threatens to destroy not only our major principle of equality, but our very lives as a potential people of God.

Since about 1775 a blend of poor theology and poorer biology has crystallized in our minds to form the claims of false racism.[30] These claims in turn focus into five principles of racism. They are as false as they are deadly. They all appear in the first volume of Gobineau's *Essay on the Differences in Races*, which explains why volumes two and three are still in French. We needed only one volume. Every single one of these principles has been offered by some "educator" during the past year as the fruit of his own vast research and earnest inquiry. Worse, it has been done and accepted with a straight face. What are these vaunted principles, by which and upon which racism thrives?

Its False Principles

The Negro people belong to a separate race of mankind. The Negro race has an entirely different ancestry. The Negro race is inferior in as many capacities as possible. The Negro race has a place in the biological hierarchy somewhere between the white man and the anthropoids. The Negro race is so different both in ancestry and in characteristics that all white peoples in America, in contradistinction to the Negroes, can be considered a homogeneous race. The individuals in the Negro race are comparatively similar to one another and, in any case, all of them are definitely more kin to one another than to any white man. The Negro must keep his "inferior place." [31]

This is not an unfair representation of the claims of racism, and these claims are made in the face of the confident awareness on the part of biologists and anthropologists that men are of one species. Race forms a most nebulous base for any kind of division. The word "race" can find its only technical usage in reference to large groups of people who do show a similarity in cephalic measures, appearances of skin, eye, nose, hair, and teeth. It can be used to refer to the transfer of physical characteristics biologically; it can be referred geographically only to those who have characteristics in common that are determined by com-

---

[30] Various listings of sources, especially, The Reverend Thomas Thompson, *The Trade in Negro Slaves*, etc., 1772; The Reverend Josiah Priest, *A Bible Defense of Slavery*, 1852.
[31] Myrdal, op. cit., p. 103.

mon location. With this in mind it is possible to speak of the Caucasoid, Negroid, and Mongoloid races, but there are no pure races. A study of 250 Swiss citizens revealed an ancestry of more than 40 so-called racial groups. All of us are hybrids of one sort or another. Race is not fixed; it is possible for mutation, natural selection, and environmental forces to have their effects but these are not psychic, mental, or spiritual characteristics. In spite of the decree of Pope Pius III in 1537, in spite of the vaunted German use of race as an "ordinand of God," there is no such thing as an inherent psychic superiority.

In contradistinction to this, however, and based squarely upon the work of Gobineau, in its modern setting, there have appeared five principles of Teutonic superiority. These are widely held and appear as far apart as the text of Hitler's *Mein Kampf* and the ordinary village conversation of great-aunts and other preservers of the *status quo* in the hamlets of the South, in the women's clubs, the various sororities aimed to preserve things in general, and in the metropolitan areas of the same setting. Note these five principles:

1. All cultural advance and, at bottom, all human progress are the work of and the result of the gifts of the great Aryan, primarily Germanic, predominantly Anglo-Saxon race.

2. All other races, especially the colored races of any kind, derive their advantages from the Aryan race and by nature are imitators, except where they are despoilers.

3. Race itself means the existence of certain psychic differences as pronounced as physical differences, and by these native traits some races are "hewers of wood and drawers of water," incapable of better things.

4. Human prosperity requires the presence within a culture of a race of conquerors and a race of vanquished so that all types of functions may be filled. Aryan superiority being obvious, the racial disposition of the problem is the most reasonable and the most profitable to the "superior group."

5. Any race mixture is a mongrelization which breeds out the better race qualities of each group and leaves always an inferior product.

Therefore the best protection against the mongrelization of one's own race is the preservation of the purity of one's blood lines which can best be accomplished through the worship of one's own ancestors, which explains the astounding popularity of patriotic and heraldic orders in the

138

South. One comes to sing with Sir Galahad "my strength is as the strength of ten," because my race is pure.

Tragically enough, these falsities apply to all out-groups, even other Teutonic groups, irrational as this seems. In our great melting pot, which Bishop Angus Dun has now called "the pressure cooker," the hyphenated Americans—the German-American, the Irish-American, the Polish-American, the Italian-American, and others by the score—become the victims of these distorted principles of Saxon superiority even though many of them participate in this same so-called blood line. This does not even mention the Jews, or the native Indian tribes.

So it goes. A man asked in earnest if King David were not really an Anglo Saxon, while recently in Poland an old lady was quite upset to discover that Jesus had been a Jew. She had thought all her life he was a Pole. Meanwhile, the cleavages sharpen our consciences. We cannot ignore the economic, selfish fear that provokes our poor theology of racism. We cannot close off the emotional set of automatic switches that guarantee our automatic racial reactions. Nor can we forget that haunting, throbbing undertone caused by the deep vibrations of that great hope that beckons us to freedom, the hope that in some sense men will be born with equal opportunity. We begin to suspect that the Creator wills that five sixths of the earth's millions who are "colored" in our eyes will not continue too long to co-operate with our superiority. The tensions of Asia and Africa spill over into our county-seat towns, our school boards, our deacon's meetings, our coffee houses. It does not help at all to be reminded that there are great spiritual voices which keep telling us to "bring forth fruits worthy of our repentance."

We are not all convinced of the falsity of these race views. Some educators, so-called Christian laymen, even pastors, and here and there a national church hold tenaciously to notions of innate superiority. Benjamin Marais gives a digest of the position held by the powers that be in the Dutch Reformed Church of South Africa.[32] It is a consistent and reasoned position, if only its major premise were sound:

[32] Op. cit. i.e. Evanston assembly, No. 8A, passim. For a report on churches of South Africa which protest racial discriminations see Visser 't Hooft, "The Ecumenical Movement and the Racial Problem," The Race Question and Modern Thought (France: UNESCO, 1954), pp. 30 ff. Currently, some evidence of a change in Dutch Reformed thinking is hopeful.

It is clear that God willed the existence of separate nations and that he wills to perpetuate the division into races and nations.

Because a nation (volk) is a "gottlichordnung" (divine that is ordained by God), it must be honored and guarded against every possible menace.

We learn from God's word that the solution to the problem of racial relationships cannot be found in efforts on the part of man to wipe out divinely instituted differences, but that it is possible, by faithfully preserving national identity and cultural character, to practice Christian brotherly love among nations and races in a spirit of thankfulness toward God.

The necessity for each nation to safeguard its language, ethical code and country with great reverence and loyalty against every threat [is obvious]. If a nation regards these things with indifference, it is lacking in gratitude towards God and wholly irresponsible.

The concept of apartheid, or rather the maintenance of identity of each nation . . . is a constant obligation of every nation out of respect for God's dispensation.

The easiest way to extinguish the light of the cross in South Africa would be a policy of total fusion of the races. Therefore, in order to remain faithful to his divine calling and to continue proclaiming the gospel of God's love in Christ, the Afrikaner had to retain his identity. This obligation rested on him. He had to love himself, that which he had become through the grace of God, in order to be able to love his neighbor. He had to separate himself in order to be a blessing to the millions of non-whites. Hence he derived his apartheid idea.[33]

What could be more obvious, in the light of what we know about ourselves, and what we can read of the sermons of our divines of the 1850's, than that our Dutch-Reformed friends in South Africa are preaching our 1850 theology, with a better sprinkling of missionary motive than we had ever dreamed. The white will remain apartheid "in order to be a blessing to the millions of non-whites." A blessing indeed! This sounds like strange preachment to the colored of the world's populace.

Meanwhile, are things any better here? I think that all my life I shall be able to hear Benjamin Mays, crying at Evanston: "In our time where segregation is based on color there is nothing one can do to

[33] Little, op. cit., p. 210, "The belief . . . that racial separation is ordained by God makes it possible for the believer to exclude people of another colour from his church without giving up his faith in the Fatherhood of God." Used by permission.

qualify. He cannot qualify even when he accepts the same creed, practices the same ritual, prays to the same God, and partakes of the same culture." At this point, according to my notes, Mays departed from his text and added in a poignant cry; "I can have your Ph.D., your Bible, and your God, but there is no way I can belong!"

The prejudice that prevents it is an institutionalism. "We have some values to protect," it says here, in the governor's speech.

Nationalism

There is real significance in the fact that Toynbee begins his monumental epic (not history) with a study that names nationality and industrialism as the two most powerful inherited institutions that have "exercised dominion de facto over our western society in our age." [34] The spirit of nationality he calls a "sour ferment of the new wine of democracy in the old bottles of tribalism." The study of nationalities is no valid construct for history, he says; not even the British Empire can be studied under such a label. This is because there is no way the forces that made Britain can be labeled as truly British. Such a complex of forces enters into the making of any nationality that there is no way such a national group or national entity can be studied in isolation. The states produced by the "new democratic ideal" have not become ecumenical and humanitarian but are rather "tribal and militant," a commentary on the triumph of nationalism even within the democratic ideal.

Since 1875 industrialism and nationalism have been working in opposite directions. Industrialism is headed in an expansive way toward a world-wide range and its ideas and accomplishments will dwarf great powers. Nationalism, "percolating downwards, implants a separate consciousness in peoples of so small a caliber that they are incapable of even minor statedom in the established sense of political, cultural, and economic values." The rise of the new states in Asia and Africa serves only to illustrate the mounting tide of nationalism in a world whose leaders have been committing themselves to internationalism with one hand and shoring up their own national values with the other.

In any valid study of the structures of modern prejudice it becomes inescapable that one must ask from whence came this spirit of national-

[34] Op. cit., I, 9.

141

ism and what was its channel, what is its nature, and what is its true power.

Nationalism, ancient and modern, is always produced by essentially identical causes. Forces, pressures from without colliding with protesting stimuli from within a peopled territory, produce a unity of interest, aims, philosophy, and purpose. Whether the nationalism be the developing nationalism of ancient Israel uniting to face a common lot of desert exile or that of modern tribes in Asia welding themselves into a nation to face economic invaders, the causes are essentially the same. Threats to old securities arouse protesting stimuli within which unite a people. Such forces are not always environmental or militaristic, as in the cases of ancient Israel and modern China; they are sometimes political, philosophical, or religious; often a combination of the three.

As Honorable Protest

Modern nationalism arose primarily as a protest against a spirit of universalism which men judged to be unacceptable. That evil universalism came to be expressed in the world dream of the papacy. Many movements, political, religious, and philosophical have been expressions of some sort of universalism. Indeed, Dostoevski asks, what is this cloud of dust raised by would-be conquerors that reaches almost to the moon but the dust that has followed the efforts of men who have desired to make all men one?

The apparent purpose of the papacy was the political, physical, and spiritual aggrandizement of the church of Rome. In that modern nationalism arose as a protest against the aim and methods of this universalism, modern nationalism must be called an honorable movement. Not all nationalists were honorable men nor were all means used honorable. Nevertheless, in so far as nationalism reflected a development of individuals and a protest against an evil universalism, it could be called honorable.

That evil universalism arose against the backdrop of the collapsing power of the Roman political state. There was a collapsing nationalism before there could be a rising universalism. Although the dreams of Pope Innocent I in 402 were a thousand years short of realization, this universalism was already underway. With the old nationalism dying or dead it is not hard to see how the popes eight hundred years later could further the papacy's dream with startling rapidity—for the structures of

Charlemagne's state died with his death, almost as speedily as they had arisen. In the military, political, and scholastic collapse of the empire of Charlemagne there was little left to resist the efforts of the popes. Leo IV could wall up the Leonine city. Nicolas I could further his plans to advance the independency of the papacy, overrule the King of Lorraine, veto the work of his archbishops, and lay plans of domination to be accomplished centuries ahead. Urban II could drain Europe of fighting men for a series of holy wars. Alexander III could openly struggle with the German Emperor, Barbarossa, Henry II of England, and Henry VI of Germany for political supremacy. Innocent III could dictate the imperial succession in Germany, humble the sovereigns of France, Spain, and Aragon, declare England a fief under John II, and so unify the church that the papacy was lord over all and to all.

In Innocent III the papacy reached its all-time high in the accomplishment of its dream. The fact that it went no higher is not because there were no more worlds to conquer, but rather because of the rise of an even more dynamic force—a "new sense of nationality." Men began to feel that as Frenchmen or Englishmen they had common interest against all foreigners, especially the pope. True, other forces played their part in the defeat of this universalism: the rise of the middle class in intelligence, wealth, and political influence; replacement by lay lawyers of ecclesiastics as royal advisers. There was a growing conviction that the aims of the church were inconsistent with the aims of Christ's Church, and finally, the papacy had no adequate physical forces at its disposal. It was forced to wage war with other men's armies. Each of these latter forces grows out of, is shadowed by, and is an expression of the new nationalism.

One of the important early expressions of this rise of nationalism was the desire, understandably, of rulers to control their own lands. The fact that several lost their battles for supremacy with the papacy does not in any way alter the importance of this expression of the rising spirit of nationality. Although we can hardly ascribe to Frederick Barbarossa the pure motives of a Marsilius of Padua he must nonetheless be included as one of those desiring to rule who exhibited a definite nationalistic trend even before Innocent III. With Charlemagne as model, Barbarossa was a vigorous ruler, as thoroughly master of Germany as his own genius in conflict with the strength of Pope Alexander III would permit. The fact

143

that his attempt to control the papacy was shattered does not alter the fact of his control over German bishops, nor does it affect the importance of this expression of the trend to nationalism.

Henry II of England, powerful, unscrupulous, though forced to embarrassing penance for the murder of Becket, gave expression in the "Constitutions of Clarendon" (1164) to this new force in the world. Regardless of his purely selfish motive and the fact that Alexander forced his abandonment of his "Constitutions," he continued to control England's ecclesiastical affairs and takes his place in the ranks of those who prepared for the day of nationalism.

The victory of Philip, the Fair, of France (1285) over Pope Boniface was a victory for nationalism. Philip's reply to *Unam Sanctum* was a staggering blow to the temporal papal authority. Another setback of importance came from Germany where the Reichstag, meeting at Rense in 1338, declared that the *chosen head of empire needs no approval of the papacy*. Though colored through and through with chicanery, intrigue, and deceit, the "Babylonish Captivity" of the papacy is another expression of this rising force. Few could see it as yet, but it was being helped along even by the selfishness of kings and the evil motives of rulers.

From 1250-1500 in another realm than that of jealous and warring rulers men began to arise who fought for nationalism with tools more powerful than swords. Literary defenders of the state were aroused. Personal gain or power was not their aim; they were fortified in most cases by exemplary lives, and what was more important, their minds were working. Dante Alighieri (1265-1321) began to acclaim peace as the best condition of humanity, peace as best secured by an emperor, and the emperor as a servant of God over a realm immune from papal interference. John of Paris (1265-1306) proclaimed that papal and royal powers are based on the sovereignty of the peoples, and neither has the right of interference with the other. In 1324 a rector of the University of Paris, Marsilius of Padua, was co-author of *Defensor Pacis* in which the claim is made that the basis of all power is the people. People are sovereign. William of Occam asserted that papacy and empire both are founded by God, that neither is superior to the other, and that the New Testament and not the Pope is the final authority. In 1351 the *Statute of Provisors* was enacted in England. Its enforcement was ineffective, but

144

it showed the growth of the spirit in England further illustrated by Parliament's rejection of fiefdom in 1366. Men were waking up. Nationalism, under various guises, was stirring. Here were ideas too advanced for the time, but destined to bear bloody interest in the Reformation and the French Revolution.

It is essential to note something of the influence of Martin Luther on this new power of nationalism. Wycliffe was dead, but his preachments lived on in England and Bohemia. Huss had been martyred, and Zizka and Prokop were dead. The Utraquists had been reabsorbed into Romanism, and the Taborites had become part of *Unam Fratrum*, but in Germany, a German spoke in German to Germans. Wycliffe's intense patriotism and Huss's zeal for religious autonomy cannot be discounted but Luther's effect served to eclipse them all. Luther was a mighty voice for nationalism. In the middle years of the sixteenth century, from pulpit and by pen, he was producing unprecedented changes in the civic and religious life of men. *On Good Works* holds that all normal trades are essentially good. *To the Christian Nobility of the German Nation* declares three limits of action. *On Christian Liberty* declares the true status of the believer as a man free from law enslaved to love. He spoke with passion of salvation by faith alone, but the important thing for nationalism was that he spoke with the voice of a German, in absolute mastery of the German tongue, and with such a psychological appeal for German minds that even today men of other nations have difficulty in understanding the spirit that moved him.

In the century before Luther began to speak, Europe was like a giant bull, bound horn and tail, hoof and nostril, by edicts and interdicts, taxes and indulgences, great tithes and holidays. The papacy rode an unruly prisoner, however. Deep within the hulk of bound Europe came rumblings that portended no good for this institutional universalism. The Renaissance had reached its height; humanism was spreading; Wycliffe and Huss had been seen as lights in the darkness. Then Luther spoke; the rumblings grew to a roar; the papacy squirmed in its precarious place; bound Europe literally burst into the Reformation. When the tumult was at last quieter, the bonds were broken; there was a state church among the German states which waited for Bismarck; Spain was a Spanish empire and was being challenged by clamoring England; the Holy Roman Empire was dying, and in France the beginnings of the revolution were like heat lightning flashes in the interval between two parts of one great storm—nationalism was on the throne. The papacy pulled in its shattered bowmen. Never again was she to be so near to world dominion. Innocent's dream was not dead, but it had been sadly belabored. Nationalism had overcome.

As Inversion of Value

Philosophies, systems, ideas, organizations, and institutions manufactured to meet a particular emergency or to make a particular contribution hang on, then come up again when they are no longer needed, remain long after their usefulness is over, and sometimes are reborn to restore old ghosts to power. It is so with nationalism. It arose to protest and oppose an evil universalism and did so. It then went on to become a veritable juggernaut under whose wheels millions would die. There was nothing to stop it, nor was there anything to stop the increasing prejudicial judgments with which nationalism was revered and sustained as the one passport to new life for subject peoples.

At the time of Ferdinand and Isabella, Spain, feeling virtuous under the trumpetings of a new Catholicism, and with the conquistadores as her advance forces, became the first power of her age. The gold of the Andes and world empire were hers. Portugal multiplied her boundaries and resources thousands of times by following suit. France sought world-empire and sent her colonists to Canada where they came into conflict with the English on the seaboard and with the Spaniards in the Mississippi Valley. Spain was still master of the Caribbean and the Atlantic, however. All through this period of Spanish domination the privateers of England were picking at her long communication lines. In holy wrath, the Armada of Spain was prepared and started out to crush the rising young England. Enmities were born that exist even today, for nationalism was the controlling philosophy of government, the tool of the desires for empire of mortal men.

The Armada, shaken by storms and a few ships from Britain, beat its way home, and the British Empire was aborning. Decades later Disraeli, dreaming of British dominion of many lands and all seas, was succeeded by Gladstone who centralized the gains made. He, in turn, was succeeded in the years that followed by a series of men and events that brought the British Empire to a hitherto unreached role and level of power in the control of the affairs of men.

146

It now appears that a process began with the separation of the American colonies which would one day result in the disintegration of the British Empire. Britain retains strong ties with Canada and hundreds of islands. Although she is through in India and Egypt, she still has influence in Australia and is a battered and weathered old veteran of the course of empire, only grudgingly acceding to the demands of history and the rise of new nationalisms which would push her aside. The fact remains that weak or strong nationalism is still the driving force in England as well as in every other great power.

Simultaneously with early English expansion France made her bid for power. Napoleon backed all Europe away in his blitzkrieg attacks on Italy and the Lombards, the German states, and even prepared his barges for the invasion of England. Turned by the stormy channel into the Russian campaign, he met a hard winter, the Duke of Wellington, and a French general who came up with support too late, all of which united to create Waterloo and exile for the Little Corporal. France's dream of European domination was a debacle, but that is not the fault of nationalism, for nationalism rules France under De Gaulle as completely as it ruled Britain or the growing United States.

In Germany, Bismarck was able to effect what no other could do, and the scattered states became a state. Germany was truly a nation for the first time. She waited only the maturing of her nationalism under Wilhelm to make her bid for world power. In the meantime, the United States entered the lists as a nationalist empire by slapping down sixth-rate Spain and assuming protectorate possession of islands and little republics. Perhaps justly so, by all our standards, but the fact remains that we too, by this time, had become a nationalistic empire.

In the Balkans an under noble was murdered and Wilhelm signaled that Germany's time for asserting her place had come. That act of the tragedy ended four years and millions of deaths later in the fiasco of Versailles. Men had not then heard of Wake Island, Tarawa, Dunkirk, and the hedgerows. Bloody Teutoburger Forest, where German nationalism first began to assert itself when forty-thousand troops of the Roman Augustus were massacred under Varus, is where we came in. The show never changes. Only the actors change. Even the scenery is the same, bloody Teutoburger Forest! Varus is dead, and Augustus and General Patton too, and there is no peace, for nationalism rules. In the 1950's we learned to spell new words like Pyongyang, Yangdok, Wonsan, and then had not even heard of Ghana, Nyasaland, the Rhodesian compromises, the Congo Republic, and the wars of the tribes who seek national status in a world of nations. There is a sense in which the cure, nationalism, was worse than the disease, for there seems to be operative in the mind and spirit of man an almost inevitable, certainly historically inescapable, process by which great institutions built on concepts of value judgment become, by inversion and by overevaluation, the road to prejudiced isolation and provincialism.

As the Sin of Particularity

Nationalism, then, is that spirit which makes people feel and act and think about a part of any given society as though it were the whole of that society. The preservation of its bounds and values and peoples becomes the end of existence, and the welfare, status, power, and future of its domains becomes the reason for existence. As MacNeile Dixon put it in his Gifford Lectures, one comes to see the world as an enlarged copy of his own village. He falls into the illusion that in his own present political, economic, and cultural way of looking at things he has, if not final truth, certainly the direct and only avenue of approach to it.

The difference between provincialistic nationalism and institutional nationalism is slight. It is simply that the institutional form of nationalism is more effectively incorporated, more completely embalmed into a system than the provincial kind of nationalism. Provincialism may continue in time as well as in space. Institutionalism is concerned with this time and this space, the here and the now and no other. If thought is "adjustment to one's surroundings," institutional nationalism is adjustment to one's surroundings in a superbly satisfied manner. Men live in the world of institutional nationalism; they are awake to only a portion of that whole universe that is said to slumber in the soul. If, as someone has said, we are mountaineers by nature, we are blind mountaineers and have been persuaded that the hills where we were born are the Himalayan peaks. It was said of Alexander Pope that he mistook a group of English gentlemen for all mankind. The delusion that one's own nation approaches millennial perfection if only one's own way of life can be preserved and spread is at bottom a prejudiced and provincial view. The idea that racial migrations are done with because we begin to be crowded on the earth is naïve; even the lemmings know better than this and periodically rush over the bluffs of Norway into the Fiords and drown.

At bottom, nationalism is the loss of size, it is the diminution of perspective. Said Malebranche when he saw a miscroscope for the first time, "this is the end of size." The continuation of nationalism as an end is the end of size, for size disappears in a world where everyone is in love with his own "six-penny Utopia."

Nationalism, then, is the realization of some community on too small a stage. It is the acceptance of a disciplinary order and a value system not adequate for the whole of things. It is a submission to the power of the partial and is therefore demonic. It is the substitution of an inadequate form of community for creative intercourse with other communities. It is the idolization of values that in a world community would be subjective and relative. It is at bottom the organized rejection, by reason of prejudiced localism, of other values and of other communities. Nationalism, a localism per se, is too small to hold the world together.

As Conversion of Ends into Means

Nationalism has a tremendous emotional appeal based on real values. There is, perhaps, no more vital human emotion than *patria*, the love of home. But nationalism becomes an organizational principle which seeks to harness every other valid value judgment in its own interest. All systems within a given territory become subject to the use of the spirit of nationalism. Everything, in the name of love of country, in the name of patriotism, in the name of the holy, becomes subject to the demand of the nation. Any true potential for universalism, an all-inclusive way of life for man, becomes a tool of the local, the temporary, and the partial. For example, Christianity is interpreted by many to be an aid to democracy, an ally in the winning of wars, a guaranty of the *status quo*, and a means against depression. Thus, nationalism becomes a most effective way of turning ends into means for the service of a lesser end. This is a primary illustration of the viciousness with which all prejudice works in all its basic structures. This is always the characteristic of prejudice. *It converts ends into means for local use.*

The news services recently quoted a speech by a Jewish rabbi which included sentences like these:

The only solution to this dilemma is to develop the concept of an American faith. Such a faith would articulate the fundamental moral and spiritual values of democratic living and symbolize them in observances and rituals based upon the "sancta" of American life: its great heroes, events, and literature.

Our task today is to spiritualize American civilization and to transform it into a powerful religious force, so that it may serve as the antidote to communism, fascism, and other contemporary false religions of cruelty and power.

This is a fabulously strange note in Judaism. It is not representative. The Jewish tradition has been quite clear on the premises and relationships involved. What a face-lifting operation and what a character transformation would be involved for classic Judaism if the Creator-God of the Universe must become the American Lord God Almighty, which seems to have been intended. This is no different in any way from the primitive tribal notion of a local God in Judaism's pagan days. This is no different in any way whatsoever from the "spirit of Rome" to which the early Christians were forced to pay allegiance or give up their lives.

Robert Calhoun, at the World Council of Churches in Evanston, on the other hand, took a quite different point of view:

It is perilously easy for us to identify God's promises with the peculiarly American way of life: to suppose that the Kingdom of God is, at least in principle, our republican form of Government, the economic system we call free enterprise, the social and cultural heritage we cherish. If all these assumptions were true, then the Kingdom of God would be established on earth precisely if and when our particular way of life has been imposed on all peoples.

Most of us would join Calhoun in the insistence that the kingdom of God comes neither so easily nor so soon.

Meanwhile, on the American scene in particular, and everywhere in general, there have appeared men of extreme, men who have ambitions for themselves, who are quite willing to use unscrupulously, but most effectively, the fundamental values wrapped up in love of native land. They are willing to use these values in such ways as to elevate themselves to positions of strength and influence. This way of life takes on a vocabulary, a style, and a pattern. In its demagogic extreme, certain traits appear and certain phrases work their way forward in nearly every speech. As Leo Lowenthal reported, the speech will feature such phrases as,

You've been cheated; there is a wide-spread conspiracy against us; the devils have gotten into Wall Street; look out for Jewish bankers, the internationalists, and the State Department. We must do something about all this. These conspirators against us are sexually corrupt too. Oriental erotics debauch youth for the purpose of wrecking Gentile morale. Our present government is corrupt, doom is just around the corner.[35]

From reading the literature that floods the desk of any semipublic person one can make his own list of phrases: New Deal communistic confiscatory taxation; capitalism and Communism both threaten us; we can't trust foreigners; Washington is a Bolshevik's rat nest; our enemies are reptiles, insects, sub-human; there is no middle ground; the Talmudic philosophy of Europe, Asia, Africa, and the New-Deal is directly opposite to that of Christianity; there must be no mixing of blood; disaster is just around the corner and the only thing you can do is trust us; it is too urgent for us to discuss it further; there is no time to think; trust me and send money; I'll go to martyrdom and maybe we will all just march on Washington.[36]

It has been claimed by writers in this area that one can recognize an American pro-Fascist by the following labels and verbal tools as they appear in conversations, speeches, and literature: racism, anti-Semitism, antialien, antirefugee, antiforeigner; references to master nations and master race; references to isolationism, anti-internationalism, red-baiting, antilabor; sympathy for other Fascists, anti-democracy; and the glorification of war, force, violence, and a one party system.[37]

Somewhere in his long shelf of books, Will Durant tells about the primitive peoples of Mexico, the Tarahumaras, who caught birds by stringing kernels of corn on tough fibers half buried under the ground. The birds ate the kernels swallowing the strings, and then the Tarahumaras ate the birds. It is not too far-fetched to see in nationalism a technique by which we eat not only the birds that make a life on this

[35] Lowenthal and Norbert Guterman, *Prophets of Deceit: A Study of the Techniques of the American Agitator* (New York: Harper & Brothers, 1949).
[36] *Ibid.*
[37] See Ralph Lord Roy, *Apostles of Discord* (Boston: Beacon Press, 1953).

earth worth living but turn, as Luther says, *curvatus in se* and destroy ourselves. Nationalism in its provincialistic, institutionalistic, and prejudiced extremes is a structure within which prejudice resides.

Religious Institutionalism

Monsignor Fulton Sheen, in his telecast of March 22, 1955, contrasted the works of Karl Marx and Fëdor Dostoevski as a section of his brief for the Russian people. Monsignor Sheen claimed, and correctly, that the spirit of Marx does not exhaust the spirit of the Russian people whom God loves. Monsignor did it exceptionally well. But what kind of mind does it require to do what Monsignor Sheen did to Dostoevski's Grand Inquisitor? He quoted a few lines from Ivan's poem, the immortal chapter on the Grand Inquisitor: "They will come fawning to us . . . and they shall have no secrets from us . . . . the most painful secrets of their conscience, all, all they will bring to us, and we shall have an answer for all;" and called this Dostoevski's prophecy of Communism.

These are the Grand Inquisitor's lines, spoken to Christ in the cell at Seville in fifteenth-century Spain. These are lines spoken to the prisoner Christ, who had just raised a little girl from the dead, in vindication of the Inquisitor's view of human freedom. The point was that the Catholic Church had discovered long ago that mankind does not truly desire freedom. The Grand Inquisitor was explicating the structures that had grown up on the ground of this denial of freedom. His whole point was that the Church had assumed the burden of the freedom of its people and would atone for the sins of its people. This, said Sheen, was Dostoevski's prophecy of Communism.

If the Grand Inquisitor was ever intended to represent a Communist, I am a Czarina. I did regret to see an honest Grand Inquisitor so slandered just to take the sting from what has been a most telling piece of anti-Catholic propaganda. I believe in my heart that the Monsignor knows better. But half-truth and clever turning to avoid truth is no new thing in religious institutionalism, nor in its servants.

Is not religion and its institutions particularly susceptible to being used to convey prejudice? Of them all, the capitol and the cathedral, the museum and the concert chamber, the library and the university, the cathedral more quickly houses our prejudices. Spiritual-minded people slip with striking ease from piety into prejudice. There is a paradox here:

religion is used to relieve us from prejudice, and religion is used to make us prejudiced. Religion has its creeds that are universalistic, but they are also divisive and brutal. Religion knows its sublime ideals, but the most horrible persecutions in history have been religious persecutions. Allport simply says, in summing up this phenomenon, that the adherents of religion are sometimes more prejudiced than others; sometimes they are less prejudiced than others.[38]

It must be noted that those who would or do go to their deaths defending their convictions are not by this fact necessarily prejudiced, nor are they necessarily the victims of prejudice. Further, most religions have modifying tenets that permit outgroups which live in error and darkness to come under the wire. Even the Roman Catholic faith has provided for the redemption of Protestants who remain in honest error.

Bigotry enters, as Allport said, when religious institutions become apologists for in-groups for reasons beyond the declarations of their creed. That is to say, religion becomes a focal frame for prejudice because it stands for so much more than faith. Religion becomes the pivot of a cultural tradition where our highest values center. There exists confusion between ethnocentric self-interest and religion, and religion is expected to rationalize and justify the former.[39] Anywhere religious institutions are called on for double duty, prejudices are laid, for inept, over-inclusive categories are used in place of differentiated thinking. Ministers become defenders of culture and work with invalid categories. Their faith filters the secular claims of their in-group and they never know it. Particularly these irrelevancies flock around religious banners, and then prejudice is in command. Often the pursuit of power, prestige, wealth, and ethnic self-interest uses religious frames and creates abominations for mottoes like "white, gentile, Protestant America," "cross and flag," "chosen people," "Gott mitt Uns," or the familiar "God's country."

We have now to ask what forces native to religious institutions make all forms of religion so susceptible to creating and encouraging prejudice?

A Native Authoritarianism

All prejudice rests, at bottom, on the creation of categories. Religion is a definite categorization of values, and everywhere it exists it has with-

[38] *Op. cit.*, p. 444.
[39] *Ibid.*, p. 448.

in it some appeal to authority. Archbishop Temple, in his great Gifford Lectures, speaks with pristine clarity, as usual, at this point: "Almost everyone who has any religious belief at all forms it in the first instance on the basis of authority, and, even though he may find a reason for it as years go by, this process does not weaken the element of authority in his creed but rather strengthens it." [40] Sometimes the source of this authority rests on the appeal to sacred writings. It may rest, however, just as solidly, upon tradition, the ruling of church courts and councils, precedent, or the charismatic leadership of a person. For example, the modern appearance of amazingly loyal in-groups within the framework of religion in response to men like the famous Daddy Grace demonstrates the fanatical and grandly prejudiced loyalty which can be given over as completely determinative of life, conduct, and destiny on the part of people who respond to the charismatic authority of a leader.

Further, the nascent authority that rests in all religious frames makes it almost unthinkable that a religion could exist without this fundamental and basic appeal. Tragedy enters when the church, the group, or the leader lays claim to some higher authority not readily available to the uninitiate. Almost all ministers of the Christian faith are victims of this presumptuous appeal to highest spiritual authority, and for this we have precedent. For example:

When the Council of Jerusalem introduced its decision with the bold assumption, "It seemed good to the Holy Ghost and to us," claiming divine inspiration for its own verdict, it struck a note which has been sustained throughout the history of Christendom. But that note has been as audible in the worst ecclesiastical pronouncements as in the best.[41]

This demand for and dependence upon authority in religious frameworks is nowhere more clearly seen than when some Christian group becomes so powerful that it can assume the status of an established church. When this happens there is almost altogether the loss of the notion of a voluntary assembly for the worship of God. Instead there exists a powerful

[40] *Op. cit.*, p. 18. Used by permission of Macmillan & Company, Ltd. and St. Martin's Press, Inc.
[41] Miner S. Bates, *Religious Liberty* (New York: Harper & Brothers, 1945), p. 354. Used by permission.

corporation "full of such sentiments and passions as usually distinguished those bodies . . . a dread of innovation and attachment to abuses, a propensity to tyranny and oppression." [42] Nowhere in the entire history of jurisprudence are there more vicious parliaments than those controlled by church bodies. Nowhere in the annals of statecraft are there more devious men than those elevated by established churches to positions of political leadership. When authority runs away with itself and becomes vested in the sacred tapestries and hangings of church office, the function disappears in the power of the wielder of authority and the church becomes something other than Church.

The ordinary antidote for established authority is "disestablishment," but here again the authority of piety and the intensity of uniform conviction, even in the so-called "gathered" church, where like-minded persons flock together and create for themselves the group's stamp of uniformity, even here, especially here, there is critical danger to liberty of spirit, of mind, and of independent conscience. There is, to my judgment, no more powerful authoritarianism than that exercised by the apparent will of the whole in large "gathered-church" groups such as the free churches in the United States. Whether it be the authority of the established church against which Kierkegaard was directing his "attack on Christendom," or whether it be the overt authoritarianism of the mores and manners of a village church in the deep South, the authoritarian hold exercised over the people is one and the same with the more potent influence being possibly on the side of the so-called free church.

In the more consciously authoritarian molds, one can find example almost without letup of the imposition of authority over the individual conscience. One of the famous examples of this, though not alone in its power, is the famous pastoral letter of Cardinal Mercier at the occasion of the elevation of Pius XI in 1922. The Cardinal, in a burst of ecclesiastical patriotism, almost as if he were giving a toast, exclaimed: "The Papacy, the accepted and cherished supremacy of one conscience over all other consciences, of one will over all wills." Do not make the mistake, however, of assuming that this is a Roman Catholic malady. Read the words of the great Presbyterian Thomas Edwards in 1647 as a classic example of Puritan authority. He cried, "Ministers and synods

---

[42] Robert Hall, cited in James Barr, *The United Free Church of Scotland* (London: Allenson, 1934), p. 173.

in their interpretations and decisions going according to the word of God, which is infallible, judge infallibly."

Everywhere, too, there is a tendency to desire control. In Aubrey Menen's delightful *Ramayana* one runs across the use of the phrase, "Bright shining faces, all in our places." This is the goal of Ramayana, said Menen, and this is the goal of most religious institutions. There are in the proscriptions of the Hindu faith regulations for the excretory functions of the human believer. Even this reasonably private activity must be carried on according to the regulation of authority.

A series of rulings that increased the authority of the pope so irritated the great independent Roman Catholic George Tyrell that he accused the church of teaching that "God is the Pope's Vicar in Heaven." [43] Sometimes the pope himself gives the authority of his office to truth already discovered, as if to make it legal. For example, in 1820 Pius VII finally ruled that the Copernican view of the universe might be considered established for men of faith. Luther called John Eck "The Pope's Holy Ghost," and this was a protest against the human claim to heavenly authority.[44] Not all authoritarianism is Catholic, however. Authority has a long arm. It can be made to reach from many different sources and in many different ways. Alaris of Lille said, "Authority has a wax nose; it can be twisted in many directions." The charge of authoritarianism can come very close to home.

Especially is this true of sectarian types. While we always attempt to keep authority as something external to the immediate religious life itself, we have the tool of authority to use when we wish to defend the integrity and autonomy of our way of life. The fine arts of heresy hunting, antievolution crusades, character assassination, and destruction of personal usefulness have been developed as effective tools among the sect and free-type churches. John M. Mecklin has said, "The great Baptist Church in large sections of this country, where it practically dominates the religious life of the masses, is utterly oblivious of its noble traditions of liberty formulated by Baptist heroes of the past." [45] This cannot be denied.

[43] *Medievalism: A Reply to Cardinal Mercier* (London: Longmans, Green Ltd., 1909), p. 71 ff.
[44] *Works*, Holman ed., 1915, vol. 3, p. 115.
[45] *The Story of American Dissent*, (New York: Harcourt, Brace and Company, 1934), pp. 33, 34.

A Consequent Intolerance

It is not my claim that intolerance, as such, is a required feature of religious life, as such. As a feature of group life in any form intolerance comes as standard equipment, even in the most primitive groups. In religion this predilection to intolerance has a field day. There is truth in Bertrand Russell's quip: "A great majority of the human race have religious opinions different from our own, and therefore groundless." [46] There is simply no kind of opinion which we will more quickly mark off than some opposite religious notion held by members of another group. Therefore the basic claim of this section is not that religion is the source of intolerance, it is simply that intolerance appears more powerfully and more effectively in religious groups than in any other frame within which prejudice finds itself at home.

All societies tend to reject that which attacks the foundations of those societies. This rejection is not always intolerance. But absolute liberty in matters of thought and belief has never yet truly existed. This absolute liberalism Arthur Vermeersch calls a sociological heresy, for to claim absolute freedom is to misunderstand the essential conditions of human life.[47] That is to say, all institutions are to some extent proprietary and religion is no exception. The institutions of religion require a basic loyalty on the part of their adherents, and any basic loyalty may have for its reverse an intolerance with respect to other loyalties. Ruggiero claims that "intolerance is of the essence of every church, an immediate consequence of its faith that it possesses the only effective means for the salvation of the soul." [48] Himself no stranger to Roman Catholic intolerance, Sebastian Castellio, tormentor of Calvin, who died while under trial for heresy, held it certain that

All sects hold their religion as established by the word of God and call it certain. Therefore, all sects are armed by Calvin's rule for mutual persecution. Calvin says he is certain, and they say the same. He says they are mistaken, and they say the same of him. Calvin wishes to be judge, and so do they. Who will be judge? Who made Calvin judge of all the sects, that he alone should kill? How can he prove that he alone knows? He has the word of God,

[46] *Skeptical Essays*, pp. 27 ff.
[47] *Tolerance* (London: Burns, Oates & Washbourne, 1913), p. 324.
[48] *Religious Freedom*, art., *Encyclopaedia of the Social Sciences*, XIII, p. 239.

so have they. If the matter is so certain, to whom is it certain? To Calvin? [49]

This same intolerance, to Castellio, accounted for the treatment the weaker party (the Evangelicals) had received at the hands of the stronger (Catholic party) but would now visit upon those who were weaker than they. In his *Counsel to France in Her Distress*, he said to the enraged evangelicals: "Rationalize as much as you please before men and draw as many fine distinctions as you please, nevertheless we know well, and I call your consciences to witness that you are doing to others what you would not have done unto you.[50]

Who can deny that this record of intolerance has written itself large on every page of religious history. In consideration of this record of intolerance, W. E. Garrison has pointed out that one must remember not only how intolerant and brutal the strong have been, but one must also remember how intolerant and brutal the weak would have been had they the privilege of being strong. "The cowardice of the weak [has] made their weakness a plea for tolerance which they would not have granted if they had been strong." [51] This delicate little matter of the might of the strong making it possible for them to be successfully intolerant appeared much earlier in the writings of Augustine: "You now see, therefore, I suppose, that the thing to be considered when anyone is coerced is whether it be good or bad." Augustine's conclusion, "When error prevails, it is right to invoke liberty of conscience, but when on the contrary truth predominates, it is proper to use coercion." Lord Macaulay picked this up and restated it in these words, "I am in the right, and you are in the wrong. When you are the stronger, you ought to tolerate me, for it is your duty to tolerate truth. But when I am the stronger, I shall persecute you, for it is my duty to persecute error." [52] In our own day this argument appears in sophisticated refinement as "the right of the majority" or "the solidarity of culture." The Melians addressed this identical argument to the enemy during the Peloponnesian Wars more than 2,300 years ago. The intolerance of men who are convinced in their opinions moderates but slowly.

[49] *Concerning Heretics*, trans. and ed. Roland H. Bainton (New York: Columbia University Press, 1935), pp. 281-82. Used by permission.
[50] *Ibid.*, p. 260.
[51] *Intolerance* (New York: Round Table Press, 1934), pp. 1, 4, 9. Cf. pp. 15, 144-45.
[52] "Essays on Sir James Mackintosh," *Complete Writings* (Boston: Houghton Mifflin, 1900), 13, 331.

In the South an acute reaction to our own provincialism has caused us to accuse ourselves as guilty to an exorbitant degree of this intolerance. Intolerance is not the property of the ignorant, nor of the weak, nor of the emotional, nor of the unlettered. Some of the most literate, powerful, and ancient of religious institutions exhibit this intolerance to a marked degree. For example, within our own generation the Vatican organ, *Osservatore Romano*, has affirmed that since there is only one true religion, Catholicism, it alone has martyrs, and all the other religions, which are fallacious, have swindlers.[53] Intolerance exists even among those who deserve the name of martyr, and institutions other than those at the extremes cited have their problems with intolerance, too.

Sometimes this intolerant zeal becomes so powerful a force that men begin to feel they themselves are never free until and unless they have been able to take freedom from those who have it. Milton, in *A Second Defense of the People of England*, hopes:

> That you should listen the least of all to those who never fancy that themselves are free unless they deprive others of their freedom; who labor at nothing with so much zeal and earnestness, as to enchain not the bodies only, but the consciences of their brethren, and to introduce into church and state the worst of all tyrannies . . . the tyranny of their own mis-shapen customs and opinions.[54]

Sometimes, too, one's provincial intolerance in religious framework serves negatively as a great device and motivating power to produce an expanded activity or a safe retreat. Lord Chesterfield in *Letters to His Son* is quoted as saying, "The good Protestant conviction that the Pope is both anti-Christ and the whore of Babylon is a more effectual preservative in this country against popery than all the solid and unanswerable arguments of Chillingsworth." [55]

There have been those who have insisted that this consequent intolerance was the reason Abraham Lincoln never united with a formal religious body. It is no wonder at all that the same breadth in Lincoln caused him to reply to his friend Joshua Speed with respect to the Know-Nothings as follows:

[53] Luzzatti, *God in Freedom* (New York: The Macmillan Company, 1930), p. 553.
[54] Cited by Bates, *op. cit.*, p. 414.
[55] February 7, 1749.

I am not a Know-Nothing, that is certain. How could I be? How can any man who abhors the oppression of negroes be in favor of degrading classes of white people? Our progress in degeneracy appears to me to be pretty rapid. As a nation we began by declaring that, "All men are created equal." We now practically read it, "All men are created equal, except negroes." When the Know-Nothings get control, it will read, "All men are created equal except negroes and foreigners and Catholics." When it comes to this, I shall prefer emigrating to some country where they make no pretence of loving liberty.[56]

All religion knows that there is no real place for intolerance in its tenets and practice. All religious frames in their most exalted moments would have to confess themselves the victims not only of authoritarianism but of dread intolerance. Most religious groups have within themselves spiritual resiliency enough to admit on occasion that there is no such thing as an aristocracy of knowledge or of salvation. As Berdyaev has put it, "The least admissible form of aristocracy is the aristocracy of salvation." The awful fact of intolerance, rampant and at home in the beds of religion, remains to contradict, to thwart, to distort, and even to pervert the fundamental claims to truth and salvation that religion seeks to offer. Berdyaev again claimed, "There may be an aristocracy of knowledge, of beauty, or refinement, but there cannot be one of salvation." [57] Prejudice cannot live without intolerance nor without an appeal to some authority. People who wish most desperately for an authority and people who wish most definitely to be certain of their own opinions are those who are victims of prejudice. Of these the frames of religion have more than a share, and indeed the very existence of the weight of prejudiced people on the frames of religion serves to bar many, to distort more, and to deny not a few.

A Distorted Critical Faculty

Cecil Northcutt, in a review of Billy Graham's London campaign, stated that "very few people grow in religion beyond the adolescent stage. For the majority, what happens at sixteen remains final." [58] Grown-up religious systems are really no better, however. Composed of persons who no longer have any critical faculty to exercise toward them-

[56] John G. Nicolay and John Hay (eds.), *Complete Works of Abraham Lincoln*, 2, 287; as cited by Bates, op. cit.

[57] *Destiny of Man* (London: Centenary Press, 1937), p. 294.

[58] "Billy Graham in Britain," *Christian Century* (June 2, 1954), p. 670.

selves and their beliefs, religious systems develop the attributes of their patrons. Containing the native authoritarianism we have discussed, characterized by the consequent intolerance that marks all religious institutions, religious systems and institutions chronically witness the loss of any self-critical function on the part of their adherents. The root of this inability to be self-critical rests in the positive devotion on which the whole system is founded. One loses his objectivity with respect to the object of his fanatical devotion. Religion is, as Archbishop Temple has said, "at root a fanatical devotion to uncriticized oracles." The religious man desires to be faithful and above all to be certain, and he therefore rests his faithfulness and its certainties in some sort of infallibilism. He may, if he is a Roman Catholic, believe the pope to be infallible. He will, if he is a Protestant fundamentalist, believe the Bible to be infallible. He certainly will, if he is Mohammedan, rest his faith and his certainties on the Koran. Sometimes in a burst of pseudospiritual arrogance he even learns to trust himself as infallible. His faith was born in an initial act of commitment and surrender, and at this point he instinctively passes all criticism because he knows there is no rational critique nor is there a rational support for his unrational act of faith in the very beginning. He cannot sustain himself by reason. Therefore reason, which would sit as judge, is never allowed to assume its real function but is allowed only to give witness to some fundamental belief. Temple, in a characteristic British understatement, admits that this contention about the reduction of reason in religion is not without truth.[59]

Thus reason, the gadfly, loses its sting. Reason which should exist in religion to make all religions except the best impossible loses its function in religious affairs, religious systems, and religious institutions. The self-critical faculties reason would impose wither away leaving only vestiges of their once powerful presence to expose the weaknesses in one's enemy. Reasoned theology should be a criticism of religion as it is, of religious beliefs as they are, and should have no regard for their supposed origin. For this critical faculty to do its work reason must speak undependent upon any supposed act or word of divine revelation. Reason should work in the full light of the knowledge of what it is criticizing and

[59] *Op. cit.*, p. 21.

161

should be allowed to work with the complete relentlessness and objectivity of true scientific inquiry.

Mature religion knows very well that its real enemy is bad religion. The enemy is not, and has not been for a very, very long time now, irreligion. In most cultural situations the first word a valid religious faith must speak is a word against bad religion, for this is the true enemy. Wrapped up in its illusions of success, based on its false indexes of statistical accounts of participation and stewardship, the modern religious institution is, by and large, victim of a numerical neurosis and a false pragmatic method in its work which serve to blind most effectively any remaining vestiges of self-criticism. Fed by false emphasis on our own well-being and on healing which overlooks the function and meaning of suffering and pain, fed by such distortions of partial personality traits as emotionalism, and happily diluted by the moral relativisms which are mistaken for the whole of morals, most modern religious institutions—except for the pain in the bowels of some of their more finicky prophets—go their marked-out routes like the great Baylonian processions from one temple to another bearing the giant god Nebo.

Religion is a very great power for evil as well as for good. Even young children are shocked by the claims of some of the more authoritarian brands of bad religion. It is simply not true that any religion is good, nor is it true that any religion is better than none. It is true, I think, that many religions do more harm than good, and the harm that even good churches do is incalculable. The cause of this is primarily the shrinking of the ability of the religious institution to be self-critical.

We have come now to a sorry state of affairs where honest self-criticism is frequently labeled a heresy by the established. It is a strange state wherein a man must be either fanatic in his truth or heretic with respect to that which he criticizes, for loyal self-criticism is neither fanaticism nor heresy. There is room, even in the church, for the church at the left hand of God, or in secular terms, "Her majesty's loyal opposition."

It must be most revolting to the finest denominational servants modern religion has produced to be called "fanatic." But the charge must be allowed to stick. "A religious fanatic is a man who is obsessed by his own idea and completely believes in it." [60] Those who serve blindly and

[60] Berdyaev, op. cit., p. 172.

162

devotedly their uncriticized oracle in the framework of an unquestioned denominational pattern, upholding unexamined concepts, preaching programs handed down from "above," wrapped in blind obedience to the segment as if it were the whole, are of the essence of fanaticism. They are, as Berdyaev knows, "cut off from the living God." They are fanatic. They are mad.

John Milton points out that a man also may be "heretick in the truth," "If he believes things only because his pastor says so, or the assembly so determines . . . though his belief be true, yet the very truth he holds becomes his heresy," because he received this truth uncritically.[61] Though this is heresy, the uncritical acceptance of unexamined concepts, on the other hand, the word heretic is also applied as a badge of honor to those who clear-headedly and courageously reject authority. " 'I suppose I am very heretical,' he says, and looks around for applause, for the word heresy no longer means being wrong; it practically means being clear-headed and courageous."

This is why, I suppose, in the modern world, the church that is the Church is sometimes, even if not most times, found at "God's left hand." Around every church that is honestly convinced that it is the Church there are those who stand longingly and even half-believingly but held by their lively critical faculties from committing themselves to such unexamined oracles. Whatever hope the modern church may have rests in these fringe groups, not in the fanatical devotion at the center of the body where criticism is dead. All this is to say that modern men simply have not understood Paul Tillich's Protestant principle at this point. For as Tillich has said, the Protestant churches are always in danger of forgetting their meaning, and the greatest danger lies in their claim that they have pure doctrine, because when a church claims purity at any point it tends to claim also the possession of a whole truth. This means, said Tillich, that the church has not understood what it is to stand at the boundary, for to stand in the boundary situation means not only to know one's sin but also to recognize one's errors. "A theology that has not passed through the shattering effect of the theology of crisis but has dismissed its prophetic 'no' with a polite bow or with

[61] *Areopagitica.*

163

an easy criticism of its method and form, cannot be taken very seriously." [62]

The isolating and stultifying effects of this death of self-criticism continue almost unbelievably within great institutional frameworks of religion. In this way of life men tie their tongues to no ears but their own. Men are free to allow all of the devastating negatives implicit in the concern for power to run as wild as in any other political arena. The election of bishops and officials becomes a piously covered-over religious fraud unable to conceal the machinations and maneuverings meant to go on behind the stage, the edges of which inevitably spill over onto the platforms where nominating speeches are made. Posts become plums awarded for faithful service. The man who comes to want something that is within the power of his institution to provide has sold his soul.

The institution that goes on living in spite of the criticisms of its heretics is not without retaliatory powers. The fear of such criticism on the part of loyal servants is almost a neurosis. Men squirm and twist under the threat of criticism and use such words as heretic, fanatic, unco-operative, betrayer, traitor, infidel, Unitarian—a curse word in the South—or just plain stupid, against their tormentors.

Perhaps nothing is more productive of prejudice in modern religious life than this loss of self-critical faculties. At the biennial meeting of a world religious body I had been invited to give a critique of the views that held one of the major parts of that world organization from participation in the World Council of Churches. I spoke candidly with affection, and I believe, with a measure of truth. It so happened that the editor of the best-known journal produced by the group was absent from that particular session but heard reactions expressed to my critique in the corridors outside. He cornered me with a view to having my speech printed in his journal. When I responded that perhaps he ought to analyze what I had said before he made such an offer he consented to hear a statement of three or four of the points I had made. In consternation, as I finished, he said, "Why we couldn't print that. All those points are against us!" I think this is what I mean. We lose the ability to accept even our own criticism of ourselves when we become victims of the dread provincialism implicit in religious institutions as such. This is the very

[62] Tillich, The Protestant Era, trans. James Luther Adams (Chicago: University of Chicago Press, 1948), p. 200.

power of the idea of Tillich that the Protestant principle requires this constant self-criticism of one's oracles, judgments, conceptions, and theology.

A Natural Bent Toward Reaction

At the Lund conference of the World Council of Churches, the *Christian Century* reported that Archbishop Brilioth showed up wearing his stovepipe hat. Martin Niemöller was wearing his pipe, and Athenagoras of Thyatira his purple silk. Joseph Hromadka appeared here and there speaking to old friends from behind his animated and handsome Slavic face; Father Florovsky wore, characteristically, his glasses on his forehead and a beard like Mephistopheles; while numerous gentlemen sported pink dickies under their chalk-striped suits. A Lund student was reported to have asked, "Who are all those creeps down around the university?" This was with respect to one of the most distinguished bodies of churchmen on the face of the earth.

I think we may as well face it. There is something about the church, in conference or out, that makes us look like creeps from out of the past. This is our natural bent for reaction. It appears in our attire, in our mannerisms and speech, in our architecture and symbols, in our archaic forms, ceremonies, and liturgies, and most of all in our thinking. This is precisely the point. "Those creeps down around the university" are men who are not through with the past and know that the past is not through with them. The church's concern for tradition and history is of its very essence, for it is through the traditions and history that the community has preserved its values.

This can be especially remarked in the re-emergence of some old and presumably extinct idea. This is particularly demonstrable in the constant recurrence of grand heresies such as Arianism, or Docetic Gnosticism, which have not been many moments in the last sixteen hundred years without classic exponents.

This knowledge gives us pause, for we are not only very near to history and tradition, we are also very near to darkness. There are times when some situation in the life of the Church reminds us of that strange fish reported to have been captured off the coast of Africa some twenty years ago, which according to all the textbooks had been extinct for more than fifty million years. Yet, reported *Time* magazine, there it was on the deck, embarrassing generations of scientists by being alive, and what is more it bit the captain.[63] This is terribly disconcerting, to have something come up out of the Mesozoic age and bite you! Bergen Evans enjoys this in *The Natural History of Nonsense* and asks, "Who can dare trust himself in a museum again?" "A living fossil," *Time* named it, and isn't this precisely a definition of the institutional church? It has not been long since, in some theological affray, one bishop or another has seized some old weapon discarded centuries ago and dealt his astonished opponent a blow on the head with it.[64] This, characteristically, the church does because it is concerned with tradition and history.

Legend and parable and drama, tradition and history and right liturgy, symbol and institution—these are the vehicles by which the church survives. The temptation is always to substitute the symbol for the reality it was born to reflect. This reveals our consequent natural bent for reaction and substitution.

In my very young manhood George Bernard Shaw was the prophet who spoke to me in this vein in the introduction to *Back to Methuselah*:

This does not mean that we should throw away legend and parable and drama: they are the natural vehicles of dogma but woe to the Churches and the rulers who substitute the legend for the dogma, the parable for the history, the drama for the religion! Better by far declare the throne of God empty than set a liar and a fool on it.

This is the great temptation, the great danger, and another fundamental weakness. Religion has its natural trends for reaction, and this produces the willingness to substitute the symbol of that that is ancient for the meaning of that that is real, for faith is never easy, and within institutional frameworks of religion men continue to say to constituted authority, "Show us a sign." They say, "Tell us what to believe and we shall believe that we believe it." The totalitarian church is not made a totalitarian church by the fact of its dominance over the whole world. The totalitarian church is made totalitarian by the fact of its dominance over its constituents. This, said Angus, is as great a danger to higher life

---

[63] "Living Fossil" (April 3, 1939), p. 35.
[64] This very season it was said that I "resurrected Marcion" in the chapel of a large University with one paragraph on Israel's history intended as a caricature.

as the totalitarian state, for there can be a thousand totalitarian churches if within the churches are those over whom the church has total thought control. This is as dangerous as anything in *Hidden Persuaders* or from Madison Avenue's advertising boards.

This natural bent for reaction perpetuates the confusion caused by the identification of faith with doctrine by further identifying it with symbol and history. Faith is a venture, and doctrine is the attempt to formulate the reason faith offers to our concerned inquiry; but at what particular period in history has Christianity attained the normative from which we may not depart, and from which we must not lift our eyes in determining what is Christian today? Without being conscious of it, I think, those who strive most worthily to preserve that which is most valuable in Christianity are sometimes the worst enemies of religion and betray it to its adversaries.

An Affinity for Transvaluation and a Reliance on Accessories

There are ways in which this is the most terrible burden institutional religion has to bear. There is something implicit in the human response to the religions of the time that presses the adherents of all religious systems to transvalue their values and to rely on the fringe benefits more than on the realities carried at the heart of the faith. We have built-in facilities for making superficial our values and for relying more on the accessories of faith than on its central meanings. Berdyaev claims that it is "generally supposed that the business of ethics is to teach that one ought not to be a pickpocket!" [65] Again, "How strange," said Gogol, "to see so little good in goodness." The surface moralities of religious people led Heinrich Heine to claim that

outlawed criminals often bear more humanity in their hearts than those pure reproachless town burghers of virtue, in whose white hearts the power of evil, it is true, is quenched—but with it, too, the power of good. And even vice is not always vice. I have seen women on whose cheeks red vice was painted and in whose hearts dwelt heavenly purity.[66]

What is this fantastic concern for fringe benefits that produces the denial of the fundamental aspects of the faith? This question I cannot

[65] *Op. cit.*, p. 98.
[66] *English Fragments.*

167

answer unless it be that there is within the structures of the prejudiced person an affinity for transvaluation and a reliance on accessories which spills over and becomes fundamental to the nature of religious institutions.

In effect this fundamental affinity for transvaluation and reliance on accessories causes us to flock around false beacons. That that is biggest is best, and we worship a god of colossality, a god of automatic process, a god who has control of status, or the Oriental Happy God who controls in his great fat paunch the end we seek. In this land of disenchantment we spin our wheels, preoccupied with a complete selfness and do not recognize that as with hydrangeas, sometimes called strawflowers, the beauty of the living flower may linger on long after the flower, or the institution, has lost its life. This creates a vast hunger for affirmation among the adherents of the religious faith. They live with their unresolved contradictions and their unasked questions and become subjective, brooding victims of a cultural inertia. What is worse, we become so accustomed to our surroundings that we do not see them and go on producing a people who are primarily concerned with respectability, orthodoxy, frugality, shrewdness, occasional philanthropy, and family heritages.

This issues in the chronic decadence into concern for luxury, materiality, and triviality. Within this framework people substitute trivial illusions for mighty faith and become victims of their own bored suburbia. This view of life and living is prejudiced. It is produced by and within a fundamental structure of prejudice which causes us to rely on the fringes of our faith. "Rogue clients evolve rogue lawyers to do their work; fool patients envolve fool doctors, and superstitious silly people in the pew secrete pretentious punk parties to inhabit their pulpits." [67] It has the effect that people quit living creatively. In the institutions of religion money is no longer means, but an end to power. The phrase "business is business" becomes prominent, in other language, in the councils of the governments of the churches. In our prejudiced commitment to lesser values we have come to rely on accessories.

The Fellatah ladies of Central Africa spent several hours a day over their

[67] Elbert Hubbard.

toilette. They made their fingers and toes purple by keeping them wrapped all night in henna leaves; they stained their teeth alternately with blue, yellow, and purple dyes; they colored their hair with indigo, penciled their eyelids with sulphuret of antimony. Every Bongo lady carried tweezers, hairpins, rings, bells, buttons, and clasps.[68]

She was, however, still a Bongo lady, and so it is, I think, with the church and with us. This kind of life and living finds its requiem in Kenneth Fearing's "Dirge":

> And wow he died as wow he lived,
>> going whop to the office and blooie home to sleep and
>> biff got married and bam had children and oof got
>> fired,
> Zowie did he live and zowie did he die.[69]

Life in this never-never land of prejudiced religious superficiality means that the adherents of religion have lost the power to distinguish between the expressions of their faith which are of real spiritual importance and those which have come to have only sentimental value through association with those elements which have real value. This was Dietrich Bonhoeffer's great concern in his *The Cost of Discipleship*. The whole world of Christians becomes concerned to get itself involved with "cheap grace." "Would you like to get hold of some real spiritual numbers kinda cheap like?" the announcer offered in advertisement for a "religious" radio program. This is the concern of the whole superficial mass of Christians to get some real spiritual numbers "kinda cheap like."

Because of this concern the church loses its will of its own. It goes on, as Roger Babson puts it, passing its plates when it is called to render a better service. It goes seeking not its own effectiveness but its own popularity. It slaughters lambs with Don Quixote instead of feeding them. The church sits at meat instead of waiting on tables as she was born to do.[70] Sometimes she puts so much emphasis upon the dishes

---

[68] Will Durant, op. cit.

[69] *New and Selected Poems* (Bloomington, Ind.: Indiana University Press). Used by permission.

[70] John Oman.

169

on the table that she misses the whole point of religious fidelity. For example, the diary of Samuel Pepys under the date February 27, 1660, reads: "Then I called for a dish of fish, which we had for dinner, this being the first day of Lent; and I do intend to try whether I can keep it or no." Under February 28, however, he wrote: "We dined, and not withstanding my resolution, yet for want of other victuals, I did eat flesh this Lent, but I am resolved to eat as little as I can."

Dietary concerns, heraldic prohibitions, theological shibboleths, class consciousness, competitive business enterprise, dress restrictions, ritual performance, participation in seasonal religious orgies and celebrations, family pews, church office, and even the regularity of attendance upon worship become symbolic flags one wears to show his fundamental relationship with this terrible moralism that strives to make us into automatons of virtue, with the intolerable dullness which produces the deepest kind of immorality. This is a specific consequence of the kind of ethic which knows no higher power nor any true center.

Perhaps this sums up best in connection with our ceremonies for the recently dead. Aubrey Mennen, speaking of burial ceremonies in the Indian culture, is not at all out of touch at home when he describes the ceremonies as giving, "as they were intended to give, the impression that the dead man had been comfortable and respected here on earth and was confident of being treated in the same manner beyond." [71]

Meanwhile Sunday is a long day. Without a break children become a terrible trial and a noisy nuisance; they get on peoples' nerves. So undoubtedly, a large number will continue going to Sunday church school, but God will remain something the kids get like other childhood diseases, a nebulous entity, as Babson has said, to which adults are immune. He will be forever associated vaguely with the funny papers because God and the comic section come on the same day.

[71] Op. cit., p. 27.

Chapter IX

Resolution of Institutionalism

Institutions are the structures we build to protect our values. Institutionalism is the result of an overweening regard for and evaluation of an instrumental value as if it were an intrinsic value. Institutionalism may be racistic, nationalistic, or religious. There are other strains, smaller and quite as powerful, into which our prejudiced value judgments may place us and within which they may confine us. For example, man may be confined by a theory of education, a scientific theory, some vocational workbench, a domestic relationship, a lodge, an order, or an idea which he has about medicine. No man is ever released, however, from any institutionalism as such except by one thing: *he comes into the possession of a sense of higher value in another framework which leads him to reassess the former. The resolution of institutionalism is always by the sublimating power of a higher sense of value.*

The means of release from prejudice is never another prejudice, for we seldom see our prejudices as prejudices. We are, rather, inclined to call our prejudices our "reasoned conclusion," our "basic conviction," or else, if we are quite sure of ourselves, we may go so far as to say,

171

"God said it to me." What makes it still more impossible to find release in better prejudices is that we honestly do not know we have those prejudices which affect us most. We live our lives largely on unexamined concepts; we base our daily decisions on mere and absurd delusions which frequently are sources of our most earnest expressions of life and thought.

The hope of release lies not in our convincing each other that we are all prejudiced; this is granted and is universal. Our release comes as a by-product of something else which sees us lifted to a better vantage point. The release is by the sublimation of the lower in something higher. It begins only when we come to understand the nature of relativity which marks nearly all of our values.

The Meaning of Value

On the flyleaf of the novel Green Dolphin Street, Evelyn Underhill is credited with a description of the three great human hungers: There is the craving which makes a man a pilgrim and a wanderer. This is the longing to go out of this normal world in search of a lost home, an El Dorado, a Sarras, some heavenly Syon. There is the craving of heart for heart, that craving of the soul to find its perfect mate which makes of man a lover. There is the craving for inward purity and perfection which makes man an ascetic and in the last resort, and sometimes, makes him a saint.

This list seems inadequate. Man can crave other things. He can crave staying at home instead of seeking his Syon. He can come to crave his hatred rather than his love or worse he can come to love his own indifference. Who would deny his capacity for sensualism which surely is as great as his craving for saintliness? His local home or his eternal home; his perfect mate or some substitute; inward purity and the quest for perfection—these are possibilities, but there also is the possibility that he may crave, like characters in Dostoevski, only the deepening of his own sense of guilt and his own inverted grasping after the unholy which becomes seriously and truly a grasping after another kind of holiness. Whatever he chooses is the result of a value judgment. What are these values and judgments which become so primary in our lives that we build our whole institutional system to confine us in the judgments we have previously made?

Emil Brunner is right, I think. " 'Value' is not an a priori conception . . . it is . . . something which corresponds to a definite need, or, to put it more exactly, the quality by means of which something corresponds to a need." [1] All this is to say that there are no intrinsic values. Value is not a priori. It is derived, proscribed, bestowed. Apart from the human personality in all its functions, which includes the capacity for bestowing value on lesser and greater ends, there is no such thing as value. Value is always the result of a favorable judgment with respect to the meeting of a need. No art, no science, no institution has value per se. The value rises in its relation to human-divine need and the judgment placed thereon as to its effectiveness in meeting a need. Our trouble comes, and along with it our prejudices, when relative values are overrated and so approach the absolute in our judgments.

Sorley, long ago, separated values under three heads: Values derive from judgments about quality, duration, and extent. That is to say, value is either instrumental, in which case it is descriptive of a means of getting at a quality, or it is intrinsic in that it has residing within it itself the quality one seeks. Value is either transient in that it is of relatively temporary duration, or it is permanent in which sense it carries within it the whole possibility of duration. Value is exclusive in which case it limits the extent to which value can reach, or it is catholic in which case the whole is wrapped up in the value. Under these heads, instrumental or intrinsic, transient or permanent, exclusive or catholic, the questions of quality, duration, and extent which constitute value are subsumed. [2]

The agony of prejudice expresses itself in us and in our institutions wherever there is a separation of value from fundamental human relations. That is to say, whenever value becomes depersonalized prejudice builds on its faulty base and is free to subsume under too narrow a head some value of greater extent. Nothing in the world known to me explains the prejudiced nature of churches like this transvaluation of value. When the church, which has at best an instrumental value, is given intrinsic value, the result is fatal to the church's true aim and turns into an immorality, a prejudiced exclusiveness.

For example, the Roman Church has an instrumental, transient, ex-

[1] *The Divine Imperative*, trans. Olive Wyon (Philadelphia: The Westminster Press, 1947), pp. 41 ff.
[2] *Moral Values and the Idea of God*, Gifford Lectures (3rd ed.; Cambridge, Mass.: Harvard University Press, 1924), pp. 36-53.

clusive value. Its value is a prejudiced value and is limited, but its immorality appears in its claim that its instrumental value is intrinsic, that its transient value is permanent, and that its exclusive value is catholic. That is to say, its sin lies in its name, catholic. Its catholic value could be as it teaches and dreams only if the basis of its exclusiveness were true and catholic, if its transience were permanent, and if its instrumentality were intrinsic. The same characterization fits all sectarian and exclusive religious groups who mistake their local particularity for an inclusive universal.

This is a "theological view" of value. It allows, even if it does not actually demand, the description of value as an end in itself. Whitehead refers to value as "the intrinsic reality of an event." The theological view of value claims that true value must include the person in the event and it is just this that makes it impossible to think of "absolute good" or even "highest good" except in terms of the kingdom of God, the repository of our highest values. The Christian faith knows no higher value. There are scales of value, however, relative levels of good and bad, and this introduces the lever, the means for resolution of our prejudiced institutionalism. The person must choose between various levels of value and the description of this process is as old as the work of Aristotle. Indeed, from the time of the writing of his *Ethic* men have known that value is not intrinsic often in this life, if ever, but one must always make relative choices of relative levels with respect to relative values.

That is to say, without the notion of hierarchy, the idea of ascending order in ranks, it would be impossible for the Christian to think of God. Even the Asiatic Gnostics have something to contribute to us here for the notion of hierarchy, and its concomitant, order, is innate, native to the sources of Western thought, perhaps the oldest structured form for thinking in the thought processes of man. The whole thing rests on the ability to compare; good, better, best; bad, worse, worst. This is the beginning of ethical life. Just as the religious life finds its sources in the capacity to think "other," "you," "thou"; so the ethical life begins in the ability to compare good, better, best; or bad, worse, worst. There are levels of value, and this points the way to the resolution of our less valuable institutionalisms. Before the sublimating choices

174

can be made, however, there descends upon all residents of all institutional frames the obligation to be self-critical. That is to say, judgment has to be leveled at the place where one is in the light of a recognized higher way.

The Obligation to Be Self-Critical

This, if I understand Paul Tillich, is a version of his Protestant principle. We are under obligation to bring every self-provided security (institution) under question. "Christianity is final only in so far as it has the power of criticizing and transforming each of its historical manifestations." The Protestant principle means that all our concepts, institutions, and values are to be held constantly under judgment. Taken simply, everything we hold valuable must be constantly justifying itself in the light of higher values and for Christians in the light of our understanding of ultimate value, the kingdom of God.

There is no escape from institutionalism that does not involve dissent from one's present value judgments as a permanent datum. No question can truly be asked except where there is the possibility of the negative answer of dissent. Where our limited value judgments have acquired intrinsic value the possibility of asking questions has almost disappeared, and dissent is no longer a possibility. This is the way we are trapped. One forgets his own finiteness, one becomes God, safely ensconced in a niche made up of his own unquestioned value judgments. The most shocking experience possible to young minds is connected with the realization of the finiteness and relativity of one's position. The awareness of the existence of other values which might prove superior is frightening. It is this that opens up the threat of meaninglessness, the abyss of despair that has been found so much at home in recent years in Reformed realism, though one suspects that not even the most realistic of Reformed theologians has been willing to put his final and ultimate values under judgment. One goes still further to confess that at least this attempt has been made with respect to the secondary frameworks of the institutions of race, nation, and religion.

It is just this that makes some of the modern contribution of religious thinkers of terrible importance. The realization of finiteness, of threat and peril, of the abyss of meaninglessness which yawns before us, produces the necessity for criticism and makes possible the asking

175

of questions; but again questions cannot be asked except in the possibility of there being dissent.

All the hell we moderns know arises out of this unwillingness to be self-critical, this acceptance of uncriticized oracles, this pride which lies so near the heart of any true religion. Notice what the acceptance of our oracles uncriticized may do.

Take the ancient notion of vengeance, an eye for an eye, a tooth for a tooth, blood vengeance by members of the same tribe or clan, so near the center of the morals and ethics of David's court. This ancient idea of uncriticized vengeance produces under the positive banner of a desire for the great value, justice, such a system of primitive vengeance that society feels clean and just only when it has wreaked vengeance, when retaliation is the heart of law, and when, in theology, hell becomes a place the "good" have used to avenge themselves upon the unrighteous, as Berdyaev saw.

For example, take the notion of community, without which order and hierarchy are impossible. Uncriticized, that is to say, unsubjected to questions, community creates sets of laws and institutions so involved as to become a Pharisaic code for washing hands before one eats; or the Virginia laws in colonial times requiring church attendance. All uncriticized oracles are denials of community. Freedom, so sacred to our hearts, uncriticized, becomes something other than freedom by refusing to be the same for all.

This principle of the criticism of one's oracles requires a willingness to see our most precious institutions not only judged, but junked in the interest of the higher value. There is an obligation to adopt, adapt, or abandon in the interest of a higher good. There is no escape from prejudice that does not include this obligation and willingness to re-examine. This quest for higher values, this rejection of "closed systems," must accept the fact that "the major advances of civilization are processes which all but wreck the societies in which they occur."

A wizened old educator in the processional down the long university avenue toward commencement, scowling out from under his medieval headpiece, twisting his neck under its hot burden of medieval garb, said, "All great advances of civilization are first called 'contrary to the scriptures,' then 'of no importance,' then, 'I believed it all the time and we have always taught it here.'"

176

The infiltration of uncriticized ideas is quite as valid in determining our institutional frameworks as is the refusal to examine the ideas which we have kept. For example, no religious group ever opposed more vehemently the invasion of a foreign idea than Southern Protestants of the nineteenth century opposed the invasion of "scientific" claims—unless it be the Catholic theologians at the University of Padua in the fifteenth century. Yet, what religious organizations on the face of the earth have become so pragmatic, pseudoscientific, even religiously reliant upon "process" in all of their promotional propaganda as have these great modern denominations? Or, what nation has ever become more ardent an expounder of socialism than the United States of America, even while waving its banners of idealistic capitalism? Or, what racial group has ever become more the victim of its own inner prejudices than the Negro racial group in the United States while protesting and lamenting its situation under a provincial institutional set of value judgments which have worked against it?

All racial groups, all national groups, all religious groups, can come into the fulfillment of higher values only after the acceptance of the obligation to be self-critical is alive amongst them and this leads always, if sincerely done, to the realization of the relativity of our position.

The Relativity of Our Position

No man can come into the recognition of the relativity of his own moral, social, or personal position except as he becomes aware of other values, other ends, other goals, other relative positions on the sliding scale of value. This is a *sine qua non* of the escape from limited institutionalism. One simply has to recognize that he has not reached the ultimate, that the highest good is not necessarily wrapped up in his intermediate location. This happens only after he has something of an understanding of value and can accept the obligation to be critical with respect to himself, his values, his institutions, his goals and ends. With the realization of the relativity of his position and the intermediateness of his own values, the realization that what he has judged to be intrinsic is only instrumental subjects him to another peril.

He becomes the victim of his own expert criticism to such an extent that he falls into that adolescent and sophomoric rejection of the customs and morals of his tribe. This almost always follows his discovery

177

of his tribe's relativity. This betrays the immaturity of our minds. Fortunately, given another decade, as Durant has said: "We begin to understand that there may be more wisdom in the moral code of the group, the formulated experience of generations of the race, than can be explained in a single college course. Sooner or later the disturbing realization comes to us that even that which we cannot understand may be true." [3]

The tragedy connected with institutionalism is not that the abandonment of one's native morality upon the discovery of its relativity is permanent. The true danger lies, rather, in an inclination incipient in one's return to his native morality. After his sophomoric excursion into freedom, this inclination may lead him so deeply to entrench himself in the morality he once abandoned that he loses all sight of other values. He becomes entrenched more firmly in that which he once was tempted to reject.[4] Who can deny that it is as bad for the window sash to be stuck shut as it is for it to be stuck open? The net result of the return is that one, having been exposed to other demands, other heritages, even other cultures, recognizing the relativity of his own position, and even going so far as to desire some sort of improvement, still, almost always, rests his hope for that improvement upon something which can never provide it. That is to say, he cries for more time to adjust.

All over the southern part of the United States these days one can hear this cry in essence. "Give us more time." "We are being pressed too hard, too fast, give us more time." In this connection, time changes nothing. Time is no healer. To depend upon time as a healer is to depend upon empty cisterns. It is not time that heals; it is the stimulus of new experience which time may or may not bring that provides the impetus toward change, improvement, and the elevation of the level of one's position. Bergen Evans put it succinctly when he said:

Cultural change is dependent more upon the stimulus of new experiences than upon the mere passage of time. Without such a stimulus it can be

---

[3] Op. cit., p. 47.

[4] The dean of a famous theological school said that the first-year students were shocked awake, the second-year students were all wild rebels, and the third-year students were all busily making their adjustments for life "outside" when they would rejoin the denominational patterns.

exceedingly slow, as the histories of various static civilizations testify. And the most important of all cultural experience is contact with members of a different culture. Advances of culture depend on the chances that any group has to learn from the experience of others, and the more contacts the greater the opportunities to learn.

That is to say, the realization of the relativity of our position must of itself lead us to the demand for new experience, which in other language, is the realization of our desperate need to hear. This is the essence of that most lacking of Christian graces, humility. This is the denial of all our fatal cultural feudalisms, our colossally evil assumptions of superiority, and our grossly impertinent misuses of advantage. The realization of the relativity of our position reproduces within us the Christian notion of repentance. It causes us to assume responsibility for situations our own sins did not create; it makes us realize that we have not only something to say, but we have also a desperate need to hear. This leads one beggar to share his crust of bread with another, and there can occur transference of value from one culture to another. Time heals nothing. Only the awareness of common needs, and of mutual values which can be exchanged can lead to the escape from our own institutionalistic prison.

Whitehead, in *Science and the Modern World*, long ago claimed that the problem of evolution lies in the "development of enduring harmonies of enduring shapes of value which merge into higher attainments of things beyond themselves." This, in itself, is a hierarchical structure of progress, but not an automatic structure. The Western world has had a great deal of difficulty understanding that dictum propounded by Shaw: "Religion is a great force . . . the only real motive force in the world; but what you fellows don't understand is that you must get at a man through his own religion and not through yours." [5] This in a cruder way is the essence of the meaning of our need to hear. There is always the possibility, one discovers in the relativity of his own position, of his running into higher values and therefore higher positions and more perfect institutions outside his own.

To achieve this realization of relativity is to become mobile in one's own time and in one's own culture. It is to become eligible for new

[5] *Getting Married.*

experience; it is to escape the bounds of the provincial and the institutional; it is to come to understand the true function and purpose of both education and religion.

Institutions and cultures have always raised their banners. Constantine was not the first, but certainly he was the most famous. His "In this Sign, Conquer" became an institutional banner and watchword for all institutions and banners through the centuries since. There is something incredibly wrong with all this flag waving we do. One must have his values, indeed, but he must learn that they are seldom, if ever, ultimate values. When this *"In Hoc Signo"* ceases, as Hocking has said, to be a battle cry, when we quit waving our instrumental values as if they were ultimate values, it will be the symptom and sign of another and greater conquest. It will mean that estrangement among the seekers of God has become a thing of the past, and the human race will have found indeed a façade to the kingdom of God.

In this sense, then, all our flags are sins, all our banners are immoral, and all our institutions are prisons, except as they are recognized to be lesser flags, immature ends, temporary housings, on the way to some ultimate goal as yet unnamed and "ununderstood," ahead of us. Only the realization that our present position is temporary, that our present banners are fading banners, that our present communities are too exclusive, that our own culture is too narrow, and our present position is but a temporary foothold on a very high cliff can bring us into a position where we can accept the possibility of there being available for us a true participation in a higher level of living and life. This, and always this, is prelude to any permanent release from our lesser institutionalisms of whatever kind.

In this sense, our treasured signs must be allowed to become symbols. That is to say, they must be allowed to stand for more than they are and to participate in that which they truly represent. This is to open the door to a new and valid kind of "reconstructionism," which W. E. Hocking, in his later years and later works, has called for. This is not to say that the ultimate religion, the ultimate philosophy, the ultimate state, and the ultimate value is to be a syncretistic amalgamation of lesser values. This could only produce, as it always has, some old-new monstrosity. It is to say that the opening of the door to higher value beginning in the awareness of what value actually may be, the willing-

180

ness to be self-critical, and the realization of the relativity of our position leaves the door open to the emergence by the whole race onto a plateau of institutional provincial freedom which the race has never known.

The willingness to hear, required by the realization of the relativity of our position, is actually the ultimate willingness to abandon. One has to become willing to abandon in order to have the prospect of finding the newer and the higher. One becomes willing to allow dissent as a permanent datum and hearing as a permanent soul capacity for humility to bring one to the edge of rejection of all of his own holinesses, his own truths, and his own ultimates. He becomes willing to follow a new Messiah, asking only that he be truly Messiah. This is a devastating thing. In order to accomplish this he has to be able to ask, and hope to answer, some questions. His tool is his innate power of comparison; this is basic intellectually and to ethics. He begins to escape his racism as he becomes willing to become a member of the human race; he escapes his nationalism as he becomes willing to be citizen of a larger world; he escapes his religious institutionalism only as he becomes willing to be a native of the kingdom of God. Years ago, Hocking, primarily with respect to religion, phrased some of the questions this realization of our relativity would require:

Which religion, in its account of the need and lostness of the human heart, can get farthest beyond platitudes and mere general lament, into the region of the literal struggle of human life with evil, sordidness, and that blight of meaninglessness which besets human success no less than human failure. . . .

Which religion does in fact most verifiably save men from greed, lust, and hatred, and without destroying their virility and effectiveness as members of the race and social order? Which is most proof against hypocrisy, duplicity, and pretense? Which confers most genuine zest for dangerous and principled living, releases positive moral power, abets a single-mindedness which can discount accident, hostility, and failure? Which one develops greatness without narrowness, and conviction without servility? Which one begets prophets who can get the ear of the godless, sophisticated, intelligent, sagacious, and critical, as well as the ear of the suggestible, dependent, sentimental, or committed?

Which religion is most fertile? Which best sustains that metaphysical urge which is the life of the arts, of great and new poetry, drama, architecture,

181

music? A true religion invites cosmic courage, including the belief that the human mind is called upon to know its universe—not to find its equation, but by degrees to understand it. It is not cowed by the spectacle of infinity; it is freed to see meanings in things, to play with traditional ideas, as Dante, Milton, Bunyan played, setting other men free from literalism and the planetary provincialisms of the human outlook. The order of culture is religion, art, philosophy—religion being the fruitful center, when it is alive.

When the religions realise that these are the questions which they must eventually meet, and that no charter from the Most High God will excuse them from meeting them, nor give them any dominion on the earth if they do not, the search for their own essence may become, as it is due to be, a grave and anxious search rather than any mere exercise of scholarly speculation.[6]

What humanist, what naturalist, what atheist, what fanatic, or what heretic or half-believer could fail to respond to a religion like this? Meanwhile, however, in the realization of the meaning of value, in the willingness to be self-critical, and in the realization of the relativity of our position there are other questions we must ask.

What race view permits all human beings to be human, denies the egomaniacal feelings of self-superiority by minorities, releases most men to be achieving their potential, and provides for the most equitable consideration of affections, loves, hopes, and enduring aims? What race view allows life to become the eagerly enjoyed possession of the most backward of men? What race view provides the most equitable possibility for the realization of life and light? What race view strikes the most shackles from the minds of men and provides the most *lebensraum* for all the sons of earth?

What view of nations and of the world provides for the most equitable distribution of the physical power of the earth to provide the food and the shelter and the clothing for the teeming multitudes? What economic view is least constrictive to the normal needs and hungers of all mankind? Which hemispheric solidarity opens most doors to personality values? What way of life among nations provides for the widest horizons to be seen by the narrowest eyes? What local loyalty provides for the apperception of the next widest circle of human aspiration? What re-

[6] *Living Religions and a World Faith* (New York: The Macmillan Company, 1940), pp. 202-5. Used by permission.

ligion releases us from ourselves and most clearly makes it possible for us to be brothers unto all men? This, and these, are the ways of release from institutionalism.

In *The Brothers Karamazov*, Father Zossima belongs not only to tender Alyosha, he belongs to the whole order of heaven and the kingdom of God. His saintliness is a believable saintliness because it is rooted, almost inextricably, in the soil and agonies of the Russian peasant heart. He understands the longings of the Russian soul for deliverance; he understands the incredible faith in Moscow as the third Rome and the Russian nation as the new Messiah; he understands the longing agony of the Russian peasant to escape his bondage to the land and his masters; and above all, he knows the hope that lies in the Russian heart that someone or something holy and exalted is over all this and will come to us too, one day, and rule over all the earth according to the promise.

Meanwhile, Father Zossima has achieved an escape from Russianness, from institutionalism, even from his own priesthood, that provides release for him. This can provide release for us too if we can receive it. If vision be granted of what has happened within and to a man who has escaped the plague of his own racistic, nationalistic, and religious institutions we can find release, too. It reads like a Sermon on the Mount as Father Zossima speaks to his peasants:

"Know, dear ones, that everyone of us is undoubtedly responsible for all men and everything on the earth . . . only through that knowledge our heart grows soft with infinite, universal, inexhaustible love. Then everyone of you will have the power to win over the whole world by love and to wash away the sins of the world with your tears. Each of you keep watch over your hearts and confess your sins to yourself unceasingly. Be not afraid of your sins even when perceiving them, if only there be penitence, but make no conditions with God. Again I say, be not proud . . . hate not those who reject you . . . the atheists, the teachers of evil, the materialists . . . for there are many good ones . . . hate not even the wicked ones.

"Love a man even in his sin, for that is the semblance of divine love and is the highest love on earth. Love all God's creation, the whole and every grain of sand in it . . . every leaf . . . every ray of God's light . . . the animals . . . the plants, everything . . . you will [begin to] perceive

183

the divine mystery in things . . . and do not be proud that you are superior to the animals who do not pollute the earth as men do. Love children especially . . . they live to soften and purify our hearts and to guide us . . . Love is a teacher; but one must know how to acquire it . . . it is dearly bought, it is won slowly by long labor . . . not only occasionally but forever. Even the wicked can love occasionally. Fly from dejection, children . . . pray to God for gladness . . . and make yourself responsible for all men's sins for [if] you throw your own impudence and indolence on others . . . you will end by sharing Satan's pride and murmuring against God." [7]

[7] Dostoevski, section, Conversations of Father Zossima, pp. 333-40 of Modern Library ed., condensed. Used by permission of Random House, Inc.

Part Four

INDIVIDUALISM

prejudgment of personality

Monologue at Coffee Break

"Faulkner's a screwball. His whole family's screwball. Them two old druggists that backed him—he neveh looked lak nothin'—always wearin' ol cloes—and them druggists—one of 'em is still livin' and Faulkner keeps hanging aroun' there lots if he's in Oxford—bought a big house over at Charlottesville, got a big'un in Oxford too—he's lecturin' some I guess over in Virginia, but he's a screwball. He wouldn't remember me . . . I work with the Council [1] . . . but I wuz there [University of Mississippi] when he wuz . . . firin' that furnace and writin' on scraps of paper settin' on a wheel-bah . . . but he wuz a screwball then . . . he hurts Mississippi . . .

"Maybe you ain't lookin' at it right—sure I know they put him ahead of Hemingway up East . . . and I know he's talkin' 'bout humans, but it hurts us to let people think it's Mississippi people.

"Yeh, I know 'bout Wolfe and No'th Carolina and I know ol

[1] White Citizens' Council.

185

Faulkner's a genius, but it hurts bad to be human, like him climbin' inside that idiot thataway [The Sound and the Fury]. That could as well a' been Connecticut as Mississippi. Yeh, course I know he's a Nobel prize winnah, and I know he tole Life not to push us intellectuals too fah down heah 'else we'd have to take sides, but we done took sides.

"I work with the Council some and I loan niggahs money allatime up to five dollahs . . . no interest atall—doan keep no records—they pay me evah week—sometimes I forget and I nevah lost a nickel, but Faulkner's screwball.

"Bilbo? You oughta read his book on mongrelization. You have? Misteh, it doan' make no differunce to us if Hitler did say it too, and that Gobineau—they all had sump'n. I work with the Council some.

"Yeh, the pink palace Bilbo built is still there and he still owes a bunch of Jews for the furnishin's—paid one bunch of 'em ten cents on the dollah afteh eveh lawyer in the county registered as his attorney and one or two wuz always sick so they could keep postponin' the case.

"No, he wasn't quite as mean or as smart as Huey Long. They don' come no smarter'n Huey, and he'd kill ya. You couldn' even teach school in Loosyanna if you didn't—but back to Bilbo. He told FDR if he didn't get Miz Roosevelt off his back he was goin' to—and FDR said he couldn't make her stop and old Bilbo said yes you can and if you don't I'm gonna treat her just lak she wuz a man! and he neveh heard no more from her.

"We may have to go cleah out of the schoolin' business down here . . . 'cept for a few in private schools—but we ain't gonna give. You take that Pearl River business—why theh's stuff we know the federals never will find out or tell, even if they know. But they cain't all of em! push us into this—you outside fellahs jes don'know."

This kind of man, this individualist caught up in his institutionalism, provincialism, and materialism, is obsessed with his my, and how discordant that I. "It may stir great compassion if it comes from lips compressed in the tragedy of concealed self-contradiction. It may arouse horror if it comes chaotically from lips that wildly, heedlessly, unsuspectingly, show forth the contradiction!" How discordant that I of self-contradiction! If he ever becomes aware of the contradiction, "a deeper shudder seizes him"—for there is a contradiction.

186

The Contradiction

Individualism is a fantastic impossibility. It simply cannot be, either as a way of life or as a slogan for some particular emphasis for living, but it is. It cannot do even as the explanation of psychological structures of existence, but it is and does. It lies at the bottom of capitalism and our economic structure; it is precious to the thought of that political philosophy known as democratic republicanism; it is the avowed and loved token of orthodoxy in the so-called "democratic" churches; it is both means and goal in much psychological therapy in the Western world. Yet it is a heresy, an abortion of community, a denial of democracy, a false maturity and healing, and is the ultimate spiritual error. It is the meaning of the lostness of the world, for there are as many centers of the universe as there are human beings. This is our ultimate lostness. It is a denial of personality and of God. It is impossible philosophically, psychologically, sociologically, and ethically and is the ultimate theological madness. It is of the essence of hell, for there is no hell beyond that which sees a man shut up to himself alone. At the same time, it is the nearest, most personal, and most powerful framework for prejudice. It is the most intimate channel within which and through which we become properly prejudiced people—which requires almost a half of our lives.

Herein lies a contradiction: It is impossible and prevalent; it is heretical, but everywhere received; it is absurd and sacred; it is a philosophical position no one would admit that he owns and yet, the almost universal social individualism provides the deepest and most vicious channel for the operation of human prejudice.

Individualism travels under many banners. There are other words for it—subjectivism, egoism, and, to be properly psychological, narcissism. Philosophically there is a nicely precise word for this view of life which is both an epistemology and a metaphysic. The word is sola-ipsis—self alone, or solipsism.

In philosophy this is an epistemology, for the doctrine of the self alone is an answer to our concern with the extent of our knowledge. It is also a metaphysic for it is concerned with the ultimate nature of reality. Epistemologically, individualism or solipsism is a subjectivism; metaphysically, it is an idealism. Individualism claims in its ultimate

187

that mind is reality; all else exists in mind only as idea. I am real; my self is all I can know and is the extent of reality.

This is a philosophical position that no one holds, or would admit that he holds. It is a *reductio ad absurdum* for beating subjective idealists over the head. This is precisely what makes the almost universal social solipsism so profound an anomaly. If there were philosophical solipsists the base they would occupy is the base from which our social individualism comes.

That is to say, when one acts as if he were all there is, his philosophical base, if he is logical, is solipsism. From an uncritical view, in particular, this is the base of that self view that permits him to be so much the victim of and the creator of prejudice. Such reasoning may also give a philosophical base for what we call sin, which itself rests on a faulty view of self.

There are crazier notions than this—that the root of our prejudices lies in an absurd notion of reality and a ridiculous view of ourselves. The obvious fact of its social acceptability is also the explanation for the fundamental necessity of considering an absurd epistemology and a ridiculous metaphysic as if it were a valid view of knowledge and reality. We are not critically concerned with this philosophical monstrosity; we are concerned practically, noncritically, ethically, and eventually theologically.

Chapter X

The Ethical Extension of Individualism

An improper view of the self lies somewhere near the base of all prejudice as well as at the base of all sin. If there were a philosophical base for selfish prejudiced living, it would be solipsism, for this is the only proper base for that thesis which lies at the heart of all prejudice. But it is primarily an ethical thesis. It claims that the goal and end of life is self-realization.

This self-realization is a quite different thing from that eudaemonism of the ancient Greeks and must be distinguished from this classical and ancient philosophy. It must even be distinguished from Epicureanism, which is a hedonism. This kind of self-realization is neither eudaemonic nor Epicurean. Self-realization may be self-aggrandizement or self-sacrifice. It is self-expression, which may or may not be pleasurable. In any event, what is desired is self-assertion, which may or may not be respectably ethical and psychologically normal. The concept of self-realization splits and forms a polarity. There is a kind of self-realization which can come only from some solipsistic base. There is a kind of self-realization without which both philosophical and psychological maturity is impossible. The difference is the difference that maintains

189

between assertion and realization, the difference between individuality and true personality. There is an intrinsic difference.

This polarity within self-realization may be expressed negatively in the assertion of individuality or it may be expressed positively as the realization of personality. Only the former can have a solipsistic base. The assertion of individuality reaches the limit of its ethic outside the prospect of any true communion between persons. The limit of true self-determination lies beyond this in a personality concept that includes God. This is the heresy of the assertion of individuality; this is its fundamental weakness; this is the essence of its impossibility. This is also the prime factor in its greatness; it creates new gods, as many gods as there are human beings. This provides for that awful conflict of gods which is the fundamental basis of all social, economic, political, and personal warfare; this is the essence of the denial of community; this is the meaning of our ultimate lostness and estrangement. But the assertion of individuality is also something that lies very near the root construction of personality. That is to say there is no psychological or personal wholeness that does not involve in some sense an assertion of individuality. To deny this is to deny the essence of human life and is to leave us living like slugs under rocks away from communion, sans life, love, laughter, tears, memory, hope, or communion. Therefore, the assertion of our individualness must be considered in both of these contexts—its apparent necessity and its moral impossibility.

The Assertion of Individuality

Every living human being seeks to realize himself. No human life is possible apart from this drive to self-realization. "The core of the matter seems to be that every being is trying to complete his own nature. Now he may seek an equilibrium in rejection: He will be narrow, insular, limited, circular. Or, he may find an equilibrium of relaxation and become a self trusting, self loving being also capable of trusting and being compatible with others." [1] At any rate he seeks to realize himself.

How is this perfectly valid description of life to be connected with solipsism? Given: Solipsism, a theory of knowledge which says all I know is me. This becomes a theory of reality which claims that all that

[1] From Gordon W. Allport, The Nature of Prejudice, 1954, Addison-Wesley, Reading, Mass. P. 441.

190

is real is me. This view of knowledge and reality then becomes a way of living, an ethic, in which all that is valued, indeed, all that matters is me. This issues in an aim, a self-realization if you please. Thus, the practical ethical, noncritical, psychological projection of solipsism is this negative assertion of individuality.

I believe nothing can be more important in the attempt to find the psychodynamic factors in the origins of prejudice than an understanding of this native, universal assertion of individuality. This is true, in part, because in the final analysis there are no prejudices that are not individual and personal. There is really no such thing as a group prejudice. There are only prejudices held in common by members of the group. Indeed, commonality of prejudices may be a constituent factor in the creation of a group, but prejudice is always basically individual.

Prejudice does not inhere in the fact of individuality. Prejudice is not given; it is gotten, learned, acquired. A connection between individuality and prejudice is this assertion of individuality which plays against the sociality of the individual. That is, a part of the assertion of the individual is the completion of a successful social reference. Prejudiced views of the already accepted individuals are learned by those who seek admission to a group, and these then assert and accept their way, by asserting and accepting the prejudices, into the group.

To recapitulate the argument: The source of estrangement and isolation in sin is also the source of prejudice. These pass through the aim of self-realization to that view of self deposited on self as a value judgment, the extent of reality, and the limit of knowledge. Wittingly or unwittingly, it rests on solipsism as a base. This is absurd and unthinkable, and prevalent.

Its Ethical Antecedents

This is deeper than Epicureanism because it involves more than pleasure; it rises out of some deeper *Gestalt* of the self. The assertion of individuality, however, includes egoistic hedonism and sounds as if it were only this at times. As Berdyaev put it: "Man lives in an agony, he wants to know who he is, where he comes from, and where he is going . . . he is a twofold and contradictory being . . . Godlike and beastlike, exalted and base, free and enslaved, apt both for rising and falling, capable of great love and sacrifice, of great cruelty and unlimited egoism." [2]

His attempt to resolve the contradiction Berdyaev described brings one of two answers to man. He becomes involved in *the assertion of individuality*, or he rises to *the realization of personality*. This assertion of individuality includes Epicureanism and sounds as if it were little more. The realization of personality has nothing to do with egoism, hedonism, or even utilitarianism [*infra*].

The fundamental tenets of individualism are naked egoism and self-love. According to the true individualist the way of naked egoism is the only intelligent method of living. This system knows no true virtue and has no concept of altruism. There is none of the utilitarian ethic even of Jeremy Bentham or of the Mills in this. It has no concern with what is best for the most. As Stirner put it: "I want to be and to have everything that I can be and have. Whether other people want to be and have similar things does not concern me. Everyone else is only what he is for me, namely: my object, and because he is my object he is my property." [3]

On the other hand, self-love is the base of individualism which Mandeville called the source of all human action. In this connection Bertrand Russell says, "When we think of mankind, we think primarily of ourselves as its representatives; we, therefore, think well of mankind, and consider its preservation important." [4]

Here again an Epicurean connection appears, but it is not truly Epicureanism. A look at the antecedents of the belief in naked egoism and self-love as constitutive of the individual becomes necessary.

According to Socrates virtue is insight which is equivalent to the "knowledge of the good." By not defining a universal concept of the "good" Socrates left the matter open. The Cynics and the Cyrenaics thrust very diverse views into the open end of this Socratic concept. Both attempted to define the true worth of individual life in a universal manner. Both wished to show man's true happiness—how he must act and how he must be constituted in order to be "certainly happy." Both

---

[2] *Slavery and Freedom*, p. 20. Used by permission of Charles Scribner's Sons and Geoffrey Bles, Ltd.
[3] Jodl, *Geschicte der Ethik*, I; cited by Brunner in *The Divine Imperative*, p. 576.
[4] *Sceptical Essays*, p. 32.

call this constitution and disposition through which happiness is gained virtue. They develop Socrates' notion of eudaemon in a one-sided manner so that the worth of all relations of even public life is estimated by the individual's happiness. "In cynicism [especially] the Greek spirit is proceeding to appropriate the fruit which the conditions of life brought about by civilization yield for the fortune of the individual." [5]

The Cynic Antisthenes taught that virtue is that conduct of life which makes man as independent as possible of events. The virtue that makes man independent demands suppression of desires. Therefore, virtue is freedom from wants and is the intelligent conduct of life. [6] This is good, especially for poor men. By this reduction of desires, a reduction of needs, men were to attain the ideal state of nature. This posits a negative view of civilization and culture. Wealth, refinement, fame, and honor are superfluous. Family, native land, art, science, and progress are indifferent. Diogenes, says Windelband, was popular just because of his jesting attempt to live in civilized Greece as in a state of nature. In this sort of individualism there is no respect for justice ($\delta\acute{\iota}\kappa\eta$) or reverence ($a\grave{\iota}\delta\acute{\omega}s$), which the Sophists had regarded as natural impulses. Therefore the Cynics are not unfairly pictured as seeing greed and lust necessary to complete the natural man.

To Aristippus good would be $\acute{\eta}\delta o\nu\acute{\eta}$, pleasure here, pleasure that would bring a satisfied will. It is a matter of indifference as to what is desired. Pleasure is higher than sensual bodily satisfaction in the moment, however. Man must enjoy as much and as vigorously as possible. Therefore, virtue is the equivalent to the ability for enjoyment. Wisdom means knowledge of how to enjoy selectively and rightly. That is, one stays in control in order to enjoy more.

The younger Aristippus, grandson of the founder of the Cyrenaics, was, as he claimed, mother-taught, and was concerned with feelings and emotions. For him, as well as for Theodorus the atheist, all ethical and legal institutions were valid for the masses, but the educated man enjoyed things as they came. It was of these that Eumereus said, "they stripped the gods of meaning." The recognition of no native land and no political responsibility, which among the Cynics grew out of despising the enjoyments of civilization, appears in the Cyrenaics out of the

---

[5] Windelband, op. cit., pp. 82 ff.
[6] Diogenes Laertius, VI, and Zenophon, Symp. 4, 34 ff.

egoism of their own enjoyment. So, as Windelband has said, in Cynicism we have the philosophy of beggars who will not beg at the shrine of Grecian beauty. In Cyrenaicism we see appearing the philosophy of parasites at the table of Grecian beauty. They are the same and are equally distant from the meaning of ancient Greek hedonism and Greek culture.

In classical hedonism we find almost no true antecedents of this modern kind of individualism. For Epicurus the wise man was the imperturbable man. He is independent of the world, free, like a king or a god. Whatever happens cannot really get to the wise man. His wisdom rests in himself, the world does not trouble him, happiness is in himself alone, not in creative work for great purposes. He does not intend to overcome the outer world; he means simply to be indifferent toward general ends. This is an inner mastery since no world power is involved, and here there is a distinction from individualism, for the modern individualist intends to control all of the world he can. For Epicurus a man must become master of the effects of the world upon himself. That is to say, he masters his passions by coming into apathy. This is a Stoic expression and means to rest content within oneself.

Epicurus designates pleasure as the *summum bonum* but nevertheless prefers the permanent frames of satisfaction and rest to the enjoyment of the moment. The wise man chooses on the basis of the expectation of continuing pleasure with respect to natural wants, conventional wants, and the not indispensable wants. "Complete blessedness falls to his lot who rejoices in all these good things in quiet enjoyment without stormy striving." [7]

In Epicureanism the *bon vivant* is the wise man who seeks aesthetic refinement of life, in terms of wit, sentiment, delicacy, comfortable arrangement, and daily living. The wise man knows what he can get and what he cannot get and this is his ataraxy, his impassiveness. This, the essence of individualistic hedonism in the classical world, is yet a far cry from that naked egoism and self-love implicit in the modern world.

Only a noncritical type of judgment would put Antisthenes, Aristippus, and Theodorus the atheist, under the same category as the great Epicurus. These represent a distinct tradition, that of the Cynics and Cyrenaics. These belong alongside the great skeptic Pyrrho, not Epicurus.

[7] Windleband, op. cit., p. 166.

THE ETHICAL EXTENSION OF INDIVIDUALISM

It is Pyrrho, not Epicurus, who affirms that the wise man knows nothing that can be affirmed as to things themselves. He has no opinion that may be assented to and therefore restrains himself from judgment and also from action. He withdraws into himself, in suspension of judgment, which saves him from passion and false action. He becomes imperturbable. He becomes a participant in ataraxy. This is the essence of individualism in an ancient form. Modern times would give it more energy but no better morals.

It remained for more modern minds to pick up the beginnings of Pyrrho and his antecedents. This kind of sensualism, with an addition of modern materialism, appears in Julien Offrai de Lamettrie (1709-1751), in *Histoire Naturelle de L'Ame* and in *L'Homme Machine*. Helvetius and Mandeville followed Lamettrie in the development of the totally selfish system of individualism. Especially Lamettrie himself, with tasteless cynicism, savored a desire for admiration and sought to exhibit hunger and love in their lowest meaning as the fundamental motives of all human life. This more nearly modern expression is called by Windelband a "wretched, artificial imitation of ancient Hedonism." It appears in the work of Labruyere, *Characteres*, 1680; in the work of La Rochefoucauld, *Reflections*, 1690; and in the most savage book ever written in English, *Gulliver's Travels*, by Jonathan Swift. His description of humankind in general in the *Voyage to the Houyhnhnms* is perhaps the most vicious exhibition of overt individualism in terms of naked egoism and self-love that the English language has ever seen produced. This is not classical hedonism, however. This is modern individualism and is something else.

There are other fundamental tenets of modern individualism. At this point, however, it should be interjected that our concept of man surely must be bigger than naked egoism and self-love as sources of all human action. There are other sources of human action, self-disgust for example. Nicholai Berdyaev is the teacher here. It is not true, he says, that mankind always loves himself above all. While it is true that man is an egoistical and egocentric being, this does not necessarily mean that he is in love with himself. It is quite common that people cannot love themselves at all. Indeed some people hate themselves. If it turns out that a man cannot love himself he usually cannot forgive this to anyone and vents upon other people the bitterness which is directed against himself. "The most vindictive people are those who do not love themselves." This is a source of human action, too. People who like themselves are generally kinder and more tolerant. This is a moral and psychological paradox. A man may be "a hard and heartless egoist but neither love nor like himself." Berdyaev claims that one of the sources of human suffering is this self-disgust. Therefore the inability to feel self-love is sometimes a source of human action. For that, there is a self-love that we are supposed to have in accordance with the will of God. We are expected to love God's creation and the divine image or likeness in ourselves. We are required to love our neighbors as ourselves. It is required that we must love ourselves, too, and respect God's image in us and this kind of love is opposed to egoism and egocentricity. It is opposed to the madness of putting oneself at the center of the universe which is a fundamental result of naked egoism and this kind of self-love.

There are major tenets of modern individualism other than naked egoism and self-love. There is for example the fundamental notion of atomistic individualism which, to use Emil Brunner's figure, is a *Robinsonnade*. In fact, Brunner calls the whole of modern philosophy "a 'Robinson Crusoe' affair, expressed in abstract terms; it is an attempt to interpret the individual human being solely in the light of his own personality, and society as the coalescence of such individuals." [8] Fundamentally, this is an attempt to bring sociology into correspondence with the nineteenth-century attempt to explain the world of phenomena in terms of isolated atoms. It apparently is no accident that nineteenth-century atomistic physics broke down when it was discovered that such a system could no longer explain the strange "communities" in the world of nature. Men also began to reflect anew on the nature of individual and community relations. They came to see, in the light of a newer science, that the individual does not exist at all except as he implies community. Therefore, atomistic materialism along with naked egoism and self-love becomes insufficient to explain either the greatness, the grandness, or the capacity for evil in mankind.

The fourth tenet of modern individualism has been the view that the desired maintenance of race groupings justifies individualistic views. Out of this grew Herbert Spencer's works in ethics wherein evolution, transposed falsely from biology, is used to explain even the human con-

[8] *Op. cit.*, p. 294.

196

science. He builds a norm and claims that whatever furthers the maintenance of the race is moral, and race maintenance depends upon and evolves alongside the maintenance of the individual himself.

A fifth tenet of this kind of individualism is that morals can always be accounted for under naturalistic labels. There is the deliberate junking of all notions of community and communal principles of moral life. For example, what we have called conscience, under the naturalistic tenet of individualism, becomes a guilt complex. Unselfish sacrifice is interpreted as either an inferiority, an Oedipus, or a Narcissus complex. Distinguished social service is really the result of an overdeveloped "herd instinct." Piety has no worth in itself. It is simply ignorance plus superstition. Moral integrity is a kind of hypocrisy. Saintliness is a kind of idiocy, and our dominant traits are always schizophrenia, paranoia, or sexual libido. In this kind of teaching total depravity is a good doctrine if folks would just live up to it, as Elbert Hubbard claimed a long time ago.

There is one other fundamental tenet of modern individualism which has had more power than the others in expressing this parody on true life in a true democracy. This is the notion that there is a presumptive structure of right which gives individualism a legal base. For example:

It is objectively "right" that an individual should develop his powers, whatever they are. This objective right is the true standard for legal right. Legal "rights" are, or should be, conditions under which individual powers may be presumed to develop best. . . .

The one certain element in the situation is that in the normal development of personal powers, whatever they may be, society will be a presumptive beneficiary. And this statement has an obverse, which is that the suppression or stunting of that development will involve presumptive, though unmeasurable, loss to both society and the individual.[9]

This view is the hard legal core of American individualism and supports a vast weight of the structure of modern emphasis on the individual.

A Reigning Ethic

A little later on a distinction will be made between the psychological definitions of individuality, which must be kept in the realization of

[9] Bates, *op. cit.*, p. 384.

personality, and the ethical system of individualism, which is quite the contradictory position from that of the realization of personality. What has been discussed in this section is rather an ethical view of the individual which is abortive, negative, anarchous, and utterly false. It is not intended to be claimed that what psychology knows as individuality can be done away with. Indeed, to do away with this concept of individuality is to do away with the foundation of personality.

In the discussion of modern individualism as an ethical system it has been claimed that the fundamental points of departure, the fundamental constructs out of which modern individualism has appeared, rest on Cynicism and Cyrenaicism, ancient rivals to classical humanism, which found modern expression primarily in the work of Lamettrie and Mandeville. The fundamental tenets of individualism are naked egoism and self-love as the sources of human action. It is described further as teaching a nineteenth-century kind of atomistic individualism which falls of its own weight before the learning wrapped up in the new physics. Individualism has also a fundamental tenet in its desire to see the preservation of the individual as a means of race maintenance. It further accounts for the naturalistic development of all moral values as a denial of individual integrity and sees most powerfully a legal base for its existence in a presumptive structure of right.

This type of individualism has its definite limitations. Before these limitations are delineated, however, perhaps a summary definition of modern ethical extensions of solipsism in terms of this ethical individualism should be attempted:

Individualism is a bastardized version of ancient hedonism wearing the garb of modern democratic idealism which claims for itself the same goal as that of classical Greek eudaemonism; that is, self-realization as the end of man, but does this in such a way as to eliminate community, subvert the development of personality, distort all social human values, and has as its end the cutting off of the individual from everything which constitutes personality. It is truly sola-ipsis in that it has neither values nor community that permit the individual ever to come outside the self and therefore is a definition of hell which is the ultimate in isolation. It is always isolationistic, atomistic, and seeks the center of the earth as its own which makes it a god-maker in demonic form.

The practical ethical extension of solipsism which appears in the

198

assertion of individuality in its modern form is, on a wide base, the reigning level of ethics in much of the Western world and most of modern life. It particularly adapts itself to the hurly-burly viciousness of the modern business world but it has its limitations. These limitations neither deny it nor refute it and this is why, in the warm, wet, mothering womb of this vicious individualism, we find the most powerful breeding place of human prejudice.

Chapter XI

The Limitations of Individualism

"The primary word *I-It* can never be spoken with the whole being." [1]
"Without *It* man cannot live. But he who lives with *It* alone is not a
man." [2] The rise of a man's power to mechanize, to maneuver, and to
utilize is always at the cost of his personal powers of relation.[3] Here the
individual succumbs grandly to the false categorization that is prejudiced
existence. He divides his life into neatly zoned circles or provinces—
the province of things, and the province of his own *I*. In one he has his
institutions, in the other his feelings. In the first circle he pursues his
aims, works, makes deals, organizes, institutes, manipulates, carries on
business, schemes, influences, and slaves. In the inner circle of feeling
he recovers. In a "boudoir rich in ever-changing interests" he read-
justs, rationalizes, likes, hates, enjoys, and indulges his griefs. If a man
lets *It* have the mastery, this continually growing world of *I-It*, "It over-
runs him and robs him of the reality of his own *I*, till the incubus over

[1] Martin Buber, *I and Thou*, trans. Ronald G. Smith, p. 3. Used by permission of
Charles Scribner's Sons and T. & T. Clark.
[2] *Ibid.*, p. 34.
[3] *Ibid.*, p. 43.

him and the ghost within him whisper to one another the confession of their non-salvation." [4]

This *I-It*, says Buber, appears as individuality with itself as subject of experiencing and using. It is the spiritual form of natural detachment. It lives on its detachment as individuality as differentiated from all others. Its aim is to taste, see, feel, and have—and to use. It knows itself as such-and-such, but never knows the self. Remote from his true being he revels in the fiction, the fantasy, of his special self-constructed image. He cannot learn that the image is never the person. [5] He is slave to this image, this personage. [6] "If you were to take the clothes off the one, there wouldn't be much left of him," whereas a true person would weigh as much as before. [7] This individuality always knows itself as such-and-such, and there emerges an authoritarian and obvious self capable of only contracted deceit. He speaks out of his concern for his my of his own kind, his race, his values, and his province like a man in a cage.

The Denial of Community

Individualism is limited by its incapacity for community. Community is the basic condition of personality. Individualism can never be "in communion" by definition and therefore can never achieve personality. Individuals, i.e., atoms, can never know community because there is no possibility of transition by an atom from the one to the many or from the many to the one. This is cut off in the beginning. There is no center precisely because there are so many centers—as many centers as there are individuals. This denial of community is the most effective limitation of individualism as a possible central theme for life and living.

Notice again that individualism can go high enough in ethics to see that the best available good lives on good terms with individual relationships, but individualism is powerless to transform individual relationships into personal relationships. This is true because individualism can know neither persons nor community between persons. This is because individualism simply cannot love outside itself. Therefore, individualism reaches its highest ceiling on the lower side of any conceivable social

[4] *Ibid.*, p. 46.
[5] Paul Tournier, *The Meaning of Persons*, trans. Edwin Hudson (New York: Harper & Brothers, 1957), p. 14.
[6] *Ibid.*, p. 32.
[7] *Ibid.*, pp. 81 ff.

good. It does not know the meaning of the word "social" and therefore could never think in terms of a good beyond itself.

In the end, self-realization of this sort precludes forever the next higher aim of good for society as a whole. It follows that this assertiveness of individualism can never reach even to the ethical level of universalistic hedonism (utilitarianism) in either its qualitative or its quantitative form.

If individualism can know only a bastardized egoistic hedonism as its form it can know other ethical systems only egoistically. Its solipsistic base has damned it to its own isolationism. Its naturalistic power ethic is confined to itself and cannot fly even as far or as high as Hobbes' power theory of social contract. No social contract can hold individualism. The individual is not subject to social grasps or communal obligations and therefore is not bound by any contract. This kind of individual is superman. He is antiman. He is a primitive Nietzsche; he is Thrasymachus. This is the essence of individualism. This is the sin of the world. Individualism is always proprietor, never guest. The game of individualism is always "one-eyed cat" with the self at bat. One knows nothing of teamplay. One becomes as Cain in Shaw's *Back to Methuselah* to whom Eve says: "You can feel nothing but a torment, and believe nothing but a lie. You will not raise your head to look at all the miracles of life that surround you; but you will run ten miles to see a fight or a death." In the full tide of individualism, life makes the individualist talk like Adam talks to Eve in the same play:

What! Eve: do not play with me about this. If only there may be an end some day, and yet no end! If only I can be relieved of the horror of having to endure myself for ever! If only the care of this terrible garden may pass on to some other gardener! If only the sentinel set by the Voice can be relieved! If only the rest and sleep that enabled me to bear it from day to day could grow after many days into an eternal rest, an eternal sleep, then I could face my days, however long they may last. Only, there must be some end, some end: I am not strong enough to bear eternity.

In these one sees the essence of this individualism shut up to itself alone so long and so powerfully that it learns at last that it cannot endure the prospect of having to live with itself alone forever. This is the essence of the limitation of individualism because it simply cannot live

202

with personality. As Berdyaev has put it, egoism destroys personality. This is the meaning of original sin. This "egocentric self-containment and concentration upon the self and the inability to issue forth from the self" represents the realization of the fully demonic. This is the essence, psychologically, of hysteria and means that while a hysterical man or woman is an example of egoism in the craze for self, the same odd way of referring everything to self is the essence of that hysteria known as individualism in its quieter moments. Individualism is but a calmer kind of hysteria.

Individualism as a mild hysteria is not the whole story. Individuality is of the essence of personality, too. It is individuality *sans the personna* which can know hysteria—for hysteria is the loss of communion, that is, the loss of the personal. Personality is individual and community; it is individuality-in-communion. Here, before individual can be person, individuality must go back to itself—be willing to be itself—as Sören Kierkegaard says it. Here, at the point of willingness to be the self before the self, individuality, the integer with potential for personality, enters the road of becoming person—a task to be achieved, and not a "given" factor of existence. In this process of becoming person (individual-in-communion) individuality is caught up in the higher; it is transmuted, not dropped off like a chrysalis. It remains, as an element of the personal. It is not obliterated. As Temple said, "Self-determination is the characteristic of man as a moral being." *Individuality is the psychological fundament of the personal, but it does not remain individuality in the personal.* Something new—communion—has been added. I have been speaking of the ethical limitations of individuality assuming its psychological essentiality. Its essentiality is the first word, not the last.

To follow Temple further, "[self-determination] is not the last word of human development; on the contrary it contains the sentence of endless frustration as truly as it affords the opportunity of entry upon the spiritual enterprise. For the self which determines cannot carry the self which is determined above its own level." [8]

It was something grander than individualistic genius that was being felt after when from his cubicle at the end of the hall a sensitive mathematician watched the master of his trade wheeled in his chair day after

[8] Op. cit., p. 244.

day to die alone, as he worked alone, on his electronic computer brain. This was no way for genius to die—alone, shut off, hemmed in to brilliance. The heart of even a scientist reached out for the master of his trade, and wrote, under a false name, on an inter-office memo pad:

Men, when they die
By natural right are due
That which all animals can claim:
A brake of grass, sweet smelling, gently crushed,
Cool earth beneath
With an open sky above,
Wherein the tilted gaze
Soars free in flight.

Yet Rakmann's dying is assuaged
By none of this most ancient heritage.
Daily unrelenting, he drags his body's husk,
Half-claimed already by a *rigor mortis*
Clack and scuffle down the corridor,
Deposits what remains to him—
A pain-filled carcass and a coursing mind—
Before the apparatus of his trade:
The hulking chassis of a Radix Digital Computer
(Mark XII of the species).

Daily, at the appointed time,
He assumes his scowl of concentration,
Begins the intricate maneuver
That can activate the idling mechanism
(Operational power level 1.7 megawatts),
Engages, interlocks, confines himself within
A clicking, buzzing world
Illuminated only by the cathode-glow
Of a thousand vacuum tubes.

When the last decisive relay closes
(A vicious instantaneous snap)
The memory drums leap to their whirring business
And The Brain begins to "think,"
Hurtling through the logic of its program,
Spewing transforms, differentials, variables

Precisely in accordance
With demands beyond
Its own power of devising.
(Rakmann, with wry humor, likes to say:
"It knows approximately nothing;
But It knows that exceeding well.")

He neglects to add
That what It knows
Is known by virtue of a painful, slow
Attrition of the tenuous web
Of molecules that tediously
Have knit up his own
Brain and vital tissue.
The process of disintegration is inexorable.

Being well-trained, Rakmann extrapolates,
Foresees the inevitable end.
It is here he crawls to do his dying.
Here his eventual chosen tomb
Far from the natural habitat
Of the animal he was.

In some far time he may
Receive this deference, in passing:
"It is well known
That Rakmann, in an earlier work,
Achieved a most original
And productive prototype;
But, of course, he missed
The crucial aspect
Of the human brain."

Men, when they die
By natural right are due
That which all animals can claim:
A brake of grass, sweet smelling, gently crushed
Cool earth beneath
With an open sky above,
Wherein the tilted gaze
Soars free in flight.[9]

* Milton Marney, Los Angeles, February, 1956.

There are other limitations of individualism. Its denial of communion both with the human-divine and with nature is enough to brand it a provincialism, but there are other limitations.

The Distortion of Reality

Individualism can never achieve a valid grasp of reality. The patent prejudice of individualism is demonstrated at its point of beginning by what it has already ruled to be unreal. It rules out all the grief of the world except its own and cries with Elizabeth in Shakespeare's *King Richard III*, "O, who hath any cause to mourn but I?" It rules out all the ideas and genius of its would-be compeers, as Hotspur, in *King Henry IV*, to whom Northumberland cried:

> Why, what a wasp-stung and impatient fool
> Art thou to break into this woman's mood,
> Tying thine ear to no tongue but thine own!

The individualist can never get out of his own skin, but he likes the "reality" he finds there. Unlike ancient islanders who thought man could be immortal only if he could "molt," shed his own skin, the individualist wishes no new containment. He is surprised to discover that any but his own skin is real. Simeon Stylites reports of Lord Curzon, the Exquisite, that while inspecting British troops in France during the First World War he watched the soldiers taking shower baths and exclaimed, "It is remarkable what white skins the lower orders have." [10] It could never enter the mind of the individualist to make any sense of Walt Whitman's remark during his work in Civil War hospitals: "I become the wounded man myself." He has ruled out all grief, ideas, influence, skin, and wounds that are not his own.

The fact that there is no valid reality for individualism is seen, too, in its loss of dimension. Life loses all height and depth and becomes one dimensional because the exclusively moral power of decision is atrophied. It is never used—the decisions are already made to exclude the personal and any other. No life, no love, no communion in abstraction—this is the death of the potential for the personal and the real. This is the denial of that relatedness extraneous to self-centered isolationism and

[10] *Christian Century.*

206

is therefore the denial of its own being which cannot be apart from relatedness. It denies the *Sein-woher* and the *Sein-wohin*, the being-whence and the being-whither, which is the realization of the real person.[11]

The individualist, says Hans Reichenbach, makes a fundamental mistake. He believes he can prove the existence of his own personality, but all that he can really assert is that he has experiences. He cannot go beyond this point and grasp or prove any objective reality. He is beyond reason, and therefore, "We have no logical arguments against him, because all our experiences prove is that we have experiences, and not that there is a physical world." [12]

Even those who have built a solipsist system do not really accept their own views of reality:

Though this (solipsistic) conception has scarcely ever been actually maintained, there have been some philosophers who developed it as a philosophical system; among them G. Berkeley and M. Stirner may be mentioned. When I say that even these men did not actually adhere to this theory, I refer to the fact that they wrote books setting forth their theory, which fact can scarcely be explained if they did not believe there were other persons who could read these books.[13]

This individualist has no view of reality truly. He cannot prove even his own existence, for this ego-proof is the same kind of inference that others use to "prove" an external world. He does not see this parallelism, for the solipsist loses the woods in a tree, his own tree.

This is a metaphysic so narrow, a view of reality so rigid that it is involved in all three of Kierkegaard's kinds of narrowness: intellectual, aesthetic, and spiritual. So fundamental a construct of Kierkegaard's despair lies at the base of all provincialism, institutionalism, and individualism. This follows logically from the inability of individualism to understand or wish for communion. There is also another limitation.

The Perversion of Value

Individualism cannot achieve a grasp of value. The relationship of value to persons has been shown in the section on institutionalism.

[11] See Brunner, op. cit., p. 296.
[12] Op. cit., p. 267.
[13] Ibid.

207

Apart from the personal, value simply does not exist. Individualism, a denial of personality, has therefore no equipment with which to arrive at value for it cannot arrive at the personal without the loss of its own entity in the communion of persons. To individualism, everything outside itself is object. Because nothing and no one can be subject, because all else is object—for manipulation—individualness, in its own right, is never person. Individual cannot be person without communion. It cannot know communion in the absence of some other subject with whom communion could happen. So sans subject, and therefore sans communion, and hence without the status of person, individualism cannot grasp value. This is how individualism slips into the ultimate slavery to objects. The individual becomes a thing owned by objects he has inadvertently subjectivized and therefore has personalized.

Berdyaev said:

The source of slavery is objectivization. Objectivization is always the organization of dominance, which is a contradiction of personality. It is precisely in the exteriorization and the alienation in human nature that man falls under the sway of the will to power, of money, of the thirst for pleasure, glory, etc., which are destructive of personality.[14]

Thus, individualism, enslaved by its objects of value judgment—power, money, pleasure, et cetera—invalidates its own values in its slaveries which deny its self-valuation as center.

This is why Temple could say, " 'To thine own self be true' is a piece of high class ethical futility which Shakespeare appropriately puts into the mouth of his own most priceless old dotard." [15] It is this kind of moral judgment which caused the bootblack at Simon's to say of a certain referee, "He won't cheat unless he has to." In this moral atmosphere, when Falstaff in King Henry IV is rebuked by young Prince Hal for purse-snatching he can claim, "Why, Hal, 'tis my vocation, Hal; 'tis no sin for a man to labor in his vocation."

The character Franklyn in Shaw's Back to Methuselah, is responding to something higher than his former individualism, when he passes this judgment on himself: "After twenty years of it I realized that I was

[14] Op. cit., p. 59.
[15] Op. cit., p. 26.

208

walking with my own ignorance and self-conceit, and that I was not within a hundred and fifty years of the experience and wisdom I was pretending to." A man can live his life out a less than truly person, in comparative harmony with his world, not, as Berdyaev said, "because he is better and less sinful than it," but because he is not sufficiently awake spiritually. He is not eager for a different kind of existence; he is too confined to a narrow circle of interest and is dominated by his surroundings to the point of being completely satisfied with them.[16] Such a man is no person; he stops short of personality and does not know his inability to recognize the valuable.

The proper choice of value cannot be achieved short of the status of persons. Roger Babson saw this and used a favorite phrase of William Temple to say it again: "No commonwealth of value is possible among men all devoted to the attainment of individual satisfaction." [17]

In an atmosphere where power and status make right, kings do not have to be persons; they can be power and be benign about it. Of the ruler in his *Ramayana*, Aubrey Menen said: "His one wish for his people was that they should, every one of them, enjoy all the good things of life, and he sincerely hoped that they would find some way of doing it. Meantime, he set them an example by enjoying the good things of life himself." [18]

The limitations of individualism are profound. It is a denial of community (personality), reality, and value. At no place in life can the essence of individualism be more clearly seen than in political statecraft. Here, where the personal is most clearly demanded for the sake of the whole, the individualistic has universally been more obvious. That is why the reigning philosophy of statecraft can most clearly reveal the limitations of individualism.

The Misuse of Power

One can find in statecraft the most universal and valid illustration of what happens to human personality when it is confronted by regnant individualism. Something about power depersonalizes, individualizes. The corruption of power lies in its depersonalizing influences. Men who

[16] *Destiny of Man*, p. 71.
[17] Roger Ward Babson and D. De F. Zuver, *Can These Bones Live?* (New York: Harper & Brothers, 1945), p. 14.
[18] *Op. cit.*, p. 29.

are heads of state lose "personalness" thereby; they become flags, symbols, or if powerful enough, forces, power, individuals in control. What better area could one wish in which to demonstrate the limitations of overt individualism from the standpoint of its contrast with persons in communion? With what person in the history of statecraft could the illustration better be made than with Niccolo Machiavelli, who makes it all plain for posterity in *The Prince* and in *The Discourses*?

I am perfectly willing to begin with Johann Gottfried Herder's judgment of Machiavelli as an honest and upright man, a sharp observer, a devoted friend of his country.[19] Herder holds that every line of Machiavelli's writing proves that he was no traitor to the cause of humanity. He says that it is a mistake to regard Machiavelli's *Prince* as satirical or as pernicious or as a hybrid of these. The mistake lies in the fact that nobody saw the work of Machiavelli in its right environment. *It is a political masterpiece.* It was never the intention of Machiavelli to give a general theory of politics. He simply portrayed the customs, the ways, the means of thinking and acting and governing used by political power figures in all time. Even Ernst Cassirer is ready to admit that Machiavelli is talking about the techniques of politics and that *The Prince* is a technical book and therefore amoral.[20] The writer is not expected to be speaking as a moral man concerned with the ethical principles involved. Machiavelli is a man who enunciates the principles by which individuals have been successful in the field of statecraft and can only by unfair tactics be called upon to speak as either moralist or ethicist. Let us see what the doctrines of an "honest and upright man, a sharp observer, a devoted friend of this country," who is giving a description, beyond morals, of the way individuals live in political life, looks like when put in the context of the demands of Christian personalism. The contrast, to say the least, should afford a picture of the limitations of overt individualism. Let Machiavelli the reporter, neither moralist nor devil, speak as simply as he will of how the individual can best use his political powers for his own advantage. Then we shall see what this does to personality.

Un mezzo bestia e mezzo uomo, part beast and part man: this is the teacher of princes, for the prince must know the art of crime. He must

---

[19] *Briefs zur Beforderung der Humanitat*, 58.
[20] *The Myth of the State* (Toronto: Anchor Press), p. 191 q.v.

be a fox to find the snares and a lion to terrify the wolves.[21] With Machiavelli it is always Caesar or nothing. Talleyrand takes directly from Machiavelli his famous statement, "It is this which is a great crime, to make a mistake." The very term "duty" is missing in *The Prince*, said Cassirer, and about the right use of power it does not say a word. Machiavelli's concern is how to play the political game, and he knew it was always played successfully by means of treachery, felony, fraud, and deception. He neither blamed nor recommended. He sought to make the best move, as if it were some game played on a board. In *Discourses* I, xxcii, Machiavelli speaks of "splendid wickedness," and the only mistakes that he will forgive are very minor ones. His only word against Caesar Borgia was for a mistake; mass murder is able to overcome its own shame by its very magnitude. The only time prophets can succeed is by the use of armed force. The best foundation for states rests on good laws and plenty of armor, but since the weight of good arms will make any kind of law acceptable, Machiavelli wishes the weight placed on having plenty of arms.[22]

The first condition by which men can be ruled requires the understanding of man himself. Here Machiavelli overthrows wholly the illusion of man's original goodness. This is a political absurdity to him. The founder of a state and the lawyer for the government of a state must act on the presupposition that all men are evil by nature and that this depravity of theirs will show any time it gets the chance. How much closer to reformed realism on the doctrine of man can Machiavelli get? Humanity alone will never do in politics; humaneness is not a political virtue. In politics man is always at some point between humanity and bestiality. Anyone who understands politics will understand both how to be human and how to be a beast. This view so impressed Catherine de Medici, Richelieu, and Napoleon that they considered Machiavelli the only politicist worth reading.

Individualism in politics has its list of rules taken from *The Prince* and *The Discourses*:

1. *When the ruler takes over, he must really take over.*

Arrange to commit all his cruelties at once, so as not to have to recur to

[21]Read *The Prince*, Chapter XVIII; *Discourses*, II, 340.
[22] *The Prince*, Chapter XII.

them every day, and so as to be able, by not making fresh changes, to reassure people and win them over by benefiting them. (*The Prince*, VIII.)

2. The prince must learn how to be immoral for his own advantage.

It is necessary for a prince, who wishes to maintain himself, to learn how not to be good, and to use this knowledge and not use it, according to the necessity of the case. (*The Prince*, XV.)

3. The ruler must not worry about scandal.

He must not mind incurring the scandal of those vices . . . some . . . which appear vices result in one's greater security and wellbeing. (*The Prince*, XV.)

4. For the ruler it is better to be feared than to be loved.

It is much safer to be feared than loved. . . . Fear is maintained by a dread of punishment which never fails. (*The Prince*, XVII.)

5. Astuteness and confusion are better than faith or loyalty.

The experience of our times shows those princes to have done great things who have had little regard for good faith, and have been able by astuteness to confuse men's brains, and who have ultimately overcome those who have made loyalty their foundation. (*The Prince*, XVIII.)

6. The prince finds much power in a virtuous appearance.

It is not, therefore, necessary for a prince to have all the above named qualities [mercy, faith, integrity, humanity, religion], but it is very necessary to seem to have them . . . take great care that nothing goes out of his mouth that is not full of the above named five qualities. . . . Nothing is more necessary than to seem to have this last quality [religion]. (*The Prince*, XVIII.)

7. The one who would rule must never join a bigger man.

A prince ought never to make a common cause with one more powerful

212

than himself to injure another . . . for if he wins you rest in his power. (*The Prince*, XXI.)

8. *There is great power in accusation.*

No more useful and necessary authority can be given to those who are appointed as guardians of the liberty of a state, than the faculty of accusing the citizens. (*The Discourses*, First Book, VII.)

9. *Power results when one encourages others to accuse.*

The lawgiver of a republic, therefore, should give every citizen the right to accuse another citizen without fear or suspicion. (*The Discourses*, First Book, VIII.)

10. *The ruler must work alone.*

It never or rarely happens that a republic or monarchy is . . . entirely reformed, unless it is done by only one individual. (*The Discourses*, First Book, IX.)

11. *The ruler will seem to give them what they want.*

First of all ascertain what the people really desire, and he will always find that they want two things: one, to revenge themselves on those who have been the cause of their enslavement, and the other, to recover their liberty. (*The Discourses*, First Book, XVI.) [That is to say one must hunt Communists and shout freedom.]

12. *Power may be gained by seeking non-constitutional powers.*

Power can easily take a name, but a name cannot give power. . . . It is the magistracies and powers that are created by illegitimate means which harm a republic. . . . Before a citizen can be in a position to usurp extraordinary powers, many things must concur. (*The Discourses*, First Book, XXXIV.)

13. *The ruler must change character gradually.*

For he who for a time has seemed good, and for purposes of his own

213

wants to become bad, should do it gradually, and should seem to be brought to it by the force of circumstances; so that, before his changed nature deprives him of his former friends, he may have gained new ones. (*The Discourses*, First Book, XLI.)

14. *He must attack when secure.*

Men rise from one ambition to another: first, they seek to secure themselves against attack, and then they attack others. (*The Discourses*, First Book, XLVI.)

15. *The successful ruler will get there first.*

There is no better nor easier mode in republics . . . for successfully opposing the ambition of any citizen, than to occupy in advance of him those ways by which he expects to attain the rank he aims at. (*The Discourses*, First Book, LII.)

16. *Count on the self-destruction of the multitudes.*

The people often, deceived by an illusive good, desire their own ruin. . . . If you propose to them anything that upon its face seems profitable and courageous, though there be really a loss concealed under it which may involve the ruin of the republic, the multitude will ever be most easily persuaded to it. (*The Discourses*, First Book, LIII.)

17. *The successful ruler rides with the pressure.*

Prudent men make the best of circumstances in their actions, and, although constrained by necessity to a certain course, make it appear as if done from their own liberality. (*The Discourses*, First Book, LI.)

18. *Individuals as such can be counted on to be cowards.*

[Multitudes] are often audacious and loud in their denunciations of the decisions of their ruler, but when punishment stares them in the face, then, distrustful of each other, they rush to obey. (*The Discourses*, First Book, LVII.)

19. *Cunning is always better than force.*

Nor do I believe that force alone will ever be found to suffice, while it will often be the case that cunning alone serves the purpose. (*The Discourses*, Second Book, XIII.)

20. *The end justifies the means.*

In the actions of men, and especially of princes . . . the end justifies the means. (*The Discourses*, First Book, XVIII.)

This is individualism at its ultimate. Its limitations are profound. Let them be carried forward as a denial of personality and community; a denial of reality and value which are necessary to the understanding of the kind of world in which we have lived.

Chapter XII

The Realization of Personality

There is a kind of self-realization based in personality. This is the *I-Thou relation* of Karl Heim. There is a difference between the assertion of individuality and the realization of personality.

The *I* of the primary word *I-Thou* makes its appearance as person and becomes conscious of itself as subjectivity without any object swinging to it. A person weighs as much naked and stripped of his objects as he does dressed. A person makes his appearance by entering into relation with other persons. Person is the spiritual form of "natural solidarity of connexion." [1] The aim of the person is "life," which is a "dying that lasts the span of a man's life." The aim of relation is relation's own being, that is, contact with the *Thou*. He is genuinely aware of other persons; he is in community; he knows the personal and moral imperative; he has a sense of vocation. He shares, he exists, he co-exists, he *is*. He says *I am*, not I am this or that or such. The person's knowing himself means knowing himself to have being, not knowing himself to have something. He differentiates himself from other individuals, for personality abides in and on individuality; he is not com-

[1] Buber, op. cit., p. 62.

216

mitted to natural detachment. His aim is not to experience and use, but to be committed. He is not concerned with his own particular kind of being. Life is not wrapped up with any *my*—my kind, my race, my creative genius. He is not a victim of his own individuality; he does not know the discordant *I*; he lives above and beyond the contradiction; the deeper shudder does not rise from his individuality.

That is to say, the self-realization based in personality does not mean a giving up of the *I*. As Buber put it, "The swinging of the *I* in its lonely truth" is the genuine subjectivity that desires heightened and unconditioned relation and moves toward true maturity. In all this the *I* does not disappear.

This does not mean a giving up of, say, the *I*, as mystical writings usually suppose: the *I* is as indispensable to this, the supreme, as to every relation, since relation is only possible between *I* and *Thou*. It is not the *I*, then, that is given up, but the false self-asserting instinct that makes a man flee to the possessing of things before the unreliable, perilous world of relation which has neither density nor duration and cannot be surveyed.[2]

Just as the *I* is always present, but is a changed and transformed *I* in its relation with *Thou*, so the person will always evade us, escape us. The person as he is, pure and undimmed, will never be trapped by us. We never grasp the true reality of ourselves or of another. What we get in relation is an image, a fragmentary and deformed image in appearance, "the personage."[3] Which is to confess that our approach as persons to each other through this image is at the same time allowed and prohibited, hidden and revealed, concealed and made plain by the image, which is not even a static image. No man is pure person. No man is pure individuality. "None is wholly real, and none wholly unreal. Every man lives in the twofold *I* but there are men so defined by person that they may be called persons, and men so defined by individuality that they may be called individuals. True history is decided in the field between these two poles."[4]

I have said that the self-realization of personality does not mean a giving up of the *I*. On the contrary the stronger the *I* of the *I-Thou*

[2] *Ibid.*, p. 78.
[3] Tournier, *op. cit.*, p. 15.
[4] Buber, *op. cit.*, p. 65.

relation the stronger the relationship that is possible in a creative way between persons. Realization of personality keeps what it must of the psychological definitions of individuality. As Tournier puts it, "We do not do embroidery in the empty air." [5] This is the *I* of *dialogue*.

"Man is a world in himself." Thus preached John Donne and is followed by Professor van den Berg. By which both mean, I think, that man is more like a forest of tangled growth than he is like a small universe. Man the individual can be diagramed, shelled, and confined; he can be studied, stripped of everything living, or thinned out to where his outlines completely merge with the surrounding chaos. The man who is in dialogue, however, remains both a specific *I* and a participating person. From his individuality he has consciousness of himself in an external world from which he has already distinguished himself. In the process of dialogue as person, however, he enters again into the world of relationship out of which, Buber said, that first individual recognition of the self as self is born. That is to say, there is a double movement: there is the consciousness of being an individual with respect to other individuals, and there is the possibility of a personal relationship with other persons. With individuals there are secrets to be treasured as evidences of individuality; with persons there are secrets to be shared as evidences of communion. There is, said Tournier, both separation and relation. The individual becomes a *Thou* through this sharing of himself that is dialogue. "The whole difference is that an individual associates and the person communicates, this is the same difference as that which maintains between the personage and the person. The personage is an external appearance which touches the personage of others from outside, the person communicates inwardly with the Thou." [6] In this dialogue, this to and fro of interpersonal communion, this systole-diastole of the soul, as Unamuno calls it, we are forced to take up a responsible position. In this responsible act the person is revealed, but no idle chatter will do this. There must be the responsible act upon which dialogue is based.

The inventor of a certain system of shorthand writing recorded for four months the conversation at dinner and in the common room of his boardinghouse. Upon transcribing the notes of those endless conversa-

[5] *Op. cit.*, p. 96.
[6] *Ibid.*, p. 129.

tions weeks later he discovered that there was not a single word that had been uttered that really mattered as to whether it had been uttered at all. No one had at any point run the risk of revealing himself or his innermost being to anyone else. There was no encounter, no meeting, no responsible act, therefore, no dialogue, therefore only individuals, not persons. Life requires *involvedness*. At the moment contact is made the very style and use of language changes. Brunner is right to see the meaning of Buber's *I-Thou* in terms of encounter. This is to say, the meeting between *I* and other is constitutive of the person.

The realization of personality keeps what it must of the psychological definitions of individuality. It goes as far as it must with self-determination, psychologically. Having reached that limit which is determined by its own level. "Self-determination must fulfill itself in the recognition of an Other which may lift it to heights forever out of its own reach; self-determination fulfills itself in self-surrender [the other side of the assertiveness of individuality] to that which is entitled to receive the submission of the self." [7] It is out of the experience of encounter with this Other, this Thou, that personality finds its three major bases: the realization of personality requires *community*; the realization of personality requires a *personal imperative*; the realization of personality requires *vocation*.

Community has its primal beginnings in awareness—"the craning of the neck"—the original notice of another which one sees even in animals. The personal imperative rises out of the moral coming of age of the *I*. While vocation is a matter of relation between *Thou-It* and *I*, it is expressed in terms of "the arrangement of the scenery" in the midst of which life is lived. The sum of the whole law and gospel of community and personality is found in Buber's tremendous statement, "In the beginning is relation." [8]

Personality and Community

"In the beginning is relation."
"All real living is meeting."

Personality has its primal roots in that original "craning of the neck."

[7] Temple, op. cit., p. 244.
[8] Op. cit., p. 18.

I go out to call my horses. They are far away from me in pasture. I whistle and call; they do not hear; they graze. I walk toward them; I approach; I speak from a hundred yards away, and then there is that "craning of the neck." They suddenly are aware. They throw up heads and necks; they toss; they come toward me; the lead mare breaks and runs away. Making a wide circle, she comes back, and then they approach, stretching out the neck for their carrot and the lead-rope. The leading began in awareness, the craning of the neck.

Old-time cowboys still judge a pony by the way he "leads out of the remuda." The better the animal the more responsive he is to the light rope on his neck. The most responsive animals will lead out at the pressure of a light rope even back in the thicker parts of the neck, while the wilder horses require a tightened rope just back of the ears and, as some have said, you have to stretch their necks far enough to put a bridle on them while the horse is still in the herd. An old French manual of equitation gives page after page to a discussion of the first levels of horse training in which the trainer must begin by making the neck flexible. If there is a proper "flexion of the neck" the rest of the animal is certain to follow the lead of the neck and head (*ramener* and *rassembler*); therefore the trainer must be sure that the animal is committed to his leadership through the motions of the neck.

I have seen the wild things do this "craning of the neck." Only this year near the Pennsylvania tracks into New York City I saw a full grown doe and two yearling deer at the edge of some deep woods in the early morning sun "craning the neck" as the horn of the great diesel engine sounded for a crossroads. This is the "I see you" that marks the Kaffir greeting noticed by Buber. This is the sniffing process that goes on among animals that recognize each other by odor. One can see this in the great herds of cattle where the suckling calves have been separated from the grazing cows during the day and then are put back together in the evening time. The craning of the neck becomes a sniffing of the herd until the calves are found by the proper cows. After the young calves have been driven through a dipping vat pandemonium reigns in the corral until the odor of the medicine has gone away enough to permit the prime relational event to happen by the recovery of odor. This craning of the neck, this I see you, this I recognize you by odor,

220

seen in primitives and animals is the fundamental awareness upon which relation, and therefore personality, is based.

Among individuals there is no personality short of this "primitive relational event." In the beginning is relation. Relation is a category of being, it is the a priori of personality. Buber calls it "the inborn Thou." Therefore community properly precedes personal imperative since even the possibility of a personal existence in an imperative form rests upon this primitive relational event.

It is simply not the case, as we learn from Buber, that we first perceive objects and then seek to put ourselves in relation with them. The effort to establish relation comes first—"the hand of the child arched out so that what is over against him may nestle under it," and then comes the actual relation, "a saying of Thou without words." But the beginning is the awareness and the relation.

Dialogue: Encounter and Understanding

This craning of the neck is not enough. If so, personality would be a larger category than the category of the human, and so far as we know as yet, this is not true. In spite of the fact that we give personality to animals and in spite of the fact that some sort of community certainly seems to be established, there must rest upon this original craning of the neck, this original encounter and engagement, a prime requisite of communion which we call understanding. There is no true communion, that is to say there is no dialogue, short of this business of understanding. This, so far as we know, requires persons. "Personality can only reveal itself in persons. Consequently it is especially in human nature, in men and women, that we see God." [9] Human nature is admittedly distorted by its self-centeredness and so gives a distorted picture of God. Even this distortion requires some sort of community as a base. It is not strange that Temple's doctrine of church is encompassed under the phrase "Commonwealth of Value." [10] For the isolated self any kind of existence, much less everlasting existence, becomes unthinkable, even unendurable. Shaw understands this most clearly of all moderns, I think, in Back to Methuselah. For the self-in-fellowship, everlasting existence becomes desirable. The difference seems to lie in the essentially social

[9] Temple, op. cit., p. 266.
[10] Gifford Lectures, op. cit., pp. 405-26.

character of finite mind. This social character is the backdrop of communion with God but expresses itself in essential dialogue. The self alienates itself from any desire for continued existence by its unwillingness to be the self-in-relation. This is Kierkegaard's classic definition of despair offered against the backdrop of the ground of self: the willingness of the self to relate "itself to its own self and by willing to be its self, the self is grounded transparently in the Power which posited it." [11] Whether the relationship is with the One or with the Many, however, the ground of self proceeds from the primal relational event into the realm of dialogue, that understanding possible between persons when things disappear. "When *Thou* is spoken, the speaker has no *thing* . . . he takes his stand in relation." [12]

Karl Heim claims that personality cannot know itself to be personality apart from God. "I could know myself only if I first knew God, upon whom my being is based." [13] This means that man is made for communion, but some sort of encounter in communion is necessary to his being constituted a person. He has "a common patrimony" as Tournier sees it, but there is required a meeting. Out of the primal relation event, a consequent understanding and dialogue, personality is achieved. Man is not an isolated, self-centered individual; "his being consists in a relatedness to the origin and goal of life." [14] It is in the field of his "common patrimony" that understanding, constitutive of personality, comes to pass. That is to say, understanding is involved in what it is to know communion.

I had spent a total of four hours in a desperate attempt to be of service to one whose life was sheer and utter boredom. At length, unable to endure my failures I said in a tone that approached asperity, "I cannot help you. You do not sin, you do not hurt, you are not grieved, and you are not dying." Whether it was the tone or the words I do not know, but a light flashed between us and an agonized voice said, "My God, I am all four, I simply do not know how to say this." Understanding had come alive, and we were in communion. There is no marriage without this, there is no pastoral relationship without this, there is no personality

---

[11] *Sickness Unto Death*, p. xix.
[12] Buber, op. cit., p. 4.
[13] Cited by E. P. Dickie, *Revelation and Response* (New York: Charles Scribner's Sons, 1938), p. 32.
[14] Brunner, *The Divine Imperative*, p. 296.

without this. People live like animals with each other because there is no meeting of the *Thou* within. Men and women live their lives as marriage partners in adultery because of this. There is no meeting of the *Thou* within. When a man is together with his wife this may happen, and it may not happen. If there is a coming together of the *Thous* then everything that goes with marriage, and particularly its sex relation, becomes symbolic of the meeting that continues between these versions of the *Thou* within, for all possibility of the wife's being an object to the husband as subject, and vice versa, has disappeared. Instead we have here the holiest of human relationships where subjects become a common subject in the involved meetings of the Thou. In this case the physical relationships can become simply an altar upon which the full encounter is expressed and demonstrated. The encounter which is only between persons is being symbolized, however, not created. The encounter and the understanding are primal.

Something like this happens in any meeting of persons. We are not made for abstraction—no life, no fellowship, no love. There must be this passage back and forth. Even in the heaviest and most abstract of philosophical discussion, for Kant himself, the center of gravity is not in *The Critique of Pure Reason*, it is in the *Critique of Practical Reason* and within this work the most important section is the *dialectic*, the passage back and forth. That is to say, human personality cannot exist, even given the original craning of the neck, without the dialogue.

In dialogue the *I* does not disappear. Recall Buber's moving tribute to the "lively and impressive" *I* of Socrates:

It is the *I* of endless dialogue, and the air of dialogue is wafted around it in all its journeys, before the judges and in the last hour in prison. This *I* lived continually in the relation with man which is bodied forth in dialogue. It never ceased to believe in the reality of men, and went out to meet them. So it took its stand with them in reality, and reality forsakes it no more. Its very loneliness can never be forsakenness, and if the world of man is silent it hears the voice of the daimonion saying, *Thou*.

Recall Buber's entrancement with the "lovely and legitimate sound" of the full *I* of Goethe. But be most profoundly moved by his illustration of the unconditioned relation in Jesus of Nazareth:

223

How powerful, even to being overpowering, and how legitimate, even to being self-evident is the saying of *I* by Jesus! For it is the *I* of unconditional relation in which the man calls his *Thou* Father in such a way that he himself is simply Son, and nothing else but Son. . . . It is useless to seek to limit this *I* to a power in itself or this *Thou* to something dwelling in ourselves, and once again to empty the real, the present relation, of reality. *I* and *Thou* abide; every man can say *Thou* and is then *I*, every man can say Father and is then Son: reality abides.

This dialogue, this meeting of mind and spirit, this understanding which involves a passage to and fro in a series of comprehending encounters, is the theme of holy scriptures. In the biblical dialogue every page reflects this aspect of what it is to be person. Indeed every great culture takes its rise from some original relational event which is kept alive and reinterpreted in terms of tradition, myth, memory, historical narrative, or call it whatever you will. This is the importance of theophany in all of the classic beginnings of great religion. There is the "*What is thy Name?*"; there is the "*Who art Thou, Lord?*"; there is the "*Master, where do you live?*" in which an original relational event has come to be.

The Recovery of the Conscious

Dialogue is incomplete in terms of encounter only. Man is not object; he is subject who is "addressed and summoned to reply." To be responsible, says Tournier, is to have to reply. Frost knows this and says:

> "Home is the place where, when you have to go there,
> They have to take you in." [16]

To have to "take one in" is the responsible reply that goes with being at home among persons. This seems to require, in terms of personality, the recovery of the conscious. Almost none of the modern psychological definitions of personality require this. Allport has been able to collect fifty significantly different definitions of personality.[15] In few of such definitions is the matter of consciousness even a factor. The whole "field theory" of psychological thinking seems designed, following the lead of

[15] *The American Handbook of Psychiatry*, ed. Silvano Arieti (New York: Basic Books, Inc., 1959), I, 108.
[16] From "The Death of the Hired Man," *Complete Poems of Robert Frost*, by Robert Frost; published by Henry Holt & Co. Copyright 1930, 1949, Henry Holt & Co.

dynamics in physics, to allow a sort of professional vagueness with respect to this matter of consciousness.[17] Harry Bone thinks that because psychology feared both theology and philosophy as close neighbors and wanted to be expressly scientific, it lost first the soul, then the self, and then consciousness. A doctrine of personality which requires the craning of the neck, the primal relational event, followed by understanding, which occurs in terms of responsibility, requires the recovery of the conscious.[18]

"The unconscious is never transformed," writes Carl Jung, but neither is the less than conscious a person. Only in the realm of his consciousness is he person. It is in the realm of consciousness that both responsibility and understanding come to be constitutive of personality. While it is true that with one's wife, with one's nearest and dearest, even with one's God, one cannot truly speak until speech has died, it is because of the overwhelming inability of the conscious mind to say what it is thinking rather than due to the lack of importance of the conscious attempt to respond and understand. "We speak with Him only when speech dies within us," and all who know encounter know the depth of this, but we do not talk with God or with our wives in stupore. Man is "subject who is addressed and summoned to reply," consciously responsible for the hearing and understanding of those with whom he is in encounter. This is the genius of Harnack's great definition of humility, itself constitutive of Christian personality, as "one who is willing to hear." The hearing and the replying have to do with the understanding.

Karl Jaspers recognizes that the reality of the world cannot be evaded and that the breakdown of various communities and the loss of constituent personality is responsible for much of the "harshness of the real." By this phrase he refers to life as it is in this present human existence. The harshness of the real is not enough to divert man from the task in which he has "to win for himself a new home." Jaspers brings a beautiful psychological understanding to this matter of community which he names as primal. "What is requisite is that a man, in conjunction with other men, should merge himself in the world as a historically concrete entity, so that, amid the universal homelessness, he may win for him-

[17] Arieti, op. cit., p. 111.
[18] Among moderns none has sensed this better than Paul Tournier, in *The Meaning of Persons*, q.v.

self a new home." [19] All of which, I think, is a way of saying that the quality of one's community—home, personality, and religion—is determined by the quality of his relation with fellow prisoners, subjects, the fellowship of those able to commune. This sounds strangely like "the return of the soul" used as synonomous with the self, first by those philosophers and European psychologists who made no sharp break with philosophy and now by prominent American psychologists in terms of the emergence of the psychology of personality as a field of scientific endeavor.[20] In any event, there seems to be no refuge behind scientific terminology and analysis of the depth levels of being that does not include the conscious expressions of the inner motivations. Some find in psychology a substitute for love, intimacy, union with others, and one's self. As Fromm has put it, psychology can become "the refuge for the lonely, alienated man instead of being a step toward the act of union." This "act of union" becomes a conscious affair involving "souls," by which we mean living and conscious personalities. That is to say, there is a cosmos for man only if he accepts the obligation to discover his real and new home in terms of the conscious and participating response he has made in the direction of understanding, which is constitutive of a dialogue of encounter which rests in turn on the primal craning of the neck, the relation which is in the beginning. Man, said Erich Fromm, is not a thing, "he cannot be dissected without being destroyed, he cannot be manipulated without being harmed, and he cannot be reproduced artificially." [21] This manhood, this essential personality, for Fromm, for Buber, for Kierkegaard, for Jaspers, for Tournier, and for that host who will still use theological and philosophical concepts in referring to that one who can both theologize and philosophize is committed to a continuous responsible understanding, in dialogue, which begins in the primal relation, "the craning of the neck," which says, "I see you," or "Thou."

Man, after his physical birth, has to go through a continuous process of birth. Emerging from the mother's womb is the first act of birth; from her

[19] *Man in the Modern Age,* trans. Eden and Cedar Paul (New York: Doubleday & Company, 1957), p. 203.

[20] *The American Handbook of Psychiatry,* I, 111.

[21] Fromm, "The Limitations and Dangers of Psychology," *Religion and Culture: Essays in honor of Paul Tillich,* p. 35.

breast, the second; from her arm, the third. . . . If he is to develop into what he potentially is as a human being he must continue to be born, that is, he must continue to dissolve the primary ties of soil and blood. He must proceed from one act of separation to the next. He must give up certainty and defenses, and take the leap into the act of commitment, concern and love.

This is constitutive of community.

Religion, said Whitehead, is what the individual does with his solitariness. Which, I think, is a way of saying that the quality of one's religion is determined by that communion to which he gives over his solitariness. No man's communion is a private affair. There is no more an escape from the lesser *Thous* than there is escape from the Great Thou who stands over against us and with whom we are eligible to commune. All this is constitutive of personality. If, as John Macmurray said, "as agent, the self is the body and as subject, the self is the mind," [22] it follows that the person is the agent-subject in relation, i.e., the person is self-in-relation. Relation involves summons and response, within a common patrimony, of conscious individuals committed to that understanding native to dialogue, all of which arises out of the primal craning of the neck. All real living is meeting. In the beginning is relation.

The Personal Imperative

Since Buber all is the same; everyone talks of commitment and choice, responsibility and community, the distinction between things and thou, and the contrast between individuals and persons. Now perhaps only some new discovery of depth psychology which can show us an underlying *I* prior to even those levels of the unconscious which rise up to haunt us can advance us beyond the psychological insights gained from the great Jew. Only incidentally is Buber dealing in terms of psychology, however. Though he knows the mysticism and has the mystical insights native to the Jewish religious consciousness he is but incidentally a mystic in I-Thou. Seen from the vantage point of the Jewish religious consciousness the mystic is swept up almost instantaneously in a set of ethical demands. Indeed, it is in the realm of the ethical that the dis-

[22] *The Self as Agent,* Gifford Lectures, 1953 (New York: Harper & Brothers, 1958), I, 91. Not available as yet is Macmurray's second volume, eagerly anticipated, *Persons in Relation.*

tinction between individual and person must Christianly be drawn and properly so, for personality in community can remain in community only with the use of ethical terms. Responsibility, love, forgiveness, communion, alienation, hate, and atonement are not mere theological terms; they are personal terms, and because they are personal terms they are ethical terms. That is to say, personality in community requires a personal imperative, which is an ethical imperative in addition to its psychological ontology. The meaning of personality rests on the worth of personality which is a value judgment and therefore an ethical judgment. In time, and in spite of the "parataxic distortions" with which all ethicists and psychologists must be concerned, man, made for community, able to commune, cannot resist the calls of communion. This is the hallmark of personality, and its realization is the realization of personality, if it involves the personal imperative.

The Failure of Introspection

Introspection has failed. We cannot arrive at personality by a beginning with the *I*. This is why person in community must be discussed before we can speak of the personal imperative. Contradictory bundles of primary response feelings make the *id* tend to ride off in all directions. The center one seeks cannot be isolated, introspectively. Nietzsche knew this in *The Joyful Wisdom* and said "everyone is furthest from himself." Paul Claudel writes "merely by looking at ourselves we falsify ourselves." [23] "I am thirty-six, and I do not know yet whether I am miserly or prodigal, sober or gluttonous." [24] Introspection, says Paul Tournier does not throw any sure light on one's self. Socrates, centuries before, in *Cratylus*, wished to steer away from the void of indefinite self-analysis. Journals and diaries are most frequently kept by adolescents, or at least in adolescent years that have continued. Jung has shown this connection with the "repression of the shadow" as the age of heaviest misunderstanding of one's self. Tournier talks of these perpetual adolescents who do not understand themselves. Yet, this insight has been most clearly arrived at not by psychologists or philosophers but by saints. Witness the confession of Francis de Sales:

[23] *The Declarations of Frederic Lefevre.*
[24] Gide, *Journal*, nrf, Paris, as cited by Tournier, op. cit.

It is not possible that the spirit of God should dwell in a mind that wishes to know too much of what is happening within itself . . . you are afraid of being afraid of being afraid. Some vexation vexes you, and then you are vexed at being vexed by that vexation. In the same way I have often seen people who, having lost their tempers, are afterwards angry at having been angry. All this is like the circles made when a stone is cast into the water—first a little circle forms and that in its turn makes a bigger one and that one makes yet another.[25]

Introspection is not the way to come at it. "We are, then, pursuing a chimera in attempting to grasp the essence of our person, completely divested of all adornments and disguises with which life has clothed it." [26] In the protection of the essential *id*, the *I-in-itself*, numerous forms of personage make willing watchdogs. We habitually guard our treasures, i.e., our prejudices, and do not dare reveal them even to ourselves.

Relation Precedes Organization

Because this seems true we are driven into another level of investigation in terms of our search for the meaning of personality. We are driven into the ethical insights which result from Buber's primacy of I-Thou. In the beginning is relation. That is to say, relation precedes experience. This is the craning of the neck previous to the submission to the organizing harness. That which relates precedes that which organizes. Indeed, to Buber, creation is relation: "In the beginning is relation." Then follows experience in the light of which the psychological *I* emerges. Only now, after the primal relational event which, without words, lives in the presence of the unsaid Thou, can we begin to talk of *I*. Only now can the process of differentiation which creates the relationship *I-It* begin to emerge. This is a devastating insight for the processes of psychological introspection. So vital is this insight, which we receive to be true, that the whole of the validity of the ethical description of personality rests upon the validity of the primacy of I-Thou over I-It. I have not seen this discussed by students of Buber: Personality does not climb to its Thou-relation through It-relations. The person begins in a Thou-relation:

---

[25] *Introduction to the Devout Life*, trans. Allan Ross (London: Burnes, Oates, and Washbourne, 1943), pp. 137-38. Cited by Tournier.
[26] Tournier, op. cit., p. 70.

Already in the original relational event he speaks the primary word *I-Thou* in a natural way that precedes what may be termed visualisation of forms— that is, before he has recognized himself as *I*. The primary word *I-It*, on the other hand, is made possible at all only by means of this recognition—by means, that is, of the separation of the *I*.

The first primary can be resolved, certainly, into *I* and *Thou*, but it did not arise from their being set together; by its nature it precedes *I*.[27]

Consciousness of the "I" is not connected with the primitive sway of the instinct for self-preservation. . . . It is not the "I" that wishes to propagate itself, but the body, that knows as yet of no "I." It is not the "I" but the body that wishes to make things, a tool or a toy, that wishes to be a "creator." Further, a *cognosco ergo sum*, in however naïve a form and however childlike a conception of an experiencing subject, cannot be found in the primitive function of knowledge. The "I" emerges as a single element out of the primal experiences, out of the vital primal words *I-affecting-Thou and Thou-affecting-I*, only after they have been split asunder.[28]

There is no proper differentiation between I and It which comes through experience until after this original relational is established.

This actual event is a separation of the human body, as the bearer of its perceptions, from the world round about it. The body comes to know and to differentiate itself in its peculiarities; the differentiation, however, remains one of pure juxtaposition, and hence cannot have the character of the state in which *I* is implied.

But when the *I* of the relation has stepped forth and taken on separate existence . . . reduced to merely functional activity, . . . awakens there the state in which *I* is properly active. Only now can the conscious act of the I take place.[29]

That is to say, before the *I* comes into view it is already so cluttered with watchdog personages that it cannot be found from within the *I*, only from within the *I-Thou* which is almost immediately an ethical point of view.

Personality as End

We will have to talk ethically; otherwise we cannot find the I of the person. That is to say, a proper value judgment by the emerging I with

[27] *Op. cit.*, p. 22.
[28] *Ibid.*, pp. 21-22.
[29] *Ibid.*, pp. 22-23.

respect to persons is required if this personal imperative can lead us to the meaning and worth of persons. A proper value judgment with respect to persons makes all share in or eligible to share in community. This contains within itself the destruction of personal prejudice *in toto*, if and as it is apprehended. In brief, it means a salute to personality everywhere it is encountered. It means Kant's Categorical Imperative in its second division. It means no person is ever means—always end—and in communion, if personality is to be realized. This involves the moral imperative of Kant so difficult of comprehension, difficult of understanding not because of Kant's clear words here but because of our previously arrived at and remained in levels of value and therefore levels of ethic.

These various levels of ethics form traps or plateaus upon which mankind frequently finds himself isolated and hence does not understand that though he may claim the idealistic manners of some superior ethic he may be acting upon levels of ethics that are inferior to the level that he claims. These levels historically have been natural drive, authority, social custom, happiness as an end, the level of duty, the level of self-realization, and that level of ethics which knows personality as an end. While this is no place to explicate the various teachings, dogma, and value judgments of each level nor to list those historical giants who belong in each level, it is sufficient at least to acknowledge the presence of various levels of ethics and to claim that the one whom we regard as our patron saint in this business of personality as an end, Immanuel Kant, actually belongs in two levels. He must be discussed in the level of ethics that is concerned with duty and the moral law and he must as seriously be discussed in the level of personality as an end in so far as his contribution to both is concerned. Personality as an end involves persons in relation but some say Kant is ineligible to discuss this matter of religion. This is not quite true. Macmurray [30] finds in his first volume of the Gifford Lectures [31] a "formal inconsistency" in Kant's distinction between the phenomenal and the noumenal. He uses this breech in Kant to introduce the philosophy of the act in which the acting person is agent and therefore bases his philosophical ground for the second

[30] To whom we look for one of the earlier discussions of religion as relation between persons, in *The Structures of Religious Experience*.
[31] *The Self As Agent.*

231

volume [32] on this concept of the actor as the agent. It would be strange if the most valuable thing in Kant's practical work, the concept of personality as end, should prove to rest upon a formal inconsistency. Be that as it may, while Kant must be most definitely considered in the philosophers of duty and morals he comes to his own, strangely, and perhaps to his own acute discomfiture, in the purely religious concept of personality as an end. Just as Jaspers' "modality of self-hood" rests on communication, just as Macmurray's concept of religion as person in relation rests on Kant's categorical imperative, so Kant's imperative of the will rests on a high view of persons that could most clearly have come from Jesus of Nazareth. Kant, after all, has not been successful in his apparent desire to remain apart from the pietism of his grandmother. Certainly he can never be claimed as "one of the flock," but any man who has his high concept of personality as a kingdom of ends rests very close to the heart of the highest interpretation of Christian ethics at which the race has yet arrived. Perhaps he would resent my baptizing him thus summarily, but he has long ago been baptized into more communions than mine.

We stand here in a holy company, then, when we begin to talk of a concept of personality resting in that relationship that maintains between conscious ends. All the Christian personalists know their indebtedness to these giants, and the holy company includes not only Immanuel Kant, but Martin Buber, William Temple, Karl Jaspers, Nikolai Berdyaev, Miguel de Unamuno, and there are others.

Personality and Vocation

The Arrangement of the Scenery

It is in this realm, the realm of relationships, that personality demonstrates its arrival. This relationship is with persons, values, communities, and material substance. The task of becoming person cannot be consummated in the realm of material stuff, nor that of community, value, nor other persons. It cannot be consummated in any one of the four—nor without any one of the four. That is to say, all persons have relations with matter, community, value, and persons. It is out of the quality of one's relations with matter, community, value, and persons that all his personages, all his roles, all his partial arrivals at personality,

---

[32] Forthcoming, entitled *Persons in Relation*.

all his denials of personality, and all of his prejudices appear. Here, then, the task is to carry forward all we have learned of the issues involved with persons and materialism, provincialism, institutionalism and individualism and subsume this under one head wherein a person can demonstrate that he is person.

The Meaning of Vocation

The relationship between the becoming-person and the stuff of this world, the communities he inhabits, the values he knows, and the persons to whom he relates himself can be subsumed under the heading "vocation." This, in the fullest sense, is a man's work. This is where he demonstrates who he is. This is his arrangement of the scenery. It is in vocation that he achieves his kingdom, and the quality of his relations is the quality of his person and his kingdom. Here, in his vocation, his work, all that comes from him in terms of matter, community, value, and persons, he arranges his scenery.

Role as Means of Relation

Role is the encrusted personage one wears to signify his relation to matter, community, value, or persons. Role is the shell that covers the presence or absence of vital relation. If it covers the absence of relation role is an assumed part one plays to achieve a certain end. If role rises out of a relation it is involuntarily worn—given—and its demands are more or less fulfilled according to the validity of the relation and the quality of the ability to wear the role resident in the recipient.

With respect to matter role expresses relation in terms like owner, agent, borrower, depositor, director, analyst, user, craftsman, prospector, engineer, or even victim. With respect to community role expresses relation in terms like member, official, citizen, bully, leader. With respect to institutions role expresses relation in terms such as priest, sheriff, manager, president. With respect to persons in relation role expresses relation in terms like friend, lover, father, confidant, adviser, teacher, disciple.

Of the terms role and vocation, the larger term is vocation. Role is essential to vocation, but vocation implies work, i.e., the totality of one's output, and requires a multiplicity of roles in each of the four areas of life structure: material, community, value, and persons.

Role is the means of relation. Every man bears a role, an encrusted

233

personage, in each area of his life structure. He is at once devourer, member, priest, and father; or he may be agent, bully, mayor, lover, husband, and deceiver. Yet none of this is the sum of vocation. Vocation as demonstration of relation is more.

Role as Denial of Relation

Role expresses relation, but role may be used to deny relation also. This is why role and vocation cannot be synonymous terms. Vocation is an undeniable expression of relation—relation to stuff, community, value, and persons. Role is not so. Role may cover up and overspread vital relations. One's fidelity to his chief role can distort and deny vital relations.

Late at night, high in the Western Rockies, warmed and fed after our hunt, he was still tense, outraged, fed-up with his year of resentments. He had vented his spleen on nearly every institutional and community symbol I know. Not even the exhilaration and exhaustion of a high hard day in the saddle had relaxed him. He preached his resentments there before the fire.

"What are you when you are not a doctor, Doctor?" I timidly offered.

"By God I'm always an M. D.," and I guess he is. Ace surgeon, keen student, recognized authority, busy, able, worthy—he had never been anything but an M. D. since he first put on the role. With it he had put on all the accompanying resentments and prejudices: against socialized medicine, inferior training, chiropractors, herb-doctors, fee agreements, splitting of referrals, and united charities. But this was not all: He hated preachers, politicians, irresponsible renters, and game-hogs.

Patiently, as well as I could, I listened to his localisms, provincialisms, and personal bigotries. In each of these a secondary role had been caught up in a major role and each expressed its relations by pressure through the major role.

"What are you when you are not a doctor, Doctor?" "I'm always an M. D." This is true. He is also and always westerner, white man, democrat, landlord, taxpayer, clubman, sportsman, husband, father, son, and rebel. These all affect the prime vocational role he wears.

"Strip it all off, Doctor! Take away all these roles and what are you, Doctor?"

"My God"—and this time it was an almost reverent confession of awe, and emptiness. When a man for the moment strips himself of his roles he can see how much he has covered over and how little is left.

234

Role can deny relation as well as express it. One's fidelity to his major role as healer can make him destroyer. One's fascination with the primary aspect of his vocational role may cause him to distort other precious relations. Sometimes this is highly desirable. As pastor a man can escape the necessity of being even Christian for a time; he can evade the responsibilities of being son, friend, father, husband, and lover, for a time. But if he does he has denied personality—with a role.

Work as Energy in Relation

Role and work have a sharp differentiation, for role can be put down, taken up, put off or changed, but work is ever the same. Work is all that comes out of a man. It is every difference his having lived makes. It is everything his life energy puts out; it is the sum totality of his having been in the world. As craftsman, dealer in the raw materials of earth, it includes what he has rejected as well as what he has kept. As communicant it includes every relation. As institutional man his work appears in what he has treasured. As person his work is personal relations. His work is his every act, which includes all his intentions as well as the consequences of his acts. His work is his every encounter, which demands a changing community. His work includes all he has valued and all to which he is related—his children, his theology, his moral judgments, his retaliations, his hates, his cursings, his prayers, his aims and his accomplishments. Everything he puts out—his humors, his ideas, his longings—these are his work. Work is the energy of a man in his relationships, and it is something he can neither put down nor destroy. There is no escape from this work—no retirement, no resignation, no release. It goes from portal to portal, womb to tomb, breath upon breath, and who can say when it is done. Work is Karma: every continuing circle in the pool which began from the living action of a moral being. This is work—energy in a context of relation. Yet vocation is the larger term. For vocation includes role and work, and something more.

Vocation: Role, Work, and End

It is in relation to the end that role and work are constitutive of vocation. It is the end in view that makes of role and work a calling. It is the end in view with respect to which work can be called good work or bad work, with respect to which role has its integrity or lacks integrity.

235

Vocation, then, is all the ways in which one offers up his domain of energy, self, and relations to his highest. One's work is always done for and in the sight of one's God. Indeed one's God can most quickly be identified by a glance at the work. This is the relation between work and worship. Work is worship (*leiturgia*). That is, the quality of work is constitutive of the quality of worship. All work is always done in the sight of and to the glory of some sort of God. The name of one's God is engraved in the work one has done. This is the essence of calling. That work must be done in the sight of and to the glory of God.

Role, work, calling—these are the constituent elements of vocation. The element of relation is contained in the element of response. What one's work may be—qualitatively—and what one's role—in its integrity —may be are determined by this element of response to relation offered in the calling. The highest God, offering a highest calling, eliciting the highest response, to the limit of one's energy in relation produces good work. Thus any good work is God's work, and God's work is good work. The goodness of the work rests in the quality of the relation of response, not in some intrinsic conformity to standard. Hence, "a little child shall lead them," for his quality of response is without flaw, and so his work.

Vocation, then, is the way one says *Thou* to God and all other *thous*. It is composed of role, work, and calling. It receives its quality from the quality of its end—its God. It is the means by which the relation that is constitutive of persons is expressed. Vocation is the arena within which role, work, and calling speak of the person who is becoming-person in terms of the quality of his relations with stuff, community, value, and persons. Here vocation is redemptive, or it is not, in terms of persons and relations within these structures.

Vocation and Matter

Can a man say *Thou* to his money? [33] Yes, a man can say thou to anything he values as a thou, but not as person. His "personhood" is determined by the quality of the *thou* to whom he gives thou-ness. This is the prime relevancy and importance of his relationships within the realm of the stuff of this present world. If he makes subject in relation out of stuff he has not only said *Thou* to his money, he has become slave

[33] Buber, *op. cit.*, p. 106.

of money. If, on the other hand, he despises the stuff of this present world he has denied his own relations as dominator, crown of creation, completing agent with respect to what God has done and will do in this present world.

The person, therefore, cannot say *Thou* to his money, but he regularly, continually, habitually, says *Thou with his money*. By means of his material substance, or by means of his lack of material substance, he says *Thou* to those to whom a "thou" is due. Thus, the stuff of this world becomes his means of witness to a relationship that goes beyond this present frame. The personal requires the perception of the invasion of this material world by the relations that lie beyond it. This is the incarnational realism of part one. This is the process of living in, alongside of, under the melange of conflicting forces, powers, and matter which make our lives at once prisoner to and master of existence. This makes of the world an arena out of which, in response to the calling of God, there appear men and women in role, work, and calling (vocation) whose quality of response is such that they matter eternally. From this high middle ground of Christian realism a man can expect new light and live on the light he has received without existing either as victim or despiser of this juggernaut of matter. In so far as he has a horizon he is redeemed from the prejudices of too narrow a view of reality, nor has he committed the idealistic prejudice of denying existence to that stuff of this world which seems very real to the Christian realist. This is a world God has made; man loves it and can offer it back to God; this is his vocation in the realm of the material.

Vocation and Provincialism

Community is related to vocation as the field of play is related to the game. Community is where the person lives out the terms of his calling by means of role and work. Only the person, conscious of every relation, can begin to experience the gradational redemption demanded by all "personhood" for us becoming-persons who are committed to churches too small, horizons too limited, and ceilings too low. This is the arena where one's calling must keep whispering that there are rooms upstairs. Indeed, it is by way of the exercise of vocation that the person finds his upper rooms and wider horizons.

Before any real awareness of and commitment to the larger whole, prejudice withers. Personhood, in its vocation, learns to give qualified loyalty to its lesser communities. Personhood lives on an expanding edge of the times and of the relations of time, looking for new and wider relations. Even here, it is not able to forsake the lesser because it has heard of a larger whole. The lesser is not despised because there is a greater. Here persons learn to live with lesser in the light of the greater. In the consciousness of the greater the relations of the lesser are made more precious by the apperception of true worth contained embryonically and prospectively within the lesser. Hence, vocation can require life to be lived within the lesser, but person is always living its life in the lesser by its consciousness of the larger whole. His loyalties are qualified loyalties, and this is devastating to prejudice.

Vocation and Institutions

It is within the field of one's province that the game of vocation is played with institutions as depositories of value. Institutions are the units of value one uses in vocation. In his vocation one uses Aristotle's "doctrine of levels," levels of value, to arrive at decision as to which game is worth which candle. Emotionally, one can have so foresworn himself to lesser values that his institutional prejudices have sealed him within a cell of prejudice. Vocation is the means personhood uses to make institutional commitments serve a higher end.

In terms of role, work, and calling the person finds himself able to recognize the difference between instrumental and intrinsic value, between transient and permanent value, between exclusive and catholic value. Within vocation one feels coming alive the possession of a sense of highest value. This response to the calling of the highest end makes it possible for him to keep placing lesser values under judgment. He finds himself able even to abandon the lesser for the higher, and what is more he is able to put his best-loved treasures under judgment, and he rules in favor of the high calling; then work and role bear him out.

Personhood does not subjectivize its institutions. Institutions remain objects to the person. Thou is said only to persons. The institution is a value unit with which one serves persons, not vice versa. To personhood, in vocation, the institution exists for persons. "I will have mercy and not sacrifice" means here that the personal value supersedes institutional value and that institutions must not be used to destroy or limit the personal. Prejudice cannot live with the relations of persons in vocation committed to highest end and recognizing that there is no intrinsic value except the person and relations of persons.

Vocation and Individuals

Here vocation runs its heaviest risk of denying its highest end, for to achieve immediate ends vocation is heavily tempted to use individuals. Even those individuals who are not yet persons can be helpful to vocation when it forgets its highest end. Sometimes vocation can rationalize its willingness to use individuals as *its* under the guise of very high purpose, such as church, for example.

The reverse is true—to such an extent that all kinds of individuals not yet persons will use the vocation of another for their own advantage. Indeed, the not-yet-person would use God if he could.

Role, work, and calling, as vocation, require particular concern at this point. The not-yet-person must be regarded as if he were person. The less-than-person must be regarded not only for his potential but for himself. Hence, vocation is a means to high relation. Vocation becomes a redemptive means to effect the personal between person and not-yet-person. The high end is justified in its vocational means, for the end is present in the means.

The solution to personal prejudice lies in vocation. This is higher than any moral imperative for this is the personal imperative in communion with persons as vocation. Vocation has become means to a valid end. The Christian vocation is the glory God gets in the Christian calling. Sometimes its fulfillment puts a man in a strange place with frightening duties and petty tasks onerous to be borne. Sometimes he seeks escape, for the sake of his prejudiced regard for himself, but he is in communion for a high end, and he cannot evade or escape.

Sometimes, as in the interview of Andrew Melville with James VI of Scotland in 1596, all the elements of what it is to be person, in proper relation with the material, the provincial, the institutional, and the personal, come alive in one moment of response to a high calling in terms of the role and work which are vocation—the means by which a man demonstrates his redemptive release from lesser prejudgments in the light of his commitment to the highest.

At Falkland Palace, Melville bore his witness to the soon-to-be James I of England, as follows:

Mr. Andrew broke off upon the King in so zealous, powerful, and unresistable a manner, that howbeit the King used his authority in a most crabbed and choleric manner, yet, Mr. Andrew bore him down, and uttered the commission as from the mighty God, calling the King but "God's silly vassal;" and, taking him by the sleeve, says this in effect, through much hot reasoning and many interruptions:

"Sir, we will humbly reverence your Majesty always, namely in public, but since we have this occasion to be with your Majesty in private, and the Country and the Church of Christ is likely to wreck for not telling you the truth and giving you a faithful counsel, we must discharge our duty therein, or else be traitors both to Christ and to you. And therefore, sir, as divers times before, so now again I must tell you, there are two Kings and two Kingdoms in Scotland. There is Christ Jesus the King, and his Kingdom the Church, whose subject King James, the Sixth, is, and of whose Kingdom not a King, nor a lord, nor a head, but a member. And, Sir, when you were in your swaddling clothes, Christ Jesus reigned freely in this land in spite of all his enemies!" [34]

The Recovery of the Personal

Somewhere along the road a man must become responsible for his own ignorance and prejudice because there will have been time enough and books enough and people enough and pain enough to teach him. On his own, he should know the agony of this fragmented world of split men who have worked under bright lights on their tiny islands, never sensing truly the surrounding illimitable darkness. He should have come to hurt for the hordes of sense-driven hive-dwellers who never will come to the tree in the midst of the garden. He should have been able to recognize how his church and himself are very great sinners, how helpless he is really to reconcile, and should have drunk deeply at least once of the sacramental wine of his own failure. He would know, by now, that cynicism is homicidal, pride is egomania, and nihilism is for sophomores. He should have had to weep over the prejudices of some village he is too small to change, but he should have outrun his own temptation to accept the call to be a bourgeois messiah. His grace for mankind should let him see that there are no seventeen-year-old anti-Christs, which gives him hope for the very young, at least; and he should have begun to recognize his allies. He should have discovered that even "among those who map

[34] Nathaniel Micklem, *The Theology of Politics* (New York: Oxford University Press, 1942), pp. 87-88. Used by permission. I have modernized the spelling.

the roads to Inferno there sometimes is to be seen a glimpse of the Damascene highway"; that those of the great church at God's left hand know of the gathered darkness, too, and by their very negation they testify to the possibility that some morning waits to let in more light. He should have sensed that revelation lies behind and flows through the revolution that now occupies his world. But have not we all been permitted to see a fantastic parade?

I have seen the parade and am still a seeker. For ten seasons, when my children were very young, we went every spring to the corner by the Governor's Mansion to see the amazing crêpe paper and wire ingenuity of the Spring Parade at our University. After it had snaked its brilliant way by us we hurried down to Congress Avenue to see it pass again! Now, at my age, I have been a seeker thirty-five of my years, a Don Quixote, and a mimic, but for more than twenty of these years I have been chasing theologians in this fantastic parade. I have small-boyed my big-eyed way into the marchers surrounding half a hundred exhibits, but the parade has gone full circle, some of the mimers and papier-mâché constructions are passing me again—and I have my bewilderments:

I saw Schleiermacher out the back door of my seminary eighteen years after Barth buried him. But great Schleiermacher did not die. He only came around the chapel and went home, as Kant used to do at commencement time, to keep from hearing some very bad sermons. Now Schleiermacher is coming back in the front door again, as indeed he must, for has Barth not replaced his bust in the lares of the gods?

My set of Harnack, imported, if you please, and paid for with grocery money, and my Troeltsch, and my Ritschl were passé, people said, when I got them. But you can buy Harnack for $2.40 in paperback, and behold, the timbers of Harnack, Troeltsch, and Ritschl lie visible in the base of Richard Niebuhr's methodology of Christian ethics, and the same great three can be felt in the prayers of Walter Rauschenbusch, now reprinted.

In my own lifetime as a seeker what was once Buttrick's heresy on atonement has become standard Presbyterian dogma, Harry Emerson Fosdick has gone a full and grand circle, Toy is revered at Louisville where he once taught, and Gezork has his host of friends in the South. The new Thomas Aquinas may have been baptized a German Protestant; Pelagius appears again among some educated bishops; Plotinus moves

241

lively now behind the pages of Karl Barth I have read; and Arius, who might have died 1,600 years ago if he had been properly appreciative of Bishop Alexander's preaching, is one ancestor to the flowering of New England. Ritschl's Christ, as having for Christians the value of God, rides, with a faint odor of Docetic Gnosticism in Bultmann's Trojan Horse, and the awful effort to evade the dreadful historicity of the gospel requires a whole cavalcade of once thought dead Docetics to animate a three-storied view of history—a metaphysical device more complicated than Augustine's hermeneutics. Everybody is back now but Spengler and Hegel, and I think they never really went away.

Under Vespasian's edicts the Christians cried "Nero reborn," but there are beneficent rebirths too. Augustine rides in a thousand exhibits. The fourth century heresy about the Father-Sufferer is at the bottom of any relevant modern soteriology. Unamuno recovers Marcus Aurelius and Kierkegaard. But by a fluke of a wild auto wheel we are denied the maturation of the new Bishop of Hippo, for the great North African, Albert Camus, was cut off just as he was climbing out of his Manichaean phase. Only Julian Huxley remains the same. Everything else changes, and most have gone the circle route which must make the shade of Oswald Spengler happy. Except for Toynbee, who restores Heraclitus, and Butterfield, who sees that all great revolutions turn in on their own middle. The parade is a cycle, and we are bogged in the traffic at the square, milling and turning. The parade has lost its form and has become a wild and vari-colored mélange. And even here a man keeps seeking, lest he lose the possibility of being found.

For up and down in the sea of faces that was a parade but is now a mélange one senses the death of form that rested on Aristotle. William Barrett sees this in *Irrational Man* and notes that there is no beginning, no middle, no end; no denouement, all edges blend, nothing cuts into new territory; no good, better, or best; no cause, no order, no shape—but a mélange, a fromage, a milling, pressured gumming-up of the parade. In this, with all its sociological manifestations, we are involved. Here we must live our lives, not as spectators, and to admit the danger is no longer heresy. Here, in this mélange, with both Athens and Jerusalem lost, some things simply never mattered less! Our threat is not heresy, it is rather that we will choke on our own exhaustion, pile up on the circle, and quit looking for a new cutting edge.

Here, now, one begins to see, there never was an ordered parade with one exhibit following another. It has always been a *fromage vert*, a mixture in a cheese vat with all sorts of ill-assorted condiments floating together in the brew. There is no longer form; this is the end of entity. So you pick up Faulkner's *The Sound and The Fury*, but you throw it down, startled, for this idiot Benjamin through whose mind there floats this hopelessly disconcatenated sequence of recollections, is no idiot at all—he is me! There is no beginning. One just falls into a mass without edges—No time, no shape—Aristotle has become Freud. The unconscious rules! Form is dead. So you hear a jazz-mass, sit in a Gothic movie-house, find the Spirit of Greece in cemeteries, Nirvana in funeral homes, see a Swastika Cross painted over the Star of David, are served pineapple juice mixed with tomato juice in Dallas, find a Mohammedan "dial-a-prayer" wheel in a Protestant church and locate the best of primitive art in public rest rooms.

The power of the figure stuns. Amos Wilder points it out in his *Theology and Modern Literature*, that Quentin, in *The Sound and The Fury*, on the day in which he was a suicide, broke the crystal on his grandfather's watch, then stripped its hands as if he would stop time, but the formless, handless monster, with its useless blood-stained face kept ticking out the droplets of his life. In this pressured fromage some things never mattered less. In a world that is eating out its innards in a revolution, could there be a revelation? The agonizing search for new symbols or for new meaning behind the old, continues, and this is our "sole, common grief," our "common weeping." This is where a man comes "to eat the flesh of his own soul." Here reason becomes, as Luther called it, "the great whore," and a matricide, for love can die here! If, after half a lifetime of searching a man can spell the name of mathematicians, physicists, theologians, and philosophers, but finds a home in neither Athens, nor Jerusalem, nor Vienna, nor Madison Avenue, may he not then be in a position to find himself with no values at all, except the personal? Is this the door to his redemption, and a life?

Is it possible that out of this agon there now emerges a clear and meaningful cry? I am profoundly moved by the agony in which the church clings to its old frames in the face of this formlessness—this death of time. I am stricken dumb, between Sundays, at my own audacity that in a shape like ours I would actually climb my stairs and call to passersby about God when I am but a befuddled man. Is there any future for this and for us? I do not *know*, but that upon which I have staked my life finds its setting in which to work *with persons in a community of inquiry*. On this I believe a man can prove his claim. Here I believe I can see an emerging hope that men can find some groves of trees in which to rest and work between their clawings at the "abyss" that threatens us with meaninglessness, for the future, any future, *has always lain with the personal*.

This is the distillate coming out of an aching center. This is not something you have to swallow hard and believe. "In the beginning is relation." The only value we have is the personal-in-relation. This is the revelation, this is the center to which everything began years ago to point and which we can now see. Here we can come together in a community of inquiry with affection even for those who have hated that to which Jesus Christ was pointing. An amazing hope for persons in relation has come to me of late. To this, Gilson, Marcel, and the Jesuit Weigel are all pointing. Camus had turned this way, preceded by Paul Tournier, Martin Buber, and a holy, holy company.

When I tried to say these things once, a grand sociologist whom I have loved for years called it "magnificently romantic." I answered in deep distress, "Doctor, do you mean 'magnificently preposterous'?" This is the surd: The unbelievable hope lies in this absurd. The future lies with the insignificant, with spirit and will, not with flesh and desire; with those who will hope and work, not with despair, acquiescence in meaninglessness, or the abomination of history. This is the surd: That the future should lie with Nels Ferré's love, which I saw once on a postcard from London to a man in trouble, more than it lies with his thought which I have seen in books. This is the surd: that the future lies with the personal and the relation that can be recovered in the personal which is centered in that blessed: I, if I be lifted up from the earth will go on drawing all men unto me.

This is what it is all about. It is not strange, is it, that Jesus Christ ahead of all the rest, should ache so to see the personal recovered? If and as it is recovered, doctors will know how to tell their patients they must die; lawyers will become human; salesmen will lose their false faces; pastors will foreswear every vestige of the professional; men will become men to each other, beholding "thy face as if it were the face of

God"; and we will see men like the man described in the Sermon on the Mount, but not by a mere ideal.

There is a work of redemption to be done, and this Jesus Christ means to us Christians. He will do this work; he has done it; he is doing it. God has come to meet us in relation. Love will do this thing, and at this point the things which never mattered less go away. We begin to hear voices, then each other, we recognize each other because redemption has come alive when persons in relation have begun to hear each other. This is the fantastic surd: That men may be so personal to persons that death is absurd. Every man who has heard you can be maintained—in relation. This is why we can not ever escape or forget the Cross where he has heard us. If we should evade this relation to our suffering we would lose any relation to resurrection, and there would be nothing left for us but to go out to his grave in the night and howl, for there is where he gives us what we have to sing about. Here relation becomes actual and makes a ministry a possibility.

I first began to suspect myself of being a professional nineteen years ago, when clutching my brand-new ordination-gift prayer book I held my first funeral for a man I did not know at Fort Knox. It was an agony to hear myself making those pre-prescribed holy noises, but I did not then know about Cross and one lifted up and moments of relation and what it is to hear a man as he dies and to die with him, if not for him. But I have tasted it now—and I decry the former emptiness. In such a man Christ does come to his people. In such a ministry a man can become all men. We do become as redeemers, frocked or not, and in this redemption of relation between persons and the Person, one can live.

Through that Thou, I am becoming a Person. Here a unique and unrepeatable event has happened. Here, in a new embodiment, a whole kingdom of hope and potential has begun to be. This relation has its tensions, and this is suffering. It has its contradictions, and this is sin. It has its paradoxes, and thus it knows of death. But it has its interruptions in the form of new appearances, and its continuity which is eternal life, and in this person-in-relation a man can serve.

If this distillate is some kind of Christian humanism, it seems inevitable, for it is all we have. Let it be, or let God be declaring us all null and void. Our hope requires the recovery of the personal in relation. Nothing else matters—much.

245

INDEX